COSTA RICA

A Global Studies Handbook

Other Titles in
ABC-CLIO's
**GLOBAL STUDIES: LATIN AMERICA
& THE CARIBBEAN**
Series

Argentina, Todd L. Edwards

Brazil, Todd L. Edwards

Chile, Lisa M. Edwards

Cuba, Ted A. Henken

Mexico, James D. Huck, Jr.

GLOBAL STUDIES: LATIN AMERICA
& THE CARIBBEAN

COSTA RICA

A Global Studies Handbook

Meg Tyler Mitchell and Scott Pentzer

A B C CLIO

Santa Barbara, California   •   Denver, Colorado   •   Oxford, England

Library of Congress Cataloging-in-Publication Data

Mitchell, Margaret T. (Margaret Tyler), 1967–
    Costa Rica : a global studies handbook / Meg Tyler Mitchell and Scott Pentzer.—1st ed.
    p.   cm.—(Global studies. Latin America & the Caribbean)
Includes bibliographical references and index.
ISBN 978-1-85109-992-4 (hard copy : alk. paper)—
ISBN 978-1-85109-993-1 (ebook)   1. Costa Rica—Handbooks, manuals, etc. I. Pentzer, Scott. II. Title.
F1543.5.M58   2008
972.86—dc22

                            2007044849

12 11 10 09 08   1 2 3 4 5 6 7 8 9 10

Production Editor: Anna A. Moore
Production Manager: Don Schmidt
Media Editor: Ellen Rasmussen
Media Resources Coordinator: Ellen Brenna Dougherty
Media Resources Manager: Caroline Price
File Management Coordinator: Paula Gerard

ABC-CLIO, Inc.
130 Cremona Drive, P.O. Box 1911
Santa Barbara, California 93116-1911

This book is also available on the World Wide Web as an ebook.
Visit www.abc-clio.com for details.

This book is printed on acid-free paper ∞

Manufactured in the United States of America

Contents

Series Editor's Foreword

In a world in which borders are blurring and cultures are blending at a dizzying pace, becoming more globally aware and knowledgeable is imperative. This is especially true regarding one's immediate neighbors, where the links are most intense and most profound. For this pragmatic reason, knowing more about Latin America is especially relevant to people living in the United States.

Beyond such a practical consideration, Latin America is a fascinating region of the world on its own terms, and it is worth the time and energy to get to know the region better simply as a matter of intellectual curiosity. By providing a readable and engaging introduction to a representative selection of the region's countries, this series hopes to engage readers and nurture their curiosity in the region and its peoples.

One point that this series will make abundantly clear is that Latin America is not a homogeneous region. For example, its population is remarkably diverse. Indigenous peoples are spread throughout the region, constituting the majority of the population in countries where the largest of the region's magnificent pre-Columbian civilizations were centered. Descendents of the Iberian European colonizers continue to dominate the region's political and economic landscape, though recently arrived immigrant populations from Europe and Asia have made significant inroads into the economic, political, and cultural aspects of these countries. The Atlantic slave trade network brought hundreds of thousands of Africans to Latin America to labor in the plantation economy. The African cultural legacy is particularly relevant to modern Brazil and the Gulf-Caribbean countries. And the process of racial mixture, or miscegenation, that occurred freely and consistently over the past 500 years of the region's history has created a unique *mestizo* identity that many modern Latin Americans embrace as their own.

Obviously, therefore, one characteristic of the region that makes it so intriguing is that it is so vastly different from one country to the next and yet, at the same time, the countries of the region bear striking similarities. In addition to sharing a physical continent and space in the Western Hemisphere, the countries of Latin America also share a basic, common history that stretches from the colonial period through the present day. And the region is also bound together in many ways by language and culture.

In terms of its geography, Latin America is a vast region, encompassing more than one-half of the entire Western Hemisphere. Further, its natural environment is one of the more diverse in the world, from the deserts in northern Chile to the lush and ecologically diverse rain forests of the Amazon River basin. It is also a region rich in natural resources, providing the world with many of its foodstuffs, energy and mineral resources, and other commodities.

A few basic statistics can help to illuminate the importance of learning more about the region. Latin Americans constitute approximately 12 percent of the world's total population, and Latin American countries make up approximately 6.5 percent of the world's landmass. By some estimates, the Spanish language is the most spoken language in the Western world and is second only to Mandarin Chinese among all linguistic groups worldwide. The vast majority of Spanish speakers reside in Latin America. Portuguese, the native language of Brazil, is among the world's 10 most spoken languages.

Among the regions of the developing world, Latin America ranks consistently at the top in terms of most economic and social indicators in aggregate terms, but the region still struggles with chronic poverty and suffers from highly skewed patterns of income distribution. A consequence of this income gap has been growing out-migration, with more and more Latin Americans each year making their way to better opportunities in wealthier and more economically developed countries. Recent efforts to promote greater economic integration by way of regional free trade agreements throughout the Western Hemisphere also illustrate the growing importance of a greater knowledge and awareness of Latin America.

In terms of politics and governments, Latin America finds itself squarely in the traditions of Western liberal democracy. Most Latin Americans embrace the values of individual freedom and liberty and expect their political systems to reflect these values. While these political aspirations have not always been the reality for Latin American countries, as of late democracy has been the norm. In fact, all of the countries of Latin America today with the exception of Cuba have democratically elected governments, and all are actively engaged globally.

The specific volumes in this series introduce Mexico, Brazil, Chile, Costa Rica, Cuba, and Argentina. They represent all of the different subregions in Latin America and they range from the smallest countries to the largest in terms of population, landmass, and economic wealth. The countries included in the series vary in terms of their ethnic and class composition, with Cuba and Brazil containing large Afro–Latin American populations and with Mexico representing a society shaped by a rich and vibrant indigenous culture. The inclusion of Cuba, which remains the region's stalwart socialist experiment, offers ideological variation within the series. Argentina, Brazil, Chile, and Mexico represent the region's top four economic regional powerhouses, whose places in the global economy are well established. These four countries are also the region's most influential actors in the international arena, serving not only as leaders within the Latin American region itself but also exercising influence in the world's premier international bodies. On the other hand, Costa Rica and Cuba demonstrate the challenges of and possibilities for the region's many less influential global actors and smaller economies.

Finally, it should be noted that Latin American culture is seeping much more into the mainstream of U.S. culture. People in the United States enjoy the foods, music, and popular culture of Latin America because they are all more readily available in and appealing to the U.S. population. In fact, one might argue that the United States itself is becoming more Latin. Evidence indicates as much, as the numbers of those who identify themselves as Hispanic or Latino in the United States are growing rapidly and disproportionately to other ethnic or racial groups. According to the 2000 U.S. Census, the Hispanic population in the United States constitutes about 12.5 percent of the total U.S. population and is now the country's largest ethnic minority group. Even more striking is the incredible growth rate of the Hispanic population in the United States relative to the total population. In just 20 years, the Hispanic population more than doubled, and if this trend continues, Hispanics will constitute a majority of the U.S. population in about 50 years. The fact that Hispanics in the United States maintain strong ties to their countries of origin and retain an affinity for the culture and lifestyles common to the region makes Latin America all the more relevant to understand.

The volumes in this series provide a basic introduction to some of the countries and peoples of Latin America. In addition to a survey of the country's history, politics, economy, and culture, each volume includes an extensive reference section to help point readers to resources that will be useful in learning more about the countries and even in planning to visit them. But above all, the hope for this series is that readers will come to a better appreciation for Latin America as a region, will want to learn more about it, and will eventually experience the richness that is Latin America.

—*James D. Huck, Jr.*
Series Editor

Preface

Costa Rica is a very small country in an out-of-the-way corner of Latin America. Costa Ricans themselves have been heard to muse on how small their population is compared with some of the giants of the Americas, how many times the 4 million Costa Ricans could fit in Mexico City, or how their economy compares with that of a prosperous county in the United States. Older people still like to recall the "millionth child" born to great fanfare in the 1950s. Perhaps these perspectives explain their habitual use of diminutive forms in their speech, giving them the self-imposed nickname "*ticos.*"

Given its size, one might legitimately ask why Costa Rica merits an entire book in a series on Latin America. Perhaps it is because the country has tended to draw disproportionate interest from foreigners. Early Spanish settlers gave the country a name promising much more in gold, silver, and indigenous subjects than it could ever make good on. In the 19th century, the country's promise was finally realized with the cultivation and export of the delightful little bean that gets many modern people through the day. Coffee brought to the country a run of prosperity and political development that was notably peaceful compared with that of the rest of Central America, perhaps because the economic benefits of coffee were more broadly shared than anywhere else in the isthmus. Of course, life was not perfect. Although Costa Rica was more prosperous and peaceful than most of its neighbors, it was still no stranger to political turmoil in the last decades of the 19th century. These disruptions were on a smaller scale than most, but they did not entirely come to an end until the Civil War of 1948. Still, this conflict resolved itself quickly and led to a new period of creative institution-building, which justifiably enhanced the country's reputation for democracy, economic development, and social stability. Costa Ricans are very nostalgic for the period from the 1950s to the 1980s, often remembering it as a heyday of almost everything: culture, stability, equality, peace, justice, prosperity, and international acclaim.

That Costa Rica reached the pinnacle of its success during this 30-year period was certainly a blessing for the country in that it provided real benefits to Costa Rican citizens in terms of education, health, and economic opportunity. But after the debt crisis of the 1980s and the subsequent pressures of the globalizing economy, Costa Rican reality has changed drastically, and it no longer matches the country's self-image or the assumptions of the millions of tourists who have visited the country in recent years. The nostalgia for the earlier successful period of the mid-20th century, and the way the tourist industry reinforces that nostalgia, may, unfortunately, be inhibiting the country's ability to address new challenges of the 21st century.

Having lived in Costa Rica for the past three years, it seems to us that this is the situation in which Costa Ricans now find themselves. The country is passing through a moment of institutional crisis and self-doubt just at the time when, paradoxically, it is again attracting the disproportionate interest of foreigners. This interest is due, in large part, to the enormous increase in tourism since the 1990s. Tourists are attracted by the country's history of effective and stable institutions, its openness to foreign investment in real estate, and its incredible natural beauty and biodiversity. Furthermore, its relatively educated population has also allowed Costa Rica to become an important offshore manufacturing and customer service center for a number of multinational corporations.

But the social tensions accompanying these "perfect" opportunities highlight the fact that not all Costa Ricans agree on where their country should be headed next. Most are aware, for example, that nearly 90 percent of coastal property available for development is owned by foreign investors and that some of those investors evade laws intended to protect delicate tropical ecosystems. Most Costa Ricans are also aware that their educational advantages are eroding in a competitive world economy. Less than one-third of Costa Ricans graduate from high school, leaving many to worry about the future of the country's economy and social stability.

These worries and tensions have become particularly focused around the debate over whether or not the country should approve a free trade agreement with the United States. The economy is growing nicely, foreign investment is flowing, and the United States is holding open the door to the largest market in the hemisphere, reassuring ticos that they are still who they think they are, while at the same time warning them that if they do not walk through the door they might lose essential economic opportunities. But Costa Ricans cannot all agree on what path their country should take.

It is a moment that calls for an honest look at the country, but conditions seem to conspire against it. Tourism demands something less than honesty in the competition for visitors in a world market, and politics in a small and fairly monopolistic media market do not lend themselves easily to a wide-ranging consideration of what the country's problems are and how to address them. On the other hand, now, as in several of the country's critical historical moments in the past, some voices are calling attention to what must be done to bring the country's reality back into a closer relationship with its image. Investigative journalists in the principal daily newspaper, *La Nación,* and committed academics in the annual *Estado de la Nación* (the State of the Nation) report, prepared by the country's public universities, have not shrunk from the truth about the deterioration of many of the country's institutions. The *Tico Times,* a longtime source of news (and real estate promotion) for the sizeable expatriate community, has done its part to point out some of the country's more urgent problems. All of these critics want Costa Rica to continue to be what it has for so long aspired to be, and seem to have concluded that it cannot do that without a large and painful dose of truth.

This book would be impossible without the work of journalists and investigators like those mentioned above. Our aim is to celebrate those things that still make the country unique; to give context to the problems that concern its citizens and admirers today; and to share in the spirit and, in our own small way, a bit of the work of these critics. This work has helped us to see Costa Rica, as small and unique as it is, as a place on the front lines of most of the major challenges to achieving something like sustainable human development. It is a different interpretation of the place than one finds in the tourist literature, but it is offered in the hope that those who read it—and those who visit Costa Rica—will pay attention to those challenges and assume their part of the work too.

Acknowledgments

We would like to thank the Associated Colleges of the Midwest (ACM) and its students for giving us the opportunity to live in Costa Rica, encouragement to write this book, and all sorts of occasions and resources to learn about the country. The ACM library in San Pedro, under the care of our colleague Judith Magnan, has been very helpful in the research for this book. Eduardo Estevanovich, the master Spanish teacher at the ACM, has been a wonderful source over the last three years for all of our questions about Costa Rican Spanish.

The ACM has given us the opportunity to meet many Costa Rican scholars, intellectuals, and artists who have in some way contributed to our understanding and appreciation of Costa Rican society. Manuel Monestel, author and founder of the band Cantoamerica, has enriched our appreciation of Latin American music, and particularly of Calypso Limonense. Carlos Sandoval, of the Institute for Social Research at the University of Costa Rica and his wife, Karina Fonseca, of the Jesuit Migration Service, have helped us in many ways to understand the phenomenon of migration in Costa Rica. Over the course of several field trips to the Arenal Volcano, Jorge Barquero introduced us to the fascinating geological history of this very new section of the planet, as well as to the challenges facing the country's national park system. Michael McCoy and Paul Hanson have both been valuable advisors to ACM students and helpful to us as we got to know the country and the people who study it. Of course, any misinterpretations, misunderstandings, or other peculiar interpretations of the place they all call home are our responsibility alone.

Finally, we would like to thank Alicia Merritt, Alex Mikaberidze, Anna Moore, and Ellen Rasmussen, our editors and contacts at ABC-CLIO, for giving us the opportunity to write this book and for their patience and guidance as we completed it.

Maps

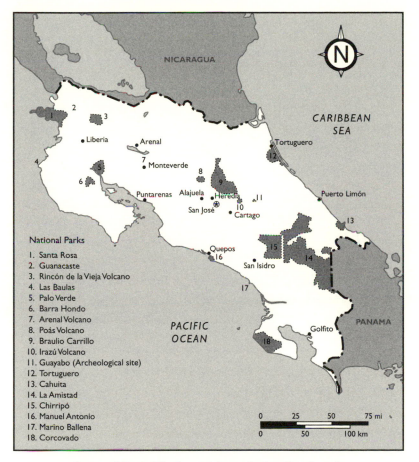

National Parks

1. Santa Rosa
2. Guanacaste
3. Rincón de la Vieja Volcano
4. Las Baulas
5. Palo Verde
6. Barra Hondo
7. Arenal Volcano
8. Poás Volcano
9. Braulio Carrillo
10. Irazú Volcano
11. Guayabo (Archeological site)
12. Tortuguero
13. Cahuita
14. La Amistad
15. Chirripó
16. Manuel Antonio
17. Marino Ballena
18. Corcovado

Some of Costa Rica's most important national parks

Political map of Costa Rica

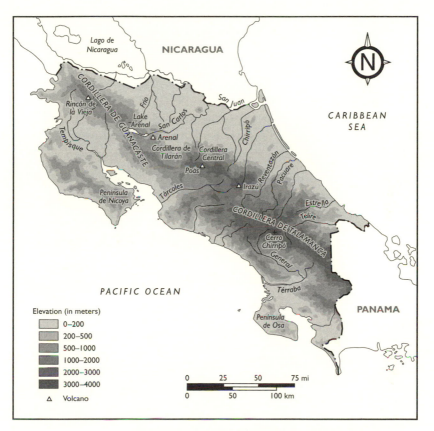

Physical map of Costa Rica

PART ONE
NARRATIVE SECTION

CHAPTER ONE

Geography and History

Costa Rica's natural beauty has impressed travelers since Christopher Columbus came ashore on his fourth voyage to the New World in 1502. His son, Hernando, wrote that the island off Costa Rica's Caribbean coast, where the ships landed, was the finest place they had yet seen. "[T]his was because the land was high with many rivers and abundant tall trees," he explained, "and because this island was so extremely leafy and filled with woodlands of huge trees, palmettos and wild almonds, as well as many other species. For this reason, the Admiral called it the Garden" (Colón 1947, 280). Yet if it was the verdant landscape that first caught the Spaniards' attention, it was their hope of finding gold there that held it. By around 1539, the Spanish invaders, still hoping (too optimistically, as it turned out) for rich deposits of gold and silver, came to call this bit of America "Costa Rica," or "Rich Coast" (Solorzano Fonseca 1992, 318).

Costa Rica still catches one's attention for many reasons, not the least of which is its spot on the map. It is a small, narrow country that occupies a very interesting geographical position: between two continents *and* between two oceans. It covers only 51,100 square kilometers and lies entirely within the tropics—between 8 and 11 degrees north of the equator. It is bounded by Nicaragua to the north and by Panama to the south. In its natural state today Costa Rica would be almost completely forested; only 30 square kilometers are above the tree line (Hall 1985, 22). There is no country whose development has been completely determined by its geographical location and climate; this would be far too simplistic. However, geography and climate are always important elements not only of the natural world but also of the social or human world. They constitute the background against which a variety of events may take place. Because the geography and climate are so particularly striking in Costa Rica, they are the logical place to begin a discussion of its history and culture.

Costa Rica was one of the last links to be formed in the land bridge that connects North and South America. At the end of the Cretaceous period 80 million years ago, the future countries of Costa Rica and Panama were only a series of volcanic islands that had been pushed up to the surface by the tectonic action of the Pacific plate sinking below the Caribbean plate. About 12 million years ago, this volcanic arc collided with South America. The passages between the islands, though, still allowed the Atlantic and Pacific oceans to flow directly into one another and separated the animal and plant species of the Northern and Southern hemispheres. About 3 million years ago, after a gradual process involving further collision of tectonic plates, volcanic activity, and erosion, the land bridge finally closed. This brought about great changes in the circulation of ocean currents, the climate, and the distribution of land and sea animals. At least one scientist has even claimed that the closing of the Central American isthmus was the "most important natural event to affect the surface of the earth in the past 60 million years" (Coates 1997, 1).

The closing of the isthmus allowed the Caribbean Sea and Pacific Ocean to develop two very different environments along the coast of what is now Central America. The Pacific Ocean in this region is more affected by seasonal changes and strong ocean currents. It developed meager coral reefs near the shore, but a larger fish population in the deep sea. The Caribbean is less affected by seasonal fluctuations, and it saw increased growth of coral reefs that supported a large population of near-shore fish. At the same time, however, the closing of the land bridge also caused certain changes in ocean currents in the Caribbean that would have striking long-term effects. Whereas the Atlantic Ocean previously flowed strongly into the Pacific, afterward it was deflected northward, creating the current we know today as the Gulf Stream. This tropical stream warmed the North Atlantic, increased precipitation in the Northern Hemisphere, and thus accelerated the creation of glaciers during the following Ice Age (Jackson and D'Croz 1997, 38).

Other changes brought about by the closing of the isthmus involved the distribution of land animals, which could now cross from south to north and north to south. Fossil records have provided scientists detailed information about which animals went where and when. Some, such as giant ground sloths (which moved north) and raccoons (which went south) were such good swimmers that they did not wait for the bridge to close completely before they began crossing from one island to another about 8 million years ago. But it was only several million years later that large numbers of animals began to migrate north and south. Fossils from Southern California, for instance, show that by 2.4 million years ago, armadillos, capybaras (large aquatic rodents), and porcupines had all arrived there from South America. At around the same time in Argentina, at the far southern end of the continent, evidence indicates the arrival of North American animals such as llamas, horses, saber cats, bears, and field mice. Over half of the land mammals still existent in South America came from North and Central America over the land bridge (Webb 1997, 101–103, 122). And in Costa Rica, species from the two hemispheres can still be found. The North American white-tailed deer lives alongside the South American brocket deer and northern rattlesnakes with southern bushmasters (Blake and Becher 2002, 16–17).

The first waves of animal migrants through what would become Costa Rica were mostly grazers and the carnivores that preyed upon them. Thus, the land bridge was not always forested, but at one time was mostly open grassland through which these animals could easily move. A second wave of animals, however, was adapted to the rain forest, which indicates that the climate and vegetation of the region had changed. This new wave included birds such as parrots and toucans, butterflies like the beautiful blue *Morpho,* and many kinds of monkeys. These animals traveled from the Amazon basin as far as central Mexico, the area north of which became too arid to suit them. A latecomer from the north was the bison, or buffalo, which had originally come to North America from Asia and never made it further south than Nicaragua. In what is today Costa Rica, the open grasslands through which earlier grazers moved had already become rain forest, through which the huge bison could not pass but which was quite suitable for monkeys and parrots (Webb 1997, 106, 107).

Costa Rica was the crossroads for these many migrations, and it is still one of the most biodiverse places on earth. An estimated 13 to 14 million different species of plants and animals exist in the world; Costa Rica contains about 4 percent of these: more than 1.5 million species. It is one of the 20 most biodiverse countries in the world. This biodiversity is even more impressive when one takes into account that Costa Rica covers only .03 percent of the earth's surface. Other countries have more different species, but none appear to have the same density of species. Costa Rica has more than 300,000 species of insects, 136 species of snakes (18 of these are poisonous), and 850 species of birds (both migrants and year-round residents), with 109 species of bats. Of the 330 known species of hummingbirds in the world, one-fifth are found in Costa Rica. The country has 1,500 species of orchids and 800 species of ferns (INBio 2007b). And every year, new species are discovered. In 2005, scientists identified 202 new species of insects, 17 new species of plants, and 1 new spider species, among others (Programa Estado de la Nación 2006, 62).

The factors that account for this diversity are Costa Rica's varied topography and the many microclimates that

Many lives were lost when Arenal unexpectedly erupted in 1968. Since then, fortunes have been gained as tourists flock to the volcano and the surrounding region. (Photo by Meg Mitchell)

such topography creates. Because of the mountains that crisscross the region, climate and vegetation can vary a great deal over very short distances. Many of these mountains are volcanic, remnants of the volcanic islands between which the isthmus was originally formed. The volcanoes in Costa Rica are part of the same arc that extends south from Mexico through Central America. Because the Pacific tectonic plate is still sinking below the Caribbean plate, compressed into the deep Middle American trench in the Pacific Ocean, many Central American volcanoes are still active. This tectonic action also explains the many earthquakes that affect the region. In Costa Rica alone, 70 percent of the population lives in areas vulnerable to earthquake and volcanic action (Coates 1997, 26; Hall 1985, 7).

Highlands run the length of the country like an asymmet-
rical backbone—narrowest in the northwest and widest in
the southeast. Beginning in the northwest, we find the range
known as the Cordillera of Guanacaste, whose highest peak
is a little more that 2,000 meters above sea level. To the
southeast, the Cordillera of Tilarán continues the volcanic
chain. This range includes the Arenal volcano (1,640 meters), one of the best known in Costa Rica. Before 1968, its
volcanic activity had been noted, but little studied, and Arenal was considered inactive. In late July of that year, a series
of earthquakes were felt in the vicinity, and then on the
morning of July 29, the volcano erupted, sending out shock
waves, poison gases, rocks, and lava. The farmers living at
the foot of the volcano were caught completely by surprise:
an entire village was destroyed, and almost 80 people were
killed (Alvarado Induni 2000, 96–98). Arenal is still dangerous; it spews red-hot lava and tosses boulders down its steep
slopes. It is, however, a national park and may be visited, but
with care. In 1988 and 2000, tourists and hikers who got too
close to the crater were killed (Blake and Becher 2002, 275).

Even further east, these ridges make the transition to the
Central Cordillera, which contains the well-known volcanoes of Poás, Barva, Irazú, and Turrialba, all visible from the
Central Valley. These are the highest volcanoes in Costa
Rica and have been designated as national parks. Poás,
Barva, and Irazú all have large, colorful lakes in their old
craters. Poás and Irazú have both shown activity over the
20th century, but nothing as destructive as Arenal. Irazú
spread a layer of ash over the Central Valley at various times
from 1963 to 1965. Turrialba has not erupted since the middle of the 19th century (although it is showing some signs of
life in 2007), and Barva has apparently not been active since
the colonial period (Alvarado Induni 2000, 175, 220).

One of the most striking aspects of Costa Rica's geography
is that because of its compact size, these mountains and volcanoes can be seen from many different parts of the country.

The lower-lying Central Valley (elevations from 600 to 1,000 meters) is surrounded by highlands. The valley is only 70 kilometers long from the north to the south and an average of about 20 kilometers wide from east to west. It contains the capital city, San José; the old colonial capital, Cartago; two other important cities, Heredia and Alajuela; and about half the country's population. The other important valleys are found in the more southerly and larger General Coto-Brus depression: the Valley of the General and the Valley of Coto-Brus, named for the rivers that drain into them. They contain the only other flat land in the central part of the country. The valleys are separated from the Central Valley by the northernmost massif of the southern Talamanca range, the "Cerro de la Muerte," or Mountain of Death. It got this name supposedly because travelers, unprepared for the high elevations, froze to death crossing from the Central Valley before the Interamerican Highway was finished in 1945.

The Talamanca range is the largest in Costa Rica and is not volcanic. The highest peaks here show evidence of glaciation during the last Ice Age, and the structure of this range is complex, containing both marine sediments and lava flows (Hall 1985, 10). Costa Rica's highest point is here—Chirripó, at 3,832 meters above sea level. All the mountains in this range are high and rugged and served in the colonial era as one of the last hiding places of the indigenous peoples after the arrival of the Spaniards. Various Indian communities can still be found in this area. The Caribbean slopes are very wet and still heavily forested in many parts. The Pacific slopes also still have some heavily forested regions, especially in the southerly Osa Peninsula, but the rate of deforestation on the Pacific side has been very rapid in recent years.

The most extensive lowlands are found in the area of the coastal plains, both on the Caribbean and Pacific coasts. The Pacific is the longer coastline (1,016 kilometers) and is striking for its peninsulas (Santa Elena and Nicoya in the

north, Osa in the south) and natural bays (the Gulf of
Nicoya and the Dulce Gulf). The Pacific coast is hilly, and its
rivers can be navigated only for short distances. The
Caribbean contains the only truly navigable rivers in Costa
Rica, the San Carlos and the Sarapiqui, which flow into the
San Juan River, which runs along the Nicaragua–Costa Rica
border and into the sea. The Caribbean coast is shorter (212
kilometers), straighter (without noticeable bays or peninsulas), and flatter. To the north of the port city of Limón we
find many swamps and lagoons as well as an intercoastal
canal. To the south, the land is very low lying and apt to
flood. Inland from the northern Caribbean coast to the
Cordilleras and from the western edge of the Cordilleras to
the Nicoya Peninsula on the Pacific are the *llanuras,* or
plains of the north. In the west, the plains have been cleared
for livestock since the colonial period, and in the east, the
plains are much wider and were only cleared in the 20th
century.

Because of its tropical location, Costa Rica experiences
little seasonal variation in temperatures. Depending on
cloud cover, temperatures may vary more at different times
of the day than they do seasonally. Temperatures also vary
depending on altitude. Since the colonial period, inhabitants
have referred broadly to three different climates in Costa
Rica by their temperatures: *tierra caliente,* the hot coastal
lowlands; *tierra templada,* the temperate Central Valley;
and *tierra fría,* the cool highlands. On the highest peaks, the
average annual temperatures are between 5 and 10 degrees
Celsius (41 to 50 degrees Fahrenheit); on the coastal lowlands, the average annual temperatures range between 25
and 30 degree Celsius (77 to 86 degrees Fahrenheit) (Hall
and Pérez Brignoli 2003, 19).

There are only two seasons in Costa Rica: wet and dry. Because of this climate, local usage of the terms "summer" and
"winter" has been reversed from what is usual in the Northern Hemisphere. Summer is the dry season, the season of

sunny, warm weather and the months when children have their longest vacations from school over Christmas holidays. This season falls during the months that in the United States are called "winter." Winter in Costa Rica is the wet season, or the rest of the year, when it is rainier and cooler. These are months that those in the United States would call "summer." And in comparison with the average rainfall in temperate countries, the amount of rain that falls in the tropics can be astounding. The yearly average rainfall in the driest areas is between 800 and 1,600 millimeters a year, while in the wettest areas, it can be between 7,000 and 9,000 millimeters (Hall and Pérez Brignoli 2003, 19).

The timing of the rainy seasons on the Pacific and Caribbean sides of the country varies with changes in the patterns of air circulation. When the air in the tropics is heated by the sun, which strikes from almost directly over-head, it rises and is replaced by cooler air from the north, creating the trade winds. Because of the direction of the ro-tation of the earth, these winds blow from the northeast across the narrow isthmus of Central America. When these winds cross the Caribbean, they warm and absorb moisture from the ocean. As this air continues to rise, it expends en-ergy and drops the moisture it has collected as rain. In Costa Rica, most of this precipitation falls on the eastern side of the central mountains. Because of the trade winds, the Caribbean has no strictly defined dry season; it may rain at any time of the year, although the months likely to be drier are March to April and September to October. In the Central Valley and on the Pacific side of the country, where the ef-fect of the trade winds is moderated by the mountains and by air currents coming from the west, the rainy season is more defined. It lasts from around May to November in the north and from April to December in the south.

Costa Ricans distinguish not only between the rainy and dry seasons but also between kinds of rain. There is the *aguacero*, or tropical downpour, which can, rather frighteningly, look like a wall of water. Aguaceros occur in the afternoons of the rainy season and although they may not last long, because of their strength they may cause great erosion, especially in areas that have become deforested. *Temporales* are more prolonged periods of rain that occur off and on during the rainy season. They are less forceful than aguaceros, but because of their duration temporales are more often responsible for flooding (Hall and Pérez Brignoli 2003, 18). Costa Ricans call the misty rain that sometimes falls between the heavier showers of the rainy season *pelo de gato,* or cat's hair.

It is the combination of tropical weather patterns and extremely varied geography that explains Costa Rica's great biodiversity. In order to study and to try to protect these diverse environments, scientists have developed systems of classification of vegetation. One system, created by biologist L. R. Holdridge, divides the regions into various "life zones." Based on the criteria of heat, precipitation, and moisture, and taking into account differences in elevations, Costa Rica may be divided into 12 major zones and 12 lesser transition zones. This creates an intricate pattern of zones and helps explain the existence of many different ecosystems over a very small area (Hall and Pérez Brignoli 2003, 22). Of the various zones, some are visually striking and likely to be seen by visitors, perhaps in one of Costa Rica's many national parks or private reserves.

The *páramo* is the highest zone and is found in the Talamanca range in the south. It is above the timberline and covered with scrubby foliage like dwarf bamboo, grasses, and mosses. The highest zones of true forest begin at a lower elevation. These are the cloud forests, so called because they are almost always covered by the clouds that rise up the Atlantic slope and shroud the trees in their moisture. They are important watersheds for areas of lower elevation. Because of the moisture, the huge trees become filled with epiphytes—plants that grow on trees but take their water

Near the continental divide, the rising cloud bank of the Pacific slope creates perfect conditions for oak trees, orchids, ferns, and birds near Santa María de Dota. (Photo by Meg Mitchell)

and nutrition from the air. Lowland forests include the wet or rain forests found in various areas on the Caribbean coast and on the Osa Peninsula on the Pacific coast. These are regions of year-round rain and extreme plant and animal diversity. Trees may reach heights of 50 meters or more and form a canopy under which smaller plants and vines must compete for sunlight. In recent years, thousands of acres of tropical lowland rain forest have been cleared in Costa Rica for the cultivation of bananas, pineapples, and oil palms. Even less acreage is left of the dry forests of the northern Pacific region, although programs such as those at Santa Rosa National Park in Guanacaste Province have attempted to conserve and regenerate them. Trees in dry forests may grow only to a height of about 20 meters, and because of seasonal rainfall patterns they are not green year-round, but lose their leaves in the dry season to conserve water. Mangrove forests, on the other hand, which are found in lowland river areas, have evolved to deal not with too little water, but with too much. They are found in the estuaries at the mouths of rivers and serve an important function in filtering the water flowing into the Pacific Ocean and the Caribbean Sea (Hall and Pérez Brignoli 2003, 20).

The system of life zones is useful for describing the environments that one *ought* to find in Costa Rica, but scientists have discovered that they also need to be able to describe those ecosystems that the country *actually* does have today. Such a system must be able to classify both natural and man-made environments and to evaluate changes in these environments over time. To understand the necessity of this classification, consider the astonishing environmental changes that have taken place in Costa Rica over the last 200 years. It is estimated that in 1800, 91.3 percent of the country was covered with forest. In 1950, that figure was 64 percent. And by 1987, only 25 percent of the country was still forested. This was the low point. By 1999, coverage had increased to 43.5 percent of the country (INBio

2007c). Although estimates vary, the Food and Agriculture Organization of the United Nations (FAO) estimates that from 2000 to 2005, the forest coverage in Costa Rica continued to increase, and in 2005, 46.8 percent of the land area was covered in forest (FAO 2007, 114).

This is very good news, but important questions remain to be answered. How was the trend toward deforestation successfully reversed? The FAO suggests that the answer to this question is not completely clear: "The turnaround may be related to innovative policies for financing forest management and paying for environmental services, although macroeconomic factors causing a reduction in agriculture may also play a part" (FAO 2007, 38). Other questions also arise. How do the reforested areas (secondary forest) compare with areas of primary forest in terms of tree size and biodiversity? Where no forest exists, what replaced it? Agriculture? Urban areas?

New technologies—aerial photographs, satellite images, global positioning devices—have helped scientists answer these kinds of questions. New methods of mapping and monitoring ecosystems allow scientists to classify vegetation and land use, to evaluate the current state of biodiversity, and to prioritize conservation areas (INBio 2007a). Although the rate of deforestation has decreased dramatically in recent years, and although Costa Rica has been one of the world's leaders in the creation of national parks and protected areas, the threats posed to the natural world by our modern way of life are constant and must never be underestimated.

PRE-HISPANIC COSTA RICA

Sometime between 30,000 and 12,000 B.C., probably in different waves, groups of hunting and gathering peoples crossed the Bering Strait from Asia and entered the New World (see Dillehay 2000). The earliest human settlements that have been found in Costa Rica date from between 12,000 and

8,000 B.C. These people seem to have made the transition to sedentary village life between 8,000 and 4,000 B.C. and to have begun to practice agriculture between 4,000 and 1,000 B.C. (Molina and Palmer 2006, 3–4). In this region of lower Central America, however, they never relied on just a few crops. Instead, using pointed digging sticks or shovels made out of large shells, they cultivated various root crops such as cassava and yuca, as well as many tree crops like guava, mamey, cacao, pejibaye (the fruit of a certain palm tree), and pineapple (Ferrero 1987, 10). Where it was not too wet, they raised corn, and they also continued to hunt and fish and use wild plants to supply their needs. One archeologist has pointed out that their "gardens" would not have looked as one might imagine: "not neat, tidy ones with straight rows and geometric beds, but unruly mixtures of herbs, shrubs, vines, and trees that were used for food, dyes, condiments, stimulants, colorants, incense, and medicines." To practice this sort of agriculture, the indigenous peoples did not have to clear-cut the forest; because they lacked metal tools, this would have been impossible. They used slash-and-burn techniques, but only over small areas. The forest was then allowed to recover for a period of time while cultivation was moved elsewhere (Cooke 1997, 147, 171).

By A.D. 500, many (though not all) of the peoples who had in earlier periods lived as dispersed clans were part of a more organized social system. Several villages with their varied resources from agriculture and hunting might be organized into a *cacicazgo,* or chiefdom. A few cacicazgos were further organized into larger groups known as *señoríos.* These were hierarchical organizations, more complicated than mere tribes or clans, but less complicated than true political entities, or states. When the Spanish arrived in the 16th century, they found an estimated 400,000 people, 18 cacicazgos, and at least two señoríos in the territory that would become Costa Rica. These groups occupied three main areas of settlement: the Gulf of Nicoya region in the

Pacific northwest; the central highlands and the Atlantic slopes; and the Diquis region of the Pacific southwest. Pre-Hispanic populations did not, of course, respect the national boundaries that we know today. Settlements in northwestern and southeastern Costa Rica overlapped with areas that are now Nicaragua and Panama (Snarskis 1981, 18; Carmack 1994, 300).

The cacicazgos possessed a degree of social and political centralization that allowed for the organization of permanent leadership, communal labor, and trade. Society was characterized by a hierarchy linked through kinship and marriage relations and cemented by ties of exchange and reciprocity. Reciprocity within each clan and between the various clans was the principle that united indigenous society. Although society functioned communally, not everyone was equal; instead, an attempt was made to maintain equilibrium in social relationships. Every social relationship was a trade off: *"Hoy por tí, mañana por mí"*—today for you, tomorrow for me. The *cacique,* or chief, of each group organized the production and the exchange of various commodities within his group, and he appropriated any surplus to distribute to his superior cacique. The most important señoríos had power over villages occupying various environments. Thus, taking advantage of the natural diversity of the region, they had access to many different kinds of goods (Fonseca Zamora 1992, 118, 189).

The groups traded agricultural products as well as materials like cotton, shells, and dyes, and manufactured goods such as ceramics, cloth, tools, weapons, and hammocks. Elite trade goods included gold, cacao, and prisoners of war (Fonseca Zamora 1992, 189, 192). These societies were, in fact, very warlike and often fought over territory, slaves, and prestige. This fact can be seen in the remains of palisaded villages they constructed for defense in some regions and in their sculptures of warriors in battle gear, often carrying the heads of their enemies taken as trophies (Stone 1977, 134, 176).

The dual nature of these societies—both warlike and given to trade—was noted in the 16th century by a Spanish observer, Fernández de Oviedo. After commenting on the Indians' weapons such as long lances made of "black palm and other trees of very good wood, [with] their thin, sharp points that can pass right through a man," he goes on to comment that "when the Indians are not making war, all their efforts go towards trading and bartering with each other; and thus, by one way or another, those who live along the coast or the rivers go in canoes to sell what they have left over. And in the same way, they barter by land and carry their loads on the backs of their slaves" (quoted in Ferrero 1987, 196–197).

Anthropologists call this region of lower Central America, along with northern South America, the Intermediate Area, that is, the region between the civilizations of Mexico to the north and the Andes to the south. But did the native cultures of Costa Rica represent the southernmost outpost of Mesoamerican culture or the northern limit of South American culture? Anthropologists have disagreed over the extent of northern and southern influences. But just as we saw that the territory was the crossroads for the migrations of plant and animal species, it is clear that it was also a crossroads for cultural influences. Evidence can be seen of trade and interaction through Costa Rica from very early periods. The earliest spear points found in Costa Rica are both in the Clovis style (from North America) and in the Magellan style (from South America). Although many archeological artifacts have been looted over the centuries or have simply deteriorated in the tropical climate, evidence exists of influence from both North and South America (Snarskis 1981, 40). The Chorotega and Nicarao people of north and northwestern Costa Rica spoke languages related to those of Mexico and, in their own stories and traditions, insisted that they had migrated south at some time in the past. When the Spanish arrived in the 16th century, they noted that these groups tended to cultivate corn and beans and to construct their villages around a plaza as the natives of Mexico did. Further south, the indigenous peoples tended to cultivate cassava, construct palisaded villages, and have a matrilineal clan structure—all reflecting South American influences. The languages of the Garabito and Guarco in the Central Valley, the Boruca and Coto on the south Pacific coast, and the Cabécar and Bribri on the south Atlantic coast were all related to the Chibcha languages of northern South America (Carmack 1994, 300; Coe 1962, 170).

Carved jade ornaments from the Olmec and Maya civilizations of Mexico, often reworked in local styles, have been found in burials in the central part of the country, as has a red-on-buff pottery very common in Mesoamerica. The influence of Panamanian and Colombian cultures is evident in, among other items, goldwork. The technology of metalworking originated in South America between 2000 and 1500 B.C. and appeared in Mexico between A.D. 700 and 900. Between A.D. 500 and 800 it began to be practiced in Costa Rica. Gold figures from Costa Rica often reflect South American styles, showing animals like frogs and double-headed birds, and a double spiral design (Bray 1981, 154, 160). Some of these gold objects were apparently traded northward to Mexico, as they have been found in the sacrificial well at Chichen-Itza in the Yucatan Peninsula (Graham 1993, 13). As regards trade to the north and to the south, one archeologist has asserted that "the fact that the rise of large ceremonial centers in Costa Rica occurred at the same time that a particular kind of long-distance trading system was in operation and [they] collapsed when that system ended strongly suggests that Costa Rican native peoples and others in between Mesoamerica and the Andes were not just passive recipients of culture but were active participants in culture change" (Quilter 2004, 197).

Yet despite varied influences and evidence of trade, there were never any great cities in the Intermediate Area, and there was no monumental architecture like the pyramids of central Mexico and the Maya area, or the urban complexes of the Inca in the South American Andes. No indigenous group in lower Central America ever developed a written language. The cacicazgos and señoríos were not nearly as complex as the states and empires of the Aztec, the Maya, or the Inca. The obvious question, one that anthropologists have frequently asked, is, Why not? Why did the peoples of the Intermediate Area in general, and of Costa Rica in particular, never develop sophisticated societies and cities? What impetus was lacking? But perhaps these are not the right questions to ask. Some anthropologists have argued that it is much more enlightening to look at the cultures of Costa Rica, and more broadly, of the whole Intermediate Area, in their own context rather than simply comparing them with more advanced civilizations. The most important questions then becomes: How did the indigenous peoples adapt to their own immediate environment? What were their unique characteristics and achievements? These questions are even more interesting when one remembers what a diversity of geography, climate, and vegetation the region possesses.

One of the most notable characteristics of these societies was their stability. There were no state-level societies, no centralized controls, and no empires. But there were also no frequent upheavals, collapses, or migrations. Archeological sites in Mesoamerica have cultural "phases," or periods of continuity between periods of great change, that lasted between 180 and 270 years. In Costa Rica, these phases lasted between 600 and 800 years. The fact that the villages existed in environments of abundant food resources may have encouraged cultural stability. As we have seen, the indigenous people took advantage of the diversity of the climate and vegetation and practiced *extensive* rather than *intensive* cultivation. They never had to rely on only one or two important crops, as was the case in more species-poor regions of Mesoamerica and the Andes (Sheets 1992, 30, 31; Carmack 1994, 289). Population density always remained low and relatively dispersed, and decentralized social and political systems were sufficient for the resolution of conflicts (either by peaceful or warlike means) and the exchange of goods among villages (Lange 1996, 315). Perhaps indigenous societies in Costa Rica failed to become more complex because social and political complexity was not necessary to maintain stability in that environment.

It is certainly evident that complicated social and political organization was not a prerequisite for sophisticated artistic development. Although many tombs and archeological sites have been looted over the centuries—not to mention the objects that were stolen or destroyed during the Spanish conquest—many beautiful pieces of goldwork, carved jade, stone sculpture, and ceramics are still intact and attest to the skills of the pre-Hispanic artisans. Some anthropologists have even suggested that in the less complex societies of Central America where artisans were only part-time specialists, they may have had more interpretive freedom to create artifacts with more individual character than in the more complex societies of Mexico and the Andes, where artisans worked in more tightly controlled workshops (Lange 1993, 297).

The study of ceramics, their decorative motifs, and how they changed over time has proved useful for understanding the prehistory and beliefs of the people of Costa Rica. All regions made ceramics, but particularly original and important ceramics have been found in the Nicoya region of the northwest Pacific coast. Up until around A.D. 500, inhabitants of this area produced ceramics more or less in the same style as the rest of Costa Rica, a style that was very similar to that of northern South America. After this date, however, there was an increase in painted polychrome (multicolored) ceramics, and various changes were seen in the iconography, apparently reflecting waves of influences from

Pre-Hispanic civilizations in Costa Rica achieved high levels of artistic development in ceramics. This is evident in this jaguar vessel from the Nicoya Culture, which dated from A.D. 1200 to 1400. (Museum of Fine Arts, Houston, Texas, Museum purchase funded by 'One Great Night in November 1991'/The Bridgeman Art Library)

Mesoamerica. The predominant motifs became an anthropomorphic jaguar, a feathered serpent, and the round goggle eyes of the Mexican rain god Tlaloc. These figures were often abstracted and simplified, repeated and reinterpreted. Just before the Spanish conquest, other motifs appeared in Nicoya ceramics, indicating renewed influences from northern South America. Many of the motifs may have originally been imported, but in Nicoya they were transformed into a style unique to that region and society (see Day 1988).

In the Atlantic slope and Central Valley regions, archeologists have discovered impressive examples of the indigenous peoples' skills as sculptors. Figures of warriors carrying trophy heads and of their captives with their hands bound are common. Large stone slabs carved around the top edge and used as tomb covers have also been found. On a smaller scale are the beautiful carved jade pieces, often in the shape of animals like alligators, bats, monkeys, frogs, and birds. But the elaborate grinding stones found at burials of this region are particularly striking. Although they resemble *metates,* or platforms for grinding corn, archeologists have suggested that with their intricate carvings they may have been only symbolic metates and, perhaps, were actually used as thrones. The edges and undersides of the stones are carved with fantastical intertwined figures of bird beaks, human heads, monkeys, snakes, and alligators. With their impressive decorations and three-legged shape, they do not much resemble any other form in pre-Columbian art. That they have been found in tombs suggests some relation to beliefs about the afterlife. Carvings sometimes show decapitated heads and zoomorphic figures that appear to be carrying corpses down to the underworld (Graham 1992, 183, 184).

Other interesting sculptural objects are the Diquis stone spheres from the Pacific southwest. They range in size from only a few centimeters to 2 meters in diameter. It is uncertain what their purpose was or how the craftsmen managed to achieve nearly perfectly spherical shapes without metal tools. The smaller spheres have been found as grave ornaments, and the larger ones may have been some kind of public monuments. They may have been symbols of the power of the caciques, as they were often placed near the mounds atop which elite residences or ceremonial buildings were constructed. The smaller spheres have been found both alone and in large groups, and they may have been used to make some sort of astronomical calculations, as archeologists have discovered them arranged in lines and in circles (Corrales Ulloa 2002, 55).

Some of the most ornate goldwork also comes from the Diquis region; it is strikingly original in its forms and skillful in its execution. Gold in this part of Central America came from river deposits and was worked in various ways. It was sometimes melted at high temperatures and pounded into very thin sheets to create large disks, bracelets, collars, masks, and even sheaths for teeth. Gold was also alloyed with copper and formed through the "lost wax" process into detailed figurines. Some of the most frequently made ornaments were pendants in the shape of animals—frogs, alligators, jaguars, eagles, lobsters, bats, and turtles, among others. Few naturalistic human forms, but many anthropomorphic ones, have been found. These objects had symbolic and supernatural meanings to those who created them and to those who wore them. Wearing gold also had a social meaning, reflecting the status or power of the person who possessed it. Gold was never merely a beautiful ornament (Bray 1981, 160).

Archeologists can never hope to understand completely the symbolism of pre-Hispanic art and its relation to religious belief and social structure. The societies that created the gold ornaments, the stone sculptures, and the ceramics left no written language to explain their meanings and context. They left only the objects themselves. Certain motifs reoccur; particularly notable are those of the animals of the tropical rain forest, and we may suppose that these had important symbolic connotations. Although the indigenous cultures were effectively dispersed and destroyed by the Spanish conquest, we may still draw upon some of the beliefs and practices of the few groups who still remain in Costa Rican territory to try to understand the beliefs and practices of their ancestors. The Bribri and Cabécar Indians of the Talamanca Mountains remained the most isolated from Spanish culture and held on to many of their ancient customs.

Pre-Hispanic peoples did not neatly divide their culture into categories of society, religion, and art. Neither was there a strict division in their thinking between human beings and nature. Pre-Hispanic cultures were "animist": they believed that not only humans but also animals and natural phenomena possessed a spirit. They had an analogical rather than a causative way of understanding the world; that is to say, the relationship *between* things was more important than their probable cause (Fonseca Zamora 1992, 166). Though people were but a part of nature, the balance between the two was very important. This balance was mediated by the shaman. He had access to both the natural and the supernatural world and used tools such as sacred stones, gold figures, and carved sticks to communicate with both worlds. He interpreted the spirit world to the human world, particularly in order to cure illness and to predict the future. The importance of the shaman can be seen in the fact that among the Bribri, the clan of the shamans is the *Tsíbriwak,* which translates as "central post" (González Chaves and González Vásquez 1989, 150).

The idea of an important central or axis post most likely comes from the construction techniques used to build the traditional Bribri house, or *u-suré.* This round house with a conical roof was not only a very effective shelter in a rainy climate but also stood as a symbol for the Bribri of their conception of the cosmos. In the past, these were

The ruins of Guayabo, near the town of Turrialba, with their systems of canals and aqueducts, indicate a pre-Hispanic civilization well adapted to the challenges of life in the tropics. (Photo by Meg Mitchell)

huge structures, up to 15 meters tall and housing up to 300 people of a single clan. The reciprocal and communal labor that made such constructions possible is no longer generally available given the demands of a modern economy, and many of the natural materials used for construction have become scarce in the forests; yet the building techniques still exist in collective memory. But technical considerations were not the only important element in constructing the house. The shaman had to know how to prepare the site and to protect the house against evil. The house had to be appropriately inaugurated with ritual dances and drinking of the local intoxicating drink, *chicha*. In the late 1980s, some indigenous groups in Talamanca built a conical house 7 meters tall for use as a cultural center, but it burned to the ground in 1988. In the Sarapiquí region of the

Caribbean coast, similar structures more recently have been built, in this case for tourism: as a hotel and indigenous museum.

The Bribri believe that the world extends upward to the heavens and downward to the underworld like two joined cones, and they build the conical house to reflect the order of the universe. The shamans undertake various rituals to cast illness, evil spirits, and other dangerous influences outside of the sacred circle of the house. The construction begins with the central pole. It is later removed and replaced with a long cord, but its symbolic meaning remains: it metaphorically connects the cone of the heavens, the home of the god Sibú, the creator of the universe, to the cone of the underworld. The underworld does not have the evil connotations one might imagine, as it is the home of Sibú's female counterpart, Surá, creator of each individual human being. The conical roof is ingeniously woven of vines and leaves. It is symbolically the vault of the heavens, and the knots in the vines that hold the thatch together stand in for the stars in the sky (see González Chaves and González Vásquez 1989).

Because they were made of perishable materials, houses dating from the pre-Hispanic period have not survived. However, as late as the 1870s, travelers in the southern parts of Costa Rica described the conical houses, as well as similar oval-shaped houses. At certain archeological sites one can imagine what settlements consisting of these dwellings might have looked like before the Spanish arrived. One important excavated site is Guayabo, near the city of Turrialba on the northeastern edge of the Central Valley. This site was occupied as early as 500 B.C., but its most important features date from about 500 or 600 years before the Spanish arrived. Certainly other archeological sites are of equal size and importance, but Guayabo is the only site that has been developed for tourists to visit (Quilter 2004, ix). Archeologists have so far uncovered at Guayabo the remains of 44 mounds and circular bases that would have provided the foundations for the sort of conical houses still seen in Talamanca. The largest of these is 28 meters in diameter. Abundant freshwater springs were channeled by the inhabitants into a complicated system of aqueducts, wells, and canals that run throughout the site. Guayabo's position on a hillside meant that it was defensible, and the buildings and plazas were obviously constructed to take advantage of the sloping ground and to create a pleasing and useful layout on various levels. Guayabo seems to be at the center of a network of paved roads, some up to 6 meters wide, which connected the site to smaller settlements, all part of the same señorío. These roads would have greatly facilitated travel and trade over very difficult terrain. According to the life zone classifications, it is located between the Premontane and Montane Rainforest zones and near the Humid Rainforest zone, which would have given its people access to many different sorts of resources. It was never as large and impressive as the pyramids of Mexico or the stone cities of the Andes, but in order to have built it, the pre-Hispanic peoples of this area needed specialized architectural and engineering skills, as well as a way to organize a great deal of communal labor. At Guayabo, it is clear that with these skills and this organization, they managed to create a small city beautifully suited to its tropical environment (see Fonseca Zamora 1981).

THE CONQUEST OF COSTA RICA AND THE COLONIAL ERA

As can be seen in the name that they gave the region, the Spaniards had high hopes of finding lots of gold in Costa Rica, and they were encouraged in these hopes by a few early expeditions. One of the earliest came north from Panama in 1522 and managed to take more than 100,000 pesos worth of gold from the indigenous people of the Pacific coast and the Nicoya Peninsula. This was a huge amount considering that the expedition had been financed for only around 8,000 pesos. But the Indians had probably collected this gold over many years, and it could only be stolen from them once. The first profitable export from Costa Rican territory was not gold, but rather captured slaves who were sent to Panama and Peru, thus decimating the indigenous population of the Nicoya Peninsula and Pacific coast (Solorzano 1992, 317).

Incursions from the Pacific coast to the interior and the Caribbean would, until the end of the 16th century, all be failures. The Spanish established their first settlement, Villa Brusellas, in the Pacific region in 1523, but the interior was not effectively controlled by the Spanish until between 1575 and 1580. Although the territory to be conquered was smaller than that subdued by Cortes in Mexico (1521) and Pizarro in Peru (1534), it proved in many ways much more difficult. Since the indigenous population lived dispersed in many small groups, there was no large city that could be taken in order to force other regions to capitulate. The conquest was also greatly complicated by Costa Rica's mountainous terrain, thick forests, rainy climate, and fierce Indian resistance. The various cacicazgos often banded together to fight the Spanish, and if they could not fight, they could flee. This form of resistance was observed by an Italian eyewitness on a 1540 expedition to the Caribbean: "The other caciques of Suerre and Quipa, seeing the bad treatment that the [Indian] prisoners received from the [Spanish] governor, burned their [own] houses, cut down the fruits and the trees, took the harvest from the fields and destroyed the country; then they immediately fled to the mountains" (quoted in Fonseca Corrales 1994, 124). The Spaniards were thus left with no supplies and no manpower.

Even before it was conquered, Costa Rican territory was nominally part of the Audiencia of Guatemala—the Spanish administrative unit that included all of what is now Central America except Panama, as well as Chiapas, which is now part of Mexico. In the middle of the 16th century, authorities in Guatemala came to fear that the Audiencia of Panama to the south would try to claim jurisdiction over the territory of Costa Rica and conquer it. Thus, new expeditions to Costa Rica were sent out from Guatemala, first under Juan de Cavallón (1560) and then under Juan Vázquez de Coronado (1562). Although they succeeded in establishing new Spanish settlements at Garcimuñoz on the Pacific slope and then at Cartago in the Central Valley, these soldiers could not be said to have conquered Costa Rica any more than their predecessors. Continued indigenous resistance, lack of Spanish manpower, and a change in the policy of the Spanish king toward the conquest of America were factors in thwarting complete conquest.

As a result of abuses committed in the conquests of the Caribbean, Mexico, and Peru, after 1542 conquerors were in theory no longer permitted, in return for a promise to Christianize and protect the Indians, to divide up villages among their soldiers as payment for services rendered. The soldiers struggling to conquer Costa Rica argued that without the right to receive this Indian tribute in goods and in labor, the *encomienda,* it was not worth their time to participate in military expeditions. Under Perafán de Ribera, the third Spanish governor sent to Central Valley in the 1560s, the soldiers complained terribly and threatened to desert Cartago, the new capital that had been founded by Vázquez de Coronado. Ribera finally broke down and distributed encomiendas, although, technically, this was illegal. Some of the villages that Ribera "handed out" to his soldiers had not even been conquered, and the Spaniards were still so obsessed with finding gold in the Caribbean that they neglected the new capital anyway. Ribera himself spent three years marching around fruitlessly in the southern mountains and jungles (Kramer, Lovell, and Lutz 1994, 39–40, 57).

It was only in the 1570s and 1580s that the Spanish ceased to see the settlements in the Central Valley as simply bases from which to depart in search of gold in the south.

The *encomenderos* (those with the right to receive Indian tribute) now found it profitable to use Indian labor to farm and raise livestock. But from the Spanish point of view, the small, dispersed Indian villages made it difficult to efficiently exploit indigenous labor. Thus, Indians were "concentrated" in new villages where they could more easily be evangelized by the Franciscan friars and made to work. At least until 1610, Indians owed tribute in goods as well as in service. They provided agricultural and household labor as well as products like cotton blankets, honey, wax, and ceramics. The sort of abuses to which the Indians were subject becomes clear in records of complaints they made to Spanish authorities. The Indians of Garabito, for instance, complained in 1590 that the Spanish governor had taken and sold corn that belonged to their village, and the Indians of Pacaca complained that the friar there forced them to spend all day long weaving mats and baskets, among other items, and the result was that the town went hungry because no men were available to work in the cornfields (Solorzano Fonseca 2002, 106–107, 127–128).

Thus it was indigenous labor and the goods collected as tribute that constituted the first sustained economic activity in colonial Costa Rica. Later, markets for wheat, corn, and pack mules and other livestock opened up in the growing settlements of Panama to the south and Nicaragua to the north, and the encomenderos took advantage of these. In the early years of the 17th century, the Spanish looked to the southeast, to the conquest of the Talamanca region, to gain new lands and more Indian labor. An Indian uprising of 1610, however, destroyed the new town of Santiago and forced the Spanish to flee back to Cartago. The southern region was to remain unconquered, but the violence there gave the Spanish the excuse they needed to declare the Indians in open rebellion and to send military expeditions to forcibly capture Indian slaves. Even with this, the encomienda as a source of labor was doomed. The population

The memory of Pablo Presbere lives on in this monument to him in the city of Limón. In San José, anti–free trade grafitti can be seen proclaiming "Pablo Presbere Lives!" (Julio Humphreys Vargas)

available to be distributed in encomienda rapidly diminished. From 69,875 in 1569, the number of Indians available to encomenderos fell to only 7,168 in 1610, a loss of 89.74 percent. And by 1691, 67.79 percent of Hispanic settlers in Cartago identified themselves as making a living off their own labor; many encomenderos and sons of encomenderos had been forced to become *campesinos*—farmers (Quiros 1990, 131).

At the beginning of the 1700s, a final effort was made to subdue and evangelize the indigenous peoples of the Talamancas. By 1709, the Franciscan friars had established 14 missions in the region. However, the Bribri, Cabécar, and Terbis Indians overcame their traditional rivalries to unite in a surprise attack under the leadership of Pablo Presbere in September 1709. Almost immediately, the Spanish authorities in Cartago organized an expedition of 200 soldiers to punish the rebellious Indians. The Spanish captured Presbere and marched him and 700 of his followers back to the capital. Two hundred Indians died or fled along the way, and the remaining 500 were divided up among the Spaniards who had participated in the expedition. Presbere was tried, condemned for treason, and executed in July 1710. Although the Spanish later sponsored other expeditions to Talamanca, after this uprising the region was never brought under their control during the colonial period, and today the Bribri still celebrate Presbere's resistance. A memorial to him stands near the central plaza in the port city of Limón.

Expeditions like these to subdue Indians fleeing from hard-driving encomenderos and intrusive Spanish priests certainly did not help to preserve the indigenous population. Much more important to understanding the decimation of the Indians, though, were the unintended and totally misunderstood effects of nearly two centuries of European presence in the New World. The Indians had no resistance to European diseases like measles, smallpox, and pneumonic fever. Trade among the Indian groups had meant that disease

The Spiritual Conquest of Costa Rica

In 1709, an uprising of indigenous groups led by Pablo Presbere killed a number of Spanish priests and soldiers in the mountains of the Talamanca region of southern Costa Rica and, although ultimately crushed, this rebellion effectively put an end to Spanish efforts to control this area during the colonial period. Despite the Spaniards' strong desire to make use of the Indians' labor and convert the Indians' souls for the Catholic Church, for almost a hundred years none of the attempts to pacify and control Talamanca had ever been very successful. This was because of the incredibly difficult geography, the inconstant financial and military support for Costa Rica from the colonial Audiencia in far-away Guatemala, and the constant and determined resistance of the indigenous inhabitants.

One of the Spanish priests killed in the 1709 rebellion was Franciscan friar Pablo de Rebullida. Whatever one may now think about the methods and motivations of the spiritual conquest, one must admit that priests like Rebullida were frightened off neither by the fierce reception they often received from the indigenous groups nor by the difficult living conditions in the mountains. Rebullida seems, however, to have been frustrated by what he felt was the lack of support from colonial authorities for his work. This frustration and the hardships he faced are clear in a letter that he wrote to his superiors in Guatemala five years before he was killed in Presbere's revolt:

> . . . Oh what pain and misfortune! That so many souls have been lost and so much silver wasted without having been made good use of, so badly have things turned out. . . . For this reason, I beg you to read this report . . . and you will see how miserable this unfortunate conquest is, and I beg those lords of the Audiencia who are pained by the loss of so many souls to see if 80 men might be sent, or any it is possible to send, so that these [Indian] nations may be saved and our lives secured.
>
> The men who are sent, if they can be, let them be men with axes and machetes and not comfort-loving men, nor

used to meat and sugar, because [here] the food often runs out and the Spaniards do not want to work, saying "a soldier does not work." This might be an appropriate response somewhere there is plenty of food. . . .

The last time I visited the Talamanca and Cabécar [Indians] I baptized 700 souls . . . ; this last time I visited the Talamancas, they rose up against me three times and another time threw stones at me. See how tame these Indians are, but I am going to return. . . . I got as far as San Miguel, and I baptized 40 souls.

Idolatry is very well rooted, and although I ask them for their idols, they respond that they don't want to hand them over; there are no marriages to speak of because they don't want to get married. . . .

May God keep me in his holy grace as He sees fit. Amen. August 18, 1704.

Source: Lázaro Lamadrid, "Letter of Fray Pablo de Rebullida, O.F.M. to Venerable Antonio Margil de Jesús, O.F.M., Urinama, Costa Rica, August 18, 1704." *The Americas,* 10:1(July 1953): 89–92.

was easily carried from place to place and affected areas like Costa Rica even before they were effectively settled by Europeans. The Indian population of Costa Rica continuously declined throughout the colonial period. Of the estimated 400,000 people when Columbus arrived in 1502, by 1569 perhaps only 120,000 remained. By 1611, only an estimated 10,000 were left (Molina and Palmer 2006, 19). In 1700, the official Spanish count was only 1,300 Indians living in 14 villages (Pinto Soria 1994, 14). While some indigenous people were living outside the villages at that time, particularly in the zones of refuge in the northern plains and the southern Talamancas, there were never many.

Once the indigenous "resource" exploited by the encomienda was exhausted, the colony had to wait until the second half of the 17th century and the first years of the

18th century for a new burst of economic activity. The boom came in the form of production of cacao—the plant from which chocolate is made—on the Atlantic slope. For twenty-five years, the Indians captured in the Talamanca region were forced to work on the cacao plantations. When this practice was finally ended, more African slaves, free blacks, and mulattoes were brought to work the cacao. Since the groves were on the Caribbean side of the country, it was relatively easy to export the cacao to the Caribbean and then to Europe through the port of Matina. But this convenience meant they were also easily attacked by British pirates and the hostile Zambo Mosquito Indians from the coastal areas north of Costa Rica. Because of these dangers, combined with high taxes and transport costs, owners of cacao plantations found that they could make more money trading illegally with British ships from Jamaica, and smuggling became widespread by the middle 1700s (see MacLeod 1985, 330–340). Yet during the colonial era, Costa Rica's economy never consistently prospered. Transportation was always difficult and labor was always scarce. The Indian population declined disastrously, and there were never very many African slaves because they were very expensive and few Spaniards could afford to import them. Near the end of the 18th century, a period of profitable tobacco farming began in the Central Valley around the town of San José, which was briefly granted a monopoly on that product by officials in Guatemala. Sugarcane was also grown commercially, and at the beginning of the 19th century, a short boom arose in brazilwood and in mining. Despite these gains, the colony always remained one of the backwaters of the Spanish Empire. So little silver money was in circulation that cacao beans came to be used as legal tender in the 18th century.

The population of Costa Rica was never large, and despite popular ideas to the contrary, it was never mostly "white." In 1801, the total population, 83 percent of which lived in the Central Valley, was only about 50,000. Of that, 6 to 9 percent was European; 60 percent was *mestizo* (of mixed blood); 14 percent was Indian; 17 percent was mulatto; and 1 percent was black (Molina and Palmer 2006, 45). Although the territory was small, there was a lot of land relative to the number of inhabitants; if a colonist wanted to farm his own piece of land, he could move to the frontier and begin to clear it. After 10 years, he could apply to the Spanish Crown for legal title (Augelli 1987, 5). Thus, although the region had a few large landowners (the owners of cattle haciendas on the Pacific coast, for example), it had many small landholders who worked family farms, or *chácaras,* from the colonial period on. Some have looked to this fact to explain Costa Rica's later relatively peaceful and democratic political development, while others have pointed out that despite the large number of small landowners, social and economic differentiation always existed.

Because of the small size of the chácaras and the low level of agricultural technology available, it was not in farming that money was to be made. It was in commerce. Merchants bought agricultural products at a relatively low price from the small farmers and exported them to Panama and Nicaragua, where they sold them in order to buy manufactured goods. These goods were then sold to the farmers and artisans of the Central Valley at a relatively high price. The small farmers were not entirely at the mercy of the merchants because they sold only their excess production— what was not needed for their family's survival. And Costa Rican merchants were often at the mercy of the foreigners from whom they obtained the expensive manufactured products. They could not reduce the prices of these useful and desirable goods to the farmers because they themselves had to pay market prices abroad. But neither was it really in the merchants' interest to do so: it was to this system of unequal exchange that they owed their modest fortunes (Molina and Palmer 2006, 41–42).

One interesting place where economic differences can be observed and even quantified is in the wills left by citizens of Cartago in the late colonial period. These wills carefully document the belongings of the deceased and clearly show that some had much more than others. In comparison with the colonial capitals of Mexico or Guatemala, Cartago may have seemed poor. In 1778, it had a population of only 7,946 and, by the beginning of the 19th century, still covered a mere 40 blocks. Yet some of its wealthiest residents had valuable possessions. Even the houses nearest the plaza, which had always belonged to the most important citizens, varied greatly in value. The most modest houses were valued at less than 400 silver pesos, the majority were valued between 400 and 800 pesos, and 17 were valued at more than 800 pesos. The finest house in town, that of Colonel Juan Francisco de Bonilla, was worth 3,000 pesos. The wealth and social standing of the elite was also reflected in their possession of African slaves, an expensive commodity, and their luxurious household furnishings. Luxurious clothing for men and women also distinguished the wealthy citizens from the commoners. Costa Rica was never a wealthy colony, but neither was it some kind of an egalitarian paradise (see Moya Gutiérrez 2002).

On September 15, 1821, Mexico and Central America declared independence from Spain. Costa Rica had avoided the violent conflicts that wracked many areas of Latin America in the years leading up to independence. In fact, it was so isolated from the important centers of Spanish power that residents did not even find out that independence had been declared until a month after the fact when the mail arrived from Guatemala. After independence, Costa Rica's first important decision was whether to become part of the empire stretching down the length of Central America that Mexico envisioned for itself or to establish its own independent republic. In 1823, the conflict between the "imperialists" and the "republicans" broke out briefly into violence at

Ochomogo, the mountain dividing the colonial capital of Cartago from the newer and more prosperous town of San José to the west. After a few hours and 20 deaths, the republican forces from San José were victorious. Little did they realize that the point was moot: the Mexicans themselves had revolted against their self-proclaimed emperor and sent him into exile a month before the battle at Ochomogo, but the news had yet to reach Costa Rica. This conflict, however, did serve to shift the balance of power in Costa Rica; San José became the new capital in 1823.

The vacuum left by the aborted Mexican empire was filled by another effort to unify the isthmus. From 1823 to 1840, Costa Rica became part of the United Provinces of Central America. This attempt to unite the republics of Guatemala, Honduras, El Salvador, Nicaragua, and Costa Rica began optimistically but did not end well. Ideological differences within and among the various countries frequently became armed conflicts, and little peace or prosperity was to be found in most of Central America during the first half of the 19th century. One of the most important differences of opinion between the opposing groups—the modernizing "liberals" and the "conservatives" who tended to hark back to the social and political structures of the colonial period—was over the role of the Catholic Church and the prerogatives of other privileged groups in colonial society. The liberals favored removing any special privileges and curbing the church's economic and social power. The conservatives defended the church and special privileges for priests, merchants, the military, and even indigenous communities. Costa Rica, where the colonial bureaucracy was weak, Indians were scarce, and the Catholic Church was without a resident bishop until the middle of the 19th century, managed to avoid many of the bloody liberal/conservative conflicts.

This is not to say that Costa Ricans had no ideological differences. Colonial political power had rested in the *cabildos,* or town councils, and after independence several conflicts erupted between the towns of the Central Valley. Costa Ricans in this period felt stronger loyalties to their town or region than to any idea of a centralized state. Cartago, the colonial capital, tended to defend the privileges it had reserved for itself over the previous 200 years. The new capital of San José, center of the 18th-century tobacco monopoly and the 19th-century coffee boom, was more forward looking and eager to add political power to its commercial power. This created tensions not only between San José and Cartago but also with the other towns of the Central Valley, Alajuela and Heredia, particularly over the issue of where the capital should be located.

The towns returned to the battlefield over this question in 1835 in the War of the League. San José emerged victorious. The hero of that battle, Braulio Carrillo, made himself dictator from 1838 to 1842 and decisively centralized political power in the new capital. He withdrew Costa Rica from the Central American federation, in which it had never participated much anyway. Carrillo pleased British creditors and avoided foreign intervention by taking the trouble to pay Costa Rica's portion of the failed federation's debt. Then he turned his attention toward making much-needed institutional reforms at home. He created a customs house, new rules for the public treasury, and new civil and penal codes.

But perhaps Carrillo's most long-lasting contribution was his enthusiastic promotion of the coffee industry, which began to flourish in the 1830s. It would not be too much to say that after the War of the League, people in the Central Valley were too busy growing and exporting coffee to stray into the sort of civil conflict that might threaten the "golden bean," as it was called. It was the common cause of coffee that really put an end to Costa Rica's persistent localism. People in all parts of the Central Valley participated and profited. Of course, some profited more than others: it was coffee that finally created an enduring dominant social class.

Yet the principal *cafetaleros,* or coffee growers, were able to plausibly argue for nearly a century that what was good for coffee was good for everyone.

ECONOMIC DEVELOPMENT IN THE CENTRAL VALLEY: COFFEE AND RAILROADS

In early 19th-century Costa Rica, very few people could be called economic or political conservatives: at the time of independence, there was hardly anything to conserve (Picado 1989, 53). The colonial period had been all about *not* changing, whereas the 19th and early 20th centuries were all about *change.* Not everyone benefited from every change, and by 1940, various groups had it in their interest to conserve the privileges they had accumulated over the previous hundred years. Over these years, Costa Rica became "modern," which on the whole benefited those in power. But in order to modernize, it increasingly tied its economy to just two export crops—coffee and bananas. This sort of dependence was risky: if world demand fell sharply, Costa Rica's economy could be ruined. As we will see, the production of these crops changed both the social environment in which they were produced and marketed and the natural environment, which was so necessary for their production in the first place.

Coffee was just the product that Costa Rica had been looking for as it entered the 19th century. The Central Valley has the right temperature and amount of rainfall, as well as the rich volcanic soil in which coffee plants thrive. Other parts of Central America would turn out to have conditions that were just as good, but it was Costa Rica that was first able to take advantage of these natural blessings. One reason was that because Costa Rica never had any real economic success in the colonial era, no vested interests stood in the way of a risky new crop. At the beginning of the 19th century, other countries in Central America still had a great deal of land and resources tied up in colonial commodities—

Until very recently, coffee was the engine of the Costa Rican economy. Today, coffee exporters aim for the high prices awarded for quality and environmental certification. (Library of Congress)

dyestuffs, for instance, like cochineal (a red dye produced by an insect) in Guatemala and indigo (a blue plant dye) in El Salvador and Nicaragua. Beginning in the 1820s, Costa Rican towns, first San José and then the others in the Central Valley, pressed their advantage by giving away municipal land to anyone who would agree to fence it and plant coffee. While this approach created a new opportunity for many farmers, it also meant that others lost access to communal pasture and forest lands. The central government was soon giving away national land under the same philosophy. Because coffee plants take three to five years to produce coffee beans, it was in farmers' interest to have clear title to the land if they were going to establish a profitable farm. Just as in the colonial period, more land was available than population to occupy it, and the coffee boom encouraged farmers to expand the frontiers within the Central Valley, looking for more land suitable for cultivation.

The pattern of landholding created by these policies was of many small- to medium-size coffee farms in the Central Valley. The only exception was the region east of the colonial capital of Cartago, where large haciendas had been established in the colonial era and where a few Indian communities still held communal land. Without the support of either the national or the municipal government, the Indians lost this land to individual coffee growers by the end of the 19th century. But in Costa Rica, this situation was the exception rather than the rule. In countries with large indigenous populations such as Guatemala or El Salvador, conflict over land was prolonged, and the Indians almost always came out on the losing side. In Costa Rica, before the coffee boom even began, the Indian population had diminished to such a point that it could offer little or no resistance to the expansion of the coffee economy.

Because in most parts of Costa Rica coffee was grown on relatively small farms, the most efficient way to organize labor turned out to be the family unit itself. Large amounts of labor were needed only when first planting the coffee trees and then each year at harvest time. With the family unit cooperating and exchanging labor with their relatives and neighbors, Costa Rica avoided the antagonistic labor relations of other Central American countries—those that lacked a frontier in which to expand (like El Salvador) or that chose to coerce coffee labor from Indians or peasants made landless by land reform laws (like Guatemala or El Salvador). In Costa Rica the tradition of the chácaras had existed since the colonial period, and with the boom in coffee production, these small family farms now grew not only their subsistence crops but also a profitable commercial crop. (For a comparative discussion of coffee development in Central America, see Williams 1994.)

Thus, unlike elites in much of the rest of Central America, Costa Rican elites, at least at first, tried neither to buy up and control large plots of land nor, consequently, to conscript wage labor from a land-starved peasantry. They found that the largest slice of the coffee profits was not to be made in production, but rather in processing and export. Using merchant profits accumulated in the colonial period, mining profits from the 1820s and 1830s, and, increasingly, British capital attracted to Costa Rica's political stability, elites invested in the expensive equipment needed for efficiently processing the coffee and shipping it to Europe. They made more money buying coffee from many small producers and processing and shipping it than they could have made by assuming the risks inherent in cultivation. Thus, the same sort of pattern that was seen in the colonial period of "buying cheap and selling dear" prevailed in the national period as well (Molina Jiménez 2002, 452).

There were 35 export houses in Costa Rica by the mid-1840s and 29 sailing ships that carried coffee from the Pacific port of Puntarenas to sell in Europe. By the 1850s, steamships were providing better and faster transportation, and Costa Rican coffee exports increased from 2.5 million pounds in 1843 to 7 million pounds in 1853. Costa Rica was the only significant coffee producer in Central America until 1873, by which time El Salvador and Guatemala were also exporting coffee. In 1890, coffee represented 91 percent of all Costa Rican export earnings (Williams 1994, 26, 31, 266; Bulmer-Thomas 1987, 2). Coffee provided the country with something it had always lacked in the colonial period: cash. And it united all Costa Ricans in a common project, thus diffusing some of the inevitable tensions that arose as society and economy changed over the last half of the 19th century and the first decades of the 20th century.

Although there were always many small coffee producers, during the second half of the 19th century the plots that small farmers worked in the Central Valley tended to diminish in size. The population increased, and, until the 20th century, families maintained the custom of dividing up assets among all heirs, often leaving each with only a tiny plot of land. The options left to the farmer with too little land, or no land at all, were to seek his fortune migrating to the frontier or to become a wage laborer on larger farms. Because of labor shortages, wages tended to increase, but so did the price of land and of basic commodities. Now that Costa Rica was tied to international markets, its economy could be strongly affected by downturns in the world coffee market. The owners of larger estates and processing plants took advantage of these economic downturns to buy up the property of smaller producers who could not pay their debts when the price of coffee dropped. By the beginning of the 20th century, the production and export of coffee had created three basic economic classes: the large landowners who also processed coffee; the small- and medium-size landowners who grew but did not process their own coffee; and the landless or very land-poor farmers who were also wage laborers. The boundaries between these three groups were fluid, and until the middle of the 20th century, the frontier always offered the possibility of improving one's lot

(Gudmundson 1995, 120). But an interesting set of statistics from the end of this period indicates how the productive capabilities of small and large producers balanced out. In 1940, 75 percent of coffee farmers (each with less than 2,000 trees) controlled about 12.5 million plants. Less than 1 percent of coffee farmers (each with at least 50,000 trees) worked 20 million plants (Winson 1989, 18).

The Costa Rican frontier remained an important element in national development throughout the period. Interestingly, it expanded not from one side of the country to the other but from the inside out: from the Central Valley out in all directions. This pattern makes sense considering that in the colonial period, the only area of the country to be extensively settled was the central area. It took economic expansion, first in coffee and later in bananas and livestock, to expand the boundaries of settlement. This expansion did not always happen very quickly. Even by 1930, only one-third the territory of Costa Rica was occupied (Augelli 1987, 10).

Even now in the 21st century, Costa Rica's high and irregular mountains and rainy climate make travel and transportation a challenge. In the 19th century, it was more difficult. When the export of coffee began in the 1830s, the most developed road leading out of the Central Valley was a mule trail to the Pacific port of Puntarenas. Between 1844 and 1846, this road was improved for use by wooden carts pulled by oxen. This solution still resulted in very slow transport, but it did make it much easier to take large amounts of coffee to port. Colonists took advantage of this road to head out toward the western and northwestern edges of the Central Valley because less and less land was available close to the most important towns. The men and women who migrated to other regions hoped to be independent, but also to be able to produce marketable crops once they had accomplished the onerous task of clearing the thick forest. At first, colonists might raise livestock or grain for the towns of the Central Valley (which were by then using almost all

Travel to Costa Rica in the 19th Century

Colonel George Earl Church traveled to Costa Rica in the last decade of the 19th century, and, in 1897, his geographical observations appeared in *The Geographical Journal,* a British publication. He wrote that he made his trip and his investigation of Costa Rica's geography because it was at that time one of the most poorly mapped regions in Latin America. More exact measurements might prove to be of some use, he thought, and Costa Rica of interest to the wider world, because at that time the United States and European countries were both investigating the possibility of building an interoceanic canal through the territory of either Costa Rica's northern or southern neighbor. Colonel Church's account of a day-long trip through a forested region just to the northeast of the Central Valley gives some idea of why much of the geography of Costa Rica might have still been unknown at that late date.

> My party consisted of six, besides myself. We were well mounted on excellent mules and horses. At 5.45 am, we rode north from Guapiles for a mile and a half through the *potreros* [pastures], and then plunged suddenly into the dense forests. . . . It was a tangled mass of trees, vines, undergrowth, creepers, thorn-bushes, and fallen trees—mixture of every imaginable obstacle in the shape of vegetation, and frequently so impenetrable that we were obliged to halt, to cut our way with *machetes.* . . . For miles we forced our way onward, sometimes crossing rivulets and mudholes, and one swamp through which our beasts floundered to the saddles, and where, to prevent them from disappearing, we had to dismount and also flounder through the black mud. . . . It was now past nine o'clock. Here it commenced to rain, and we put on our waterproofs. Mine was thick rubber, the best I could buy in London—"Especially made for the tropics," the dealer said. The rain went through it as if it were a rag, and for the next seven hours I might as well been under a hydrant. . . . Soon our beasts, from the top of their backs and ears to their feet, looked as if they had been painted with black slime, and their riders were almost in the same condition. We often crossed small streams with

(continues)

steep banks, so steep sometimes that we had to dismount to let the mules and horses slide down or scramble up, which they did bravely. . . .

I need not elaborate the experiences of the return journey. We arrived in Guapiles again about six o'clock in the evening, all resembling equestrian mud statues.

Source: George Earl Church. 1897. "Costa Rica." *The Geographical Journal* 10 (1): 56–84.

their land to grow coffee and had little left over for food). But later, they raised coffee themselves, or perhaps sugarcane. If in the west smaller farms prevailed, in the east, toward the town of Turrialba, the holdings were much larger. Although the crops were more or less the same, in the east haciendas utilizing paid labor would become the common means of production. But the real development of these eastern haciendas awaited the construction of the railroad (Molina Jiménez 2002, 469).

In 1870, the Costa Rican government contracted with British firms to build a railroad from San José to the Atlantic coast. This modern and relatively rapid form of transportation would be able to get the coffee efficiently to a port, where it could then easily be shipped to markets in Europe. Before the railroad, coffee shipments leaving from Puntarenas had to cross east again through Panama or travel all the way around the tip of South America. The railroad would also serve to better integrate the eastern region and the Caribbean coast with the rest of Costa Rica, an endeavor attempted since the colonial period but never accomplished. The British firms that began construction of the railroad could not accomplish it, either. Because of financial and topographical difficulties, they were unable to finish the work, and in 1884, Costa Rica contracted an American to do it.

Minor Keith promised to renegotiate the British debt and to take the railroad all the way to Puerto Limón on the Caribbean coast. In return, Keith received many concessions from the Costa Rican government, including a 99-year lease on the railroad and 800,000 acres of land in the Caribbean region (Molina and Palmer 2006, 70). The railroad began service in 1890 and continued until the early 1990s, when an earthquake damaged much of the track and the rail system was shut down.

Along with the coffee boom and the construction of the railroad, modest industrial growth occurred in the towns of the Central Valley beginning in the late 19th century. These operations were mostly small and often vulnerable to competition from imports. They fabricated consumer goods like soap, candles, beer, shoes, and textiles. Until the turn of the 20th century, workers participated in a variety of cooperative societies and clubs. After 1909, union membership became stronger and socialist influence was more widely felt. In the 1920s and 1930s, strikes became more common. A widespread strike of 1920 that involved workers as diverse as bricklayers, mechanics, typesetters, cigar makers, and electricians won the passage of a law guaranteeing the eight-hour workday (Oliva Medina 1991, 34–40, 48, 50). Those who labored in workshops or at skilled trades had developed a sense of belonging to a class of urban workers or artisans, but there was a growing class who had not developed such a sense. These included street and merchant vendors, guards, day laborers, shoe shiners, and newspaper sellers. By 1924, the municipal government of San José felt that a large enough number of these workers existed to merit a registry and a set of rules governing shoe shiners and newspaper and lottery ticket sellers (Palmer 2005, 319). Thus in the coffee boom, San José, and to some extent the other towns of the Central Valley, gained not only the prosperity that had eluded Costa Rica since the colonial era but also a more modern urban social structure.

THE REST OF THE COUNTRY: CATTLE AND BANANAS

But as coffee took over the Central Valley, what was happening in the rest of the country? The province of Guanacaste in the northern Pacific region had been an area devoted to cattle raising since the early colonial period. This was the part of the country where the Spanish had made their first incursions in the 16th century and where almost all of the Indian population had died of disease or been captured as slaves and shipped to Peru and Panama. Thus, a huge amount of land had been left open for raising livestock. The market for livestock was revitalized in the second half of the 19th century as coffee farming in the Central Valley came to displace almost all other agriculture there. The same sort of process could be seen in Guanacaste by the 1920s: all other agriculture there was driven out by cattle raising (Edelman 1992, 77).

Landholding in Guanacaste was very different from that in the Central Valley. Much of the land in Guanacaste was held in very large haciendas by absentee landlords, often North Americans or Nicaraguans. This region had, in fact, belonged to Nicaragua in the colonial period and had only been annexed to Costa Rica in 1824. In the 19th and into the 20th century, Guanacaste maintained closer ties with the city of Rivas in Nicaragua than with San José. This connection is not so surprising considering the difficulty of travel over the mountains to the Central Valley. Even in 1937, Guanacaste had no real roads and certainly no railroad. Oxcart roads predominated until the 1940s, when construction of the Pan-American Highway began (Edelman 1992, 90, 84).

Wage labor had always been the primary form of employment in Guanacaste, and labor was always scarce. Before 1930 the *peones* (day laborers) and the *sabaneros* (cowboys) had a fair amount of leverage in the labor market. But after this period, labor became more abundant, the price of beef rose, and owners and speculators began to claim and fence in land that before had appeared to belong to no one. By the turn of the 20th century, likely half of the population of Guanacaste, in many cases entire communities, depended on insecure land claims within vast haciendas.

The protests of land-hungry Guanacastecans to the government in San José resulted in a certain amount of rather ad hoc land redistribution. But the advantage was not always to the little guy. Some hacienda owners actually encouraged squatters to occupy their lands because they knew the government would compensate the landowners with land in other areas that might be even more valuable. Despite these conflicts, Guanacaste continued to supply Costa Rica with beef; the country became self-sufficient in this commodity and even began to look to export it. But as Guanacaste exported more beef, the amount and quality of beef for consumption there went down. By 1949, the residents of the region consumed 40 percent less beef and consumed beef of poorer quality than the rest of Costa Rica (Edelman 1992, 181).

If beef was the product of the Pacific region, bananas were crop of the Atlantic. When he built the railroad to the Atlantic, Minor Keith financed part of the construction by growing bananas along the line and exporting them to the United States. By 1899, his banana plantations came to be part of the United Fruit Company of Boston (UFCo). This company became one of the most powerful, profitable, and disliked of all American companies to operate in Central America and the Caribbean in the first half of the 20th century. By 1910, the value of banana exports from Costa Rica equaled the value of coffee exports. In 1913, the banana industry reached its height, exporting 11 million bunches (Cardoso 1986, 213). Though the industry declined in value in later years, its impact radically changed the life and economy of the Caribbean coast, just as coffee had changed the Central Highlands.

One of the most noticeable changes was in the population of the Caribbean region. Just as with the production of coffee, there was always a shortage of labor. As a result, many foreign workers came to the coast, first to work on the railroad and then to grow bananas. Between 1900 and 1913, an estimated 20,000 English-speaking Jamaicans came to Costa Rica. Smaller numbers of immigrants also came from other Caribbean islands, Nicaragua, Colombia, and China. The work in the banana plantations was grueling, but the wages were relatively high. The immigrants often worked with the hope that their situation was only temporary, that they would earn enough money to set up as independent farmers back in Jamaica or in Costa Rica (Chomsky 1996, 34, 43).

Although UFCo owned huge tracts of land, much of the banana crop was grown by small independent planters and then sold to the company. This is the same sort of arrangement that characterized coffee cultivation in the Central Valley. By subcontracting, the big banana company avoided much of the risk—disease, flooding, overproduction—inherent in farming. UFCo made its profit by controlling the price paid per bunch and the transport and marketing of the bananas. Subcontracting suited workers who wanted some measure of independence, but it was risky. If the price of bananas dropped, UFCo would simply not buy all that the independent growers had produced.

The first major strike in Costa Rica occurred in 1910 when the all-Jamaican Artists and Laborers Union struck against UFCo. The workers protested, among other factors, the company's practice of paying them in coupons redeemable at company stores. They created their own commissary where workers could buy goods for cash or credit, and they declared Jamaican Emancipation Day (August 1) a holiday. The banana company locked out 600 workers in retaliation. With the support of neither the Costa Rican government nor the British consulate (to which the strikers appealed for help because, being from Jamaica, they were all technically British citizens), the movement was doomed. The union had 5,000 members at its height, but by 1912 it had dissolved. This action was, however, not to be the last important strike against UFCo (Chomsky 1996, 154, 171).

Since the founding of UFCo in 1899, Limón Province had functioned as an enclave, where the banana company controlled its own plantations; docks and railways; and, only somewhat less directly, the independent farmers and workers who depended upon the company for their livelihoods. But unlike coffee workers' wages, banana workers' wages did not have much of an effect on the national economy. The United Fruit Company imported food and other necessities, which it then sold back to the workers for the wages they had just earned working for that same company. And UFCo paid no taxes on the goods it imported to sell. By the 1930s, the power of UFCo was excessive, and the abuses and harsh conditions were no longer suffered only by an immigrant Afro-Caribbean population easily ignored by the (often racist) citizenry in the Central Valley. White Hispanic workers had become a majority on the plantations, and their plight, together with the complaints of independent Costa Rican banana farmers, would finally find a more receptive audience in San José.

POLITICAL DEVELOPMENT, 1824–1870

Because Costa Rica's political and social history has been so much less violent and chaotic than the history of its Central American neighbors, it has often been assumed (or even asserted) that no serious difficulties were experienced in building Costa Rica's political democracy. Yet while the orderly and democratic transfer of power has not been interrupted since 1949, this was by no means the case from the republic's inception. Like most democracies, Costa Rica has had to struggle with the temptation to use force, rather than ballots, to transfer political power and to exclude, rather than include, important segments of the population from the benefits of citizenship. In fact, from 1824 until 1949, only 8 of 48 presidents assumed office as a result of clean and competitive elections (Lehoucq 1998, 27–28).

However, even when democratic rules were abused by leaders and citizens alike, the *idea* of democracy was always a valued aspect of Costa Rican national identity, and it often served to curb authoritarian excesses. In the first years following independence, the four principal towns elected several *juntas de gobierno,* or local councils, to govern the affairs of the community. Even as a nominal member of the Central American federation, Costa Rica adopted its own constitution that invested a popularly elected legislative assembly with much more power than the executive branch. This early experience of popular participation in government, and the negative example of authoritarianism and civil conflict elsewhere in the Central American federation, led Costa Ricans to link their national identity to the ideals of democracy and domestic tranquility. Reality often differed significantly from the ideal, but the ideal was still influential.

The unpleasant experience of Braulio Carrillo, the first Costa Rican president to baldly state that he intended to rule for life, illustrated the importance his countrymen attached to democratic appearances. When Francisco Morazán, a famous Honduran champion of Central American unity, arrived to depose Carrillo in April 1842, the very military forces Carrillo had centralized in San José would not defend the local dictator from the foreign invader. Carrillo went into exile, but Morazán's dictatorial tendencies and attempts to tax Costa Ricans and mobilize them to fight for the restoration of the Central American federation did not serve him much better. Five months after he arrived, a popular uprising in San José led to his summary trial and execution on the central plaza.

The execution of Morazán, however, would not rid the country of dictators for good. From 1842 until 1871, Costa

Rica had six constitutions. Between 1846 and 1870 there were seven *golpes de estado*—occasions when the presidential succession was determined by small groups of armed men tied to competing factions of the ruling coffee oligarchy (Vega Carballo 1981, 239; Holden 2004, 99). Typically, these events would be preceded by efforts to elicit popular discontent with whoever was in power, or with a particular candidate near election time, and would be followed by fraudulent elections to legitimate whoever had emerged victorious. But not until 1870 did any of the officers involved in the golpe install himself as president. The military plotters were under the firm control of rival factions of the coffee elite that controlled the patronage, privileges, and policies of the growing state. The limited scuffles in the capital did not prevent the coffee-laden oxcarts from making their way down to the port at Puntarenas and returning with imported (and taxed) goods from the outside world. Public lands continued to be claimed and distributed. Profitable side businesses like finance that were intricately tied to the government created ample opportunity for factional rivalries and conflicts of interest. Without a firm commitment to decide winners and losers through popular elections, however, the recourse to intrigue and revolt was inevitable.

This problem became more acute after Costa Rica's participation in the successful expulsion of the North American adventurer William Walker from Nicaragua in 1856–1857. Walker and his fellow soldiers of fortune had taken advantage of the civil wars between Nicaraguan liberals and conservatives to intervene there, first to aid the conservatives, and then to declare Walker "president for life." As president of Nicaragua, his goal was to reunite Central America and annex it to the United States as a slave state. Costa Rican president Juan Rafael Mora joined the broader Central American effort to expel the "filibusters," as they were called. Mora's army defeated Walker's troops at Santa Rosa

William Walker, self-proclaimed president of Nicaragua from 1856 to 1858, is the principal villain of Costa Rican history. His defeat by Costa Rican forces still inspires patriotism. (Library of Congress)

in northern Guanacaste and then pursued Walker across the border to win a second decisive battle at Rivas.

The battle against Walker produced Costa Rica's first national hero, the humble Juan Santamaría, who died setting fire to a building where the invaders had holed up. Since Costa Rica had fought no wars for independence, until 1856 it had no national struggle and no heroes around whom to construct a patriotic ideal. The war against Walker provided both of these. But wartime conditions and poor hygiene also sparked a cholera epidemic that killed roughly 10 percent of the already scarce national population and aggravated the problem of military intervention in politics. Less humble war heroes returned with greater enthusiasm for the military than was customary in a country that was notoriously slack in arming, training, and even clothing its troops. Despite the country's exhaustion from the war and the disease that followed, the golpes intensified until one of those heroes, Colonel Tomás Guardia, gained control of the government in 1870 and ruled as a virtual dictator until his death in 1882.

ORDER AND PROGRESS: THE CONSTITUTION OF 1871 AND THE LIBERAL STATE

Although he ruled as a dictator, ironically, Guardia contributed to the consolidation of a more truly liberal and, eventually, more democratic state. Most importantly, Guardia's dominance of the military made it possible to bring the barracks under his firm personal control, thus ending the chaotic military interventions in politics of his time. As a military man, and as a leader responding to a series of real threats in the region, Guardia increased the size of the army and modernized it with new weapons and training. Spending on the military increased notably, but most of Costa Rica's potential soldiers (nearly 30,000, including militia and reserve forces) were not on active duty (Vega Carballo 1981, 269). Indeed, at the height of Guardia's power in 1880, only 353 active-duty soldiers manned the nation's garrisons, outnumbered by the 628 schoolteachers in the nation's public school system (Holden 2004, 100).

As the army was brought under control, a constitution drafted in 1871 established new rules of the political and economic game, many of which are still in effect today. The new constitution concentrated a great deal of power in the executive branch, giving the president the right to name and remove all cabinet ministers, to convoke the legislature (and to suspend constitutional guarantees during the nine months of the year when it was not in session), and to name provincial governors and other local government officials. Local government officials supervised elections. The power to name these officials, together with control of the armed forces, put at the disposal of future presidents a political machine that made it very difficult for opposition candidates to win elections.

Suffrage was not universal, secret, or direct at this time, and the president's ability to manipulate elections further limited citizens' rights to choose their leaders. However, the 1871 Constitution firmly guaranteed other rights that limited the state's ability to interfere in private affairs. Costa Ricans were guaranteed equality before the law, freedom of transit, the right to peaceful association, privacy in one's home and correspondence, freedom of speech, protection against arbitrary arrest (*habeas corpus*), and protection against retroactive laws. And, above all else in an enthusiastically liberal society, Costa Ricans were guaranteed the right to private property (Vargas Arias 2002, 304).

According to the liberal belief of the time, "order" of the sort established by Guardia and "liberty" of the sort guaranteed in the Constitution of 1871 would pave the way for "progress." Above all, progress meant scientific thinking and economic development. Such ideas were influential throughout Latin America at the time. Costa Rica, however, was luckier than many of its Central American neighbors in that by the late 19th century it actually enjoyed economic advancement, thanks to its early promotion of coffee exports. It would soon be on its way to constructing that all-important symbol of 19th-century progress: the railroad. Unfortunately for Guardia, he did not live to see the railroad completed; he died of natural causes during the last months of his second term as president as he awaited the results of the elections that were to produce his successor.

Próspero Fernández, who was elected president soon after Guardia's death in 1882, furthered the liberal agenda with such arrogant confidence that his cohort of politicians became known as the "Olympus Generation." This generation would consolidate its political power by attacking its strongest rival for influence in Costa Rican society: the Catholic Church. It would reform the education system to try to create the mentality necessary, as they saw it, to make Costa Rica even more peaceful and prosperous. And it would use the country's economic success to modernize the cities of the Central Valley.

Even in a country where the Catholic Church was weak, anticlericalism was a reliable way to rally liberal forces. In July and August 1884, Fernández expelled the bishop of San José and the entire Jesuit order from the country, secularized the cemeteries, prohibited monastic orders, canceled the republic's special relationship with the Vatican, prohibited the collection of funds for the church without government authorization, forbade priests to collect fees for conducting funerals, and prohibited religious processions outside of church sanctuaries (Vargas Arias 2002, 312). Religious education was also removed from public schools. These measures were very much in the spirit of the time in Latin America, and the liberals saw them as necessary in order to create a modern citizenry free of what they believed were the ignorance and prejudice perpetuated by popular

Christianity. Most of these measures were, however, later moderated or reversed (although the Jesuits never returned to Costa Rica). Still, they indicated that the construction of a nation governed by law and "progressive" public opinion would come at the initial expense of the church.

Establishing the supremacy of the state in a country that had become tired of Guardia's military also meant strengthening Costa Ricans' respect for the law (and lawyers). While it might be difficult today to share the excitement that attended the publication of modernized civil, penal, and procedural codes, they were seen by 19th-century liberals as revolutionary steps forward into a world governed by reason. Próspero Fernández and his successor, Bernardo Soto, oversaw the completion of these legal reforms in the 1880s. With their completion came some very practical changes in daily life. Marriage required only a civil ceremony recorded in the Civil Registry, and divorce became a legal right. Transfers of property required (and still require) the services of a lawyer and notary, and property rights were only secure if they were properly recorded in the Public Registry in San José. In a more general sense, these changes meant that, in the words of one historian, "the future belonged more to the lawyer than to the priest" (Molina Jiménez 1991, 327).

Unsurprisingly, the aggressive reforms of the Olympians generated resistance from the priests. The silent majority of Costa Ricans also resented these reforms, because they still looked to popular Catholicism to make sense of life and to parish priests to defend them from manipulation by the powerful. This resistance found political expression in the elections of 1889, which official history books mark as a sort of "second birth" of democracy in Costa Rica. The election pitted outgoing President Bernardo Soto and his political machine against an opposition candidate supported by the Catholic Church.

The opposition candidacy of José Joaquín Rodríguez attracted those who thought the attacks on the church had gone too far. Later developments suggest that Rodríguez might also have attracted those who had not benefited from the brave new world of order and progress—farmers who lost their land to those with more capital or better connections in San José and artisans unable to compete with imported goods. As the first round of elections came to a close in November 1889, it became clear that although Rodríguez had won, President Soto was preparing the usual tricks to impose his chosen successor, Ascención Esquivel. The police appeared in the streets of San José cheering Esquivel, and the official Liberal Party floated the word that the army would help to steal the election from Rodríguez. In response, armed supporters of Rodríguez converged on San José, Cartago, and Heredia from surrounding villages to defend the results of the election. After considerable tension, some sporadic violence, and negotiations, Soto acquiesced to the wishes of the armed citizenry, and the election results were respected (Molina and Palmer 2004, 146–148). The corner had not been turned, however, on authoritarianism and electoral fraud in Costa Rica.

Nor was the Catholic Church able to effectively employ the political capital gained in 1889 to force important concessions to the church or to those suffering the effects of the liberal reforms of the 1880s. Soon after his election, Rodríguez reopened the public schools to religious education, but only as an optional activity. This was far short of what Catholics had hoped for. Abandoned by a state that had given the church special status for more than 300 years, Bishop Bernardo Thiel began to develop a stronger social agenda in the early 1890s. The church briefly turned its attention toward dispossessed farmers and artisans hurt by new imports, as well as toward others made marginal and insecure by the late 19th-century export economy. With the active support of priests, the Catholic Union Party was formed soon after the events of 1889. Also, taking a cue from Pope Leo XIII, who in 1891 inaugurated the tradition of

Catholic social teaching with an encyclical letter on the plight of industrial workers in Europe, Thiel circulated a pastoral letter of his own, "On the Just Salary." The letter infuriated liberals who believed fervently that the market should be left alone to determine wages. Some even condemned Thiel as a socialist.

Thiel's letter and the popularity of the Catholic Union Party also served as an implicit warning to liberals that the church could become a troublesome voice for the poor (Picado 1989, 59–65). Indeed, in 1894 the liberal oligarchy felt compelled to intervene yet again to falsify elections that seemed to favor the Catholic Union Party. The victors in those fraudulent elections went on to reform the Costa Rican constitution in 1895 to prohibit the use of explicitly religious messages in elections. The door on direct church participation in party politics was closed (Vargas Arias 2002, 313). While this measure would seem to indicate a continuation of the aggressive tactics of the 1880s, the adversarial relationship that had developed between the Catholic Church and the liberal state had become increasingly uncomfortable for both sides. The liberals had clearly won the contest, but they also realized that further conflict with the church had become counterproductive. In 1899, a council of Latin American bishops prohibited the participation of priests in politics throughout the region. By the first decade of the 20th century, the Catholic Church had accepted the role it had been assigned by the liberal state: guarantor of the moral order upon which the broader political and economic order depended (Picado 1989, 76–77).

EDUCATION AND MODERNIZATION

The Catholic Church had always felt that one of the most important means it had to exercise influence over the population was education. The liberals, however, believed that the state must be responsible for educational reform, not only to consolidate political control but also to form more literate and economically productive citizens loyal to the state and conscious of their identity as Costa Ricans. This was a difficult task, considering that the first school had not been founded until 1814, at the very end of the colonial period. By 1828, the various municipalities were charged with improving and maintaining elementary schools, but ten years later, only fifty-eight schools had been established and no real teacher training was taking place. There was no school for girls until 1849, and even then it had a domestic (sewing, cooking, child care) rather than an academic emphasis. In 1843, the University of Santo Tomás was founded, yet even as late as the 1860s, the government was only beginning to create a system of secondary schools to prepare students to enter the university. In 1864, the illiteracy rate was around 90 percent (Quesada Camacho 1991, 45; Molina and Palmer 2006, 57).

Attempts were made to reform and consolidate the system and to improve teacher training in 1869 and again in 1886. The role of the Catholic Church, which had, since the colonial period, given all education a religious focus, was sharply curtailed in the 1880s. The state was to provide education for both boys and girls, and it was to be obligatory and free of charge. This education was based on positivist ideas—ideas of the influential 19th-century philosophy that promoted scientific thinking and practical ends. The emphasis remained on elementary education. (The university, except for a few departments, was closed in 1888, as it was poorly organized and lacked qualified professors. A new national university did not open until 1940.) In 1892, the illiteracy rate was still 65 percent, and many families still preferred not to send their children to school because they needed children's labor on the farm or in the workshop. Continued colonization also played a role in low attendance; as families moved out from established settlements, they also moved away from the schools (Molina Jiménez 2000, 28).

In 1894, three types of elementary schools were created. One offered education only through the second grade, one through the fourth, and one through the fifth. In the majority of schools outside of the Central Valley, only two years of schooling were available (Quesada Camacho 1991, 44). In that same year, 8 percent of school-age children attended school. While this figure was better than the 3 percent in Nicaragua, it was less than the 9.6 percent in Argentina (Molina Jiménez 2000, 31). The Costa Rican educational system had certainly improved over the 19th century and would continue to improve in the 20th century with the establishment of a normal school for teacher training (1914) and the founding of many more secondary schools. Yet, by the turn of the century, what educational reformers had created was an extremely hierarchical and geographically unequal system. There were always more, and more advanced, schools in the Central Valley than in the rest of the country. In reality, several school systems—not a single, unified system—served distinct social classes. By the late 1940s, nearly 100,000 students were enrolled in Costa Rican schools, but a way would have to be found to better consolidate the education system if the country was to continue to develop economically as well as politically (Quesada Camacho 1991, 41, 43). An improved education system was not only an important investment but it was also (along with the railroad) an important *symbol* of modernization in the late 19th and early 20th centuries. One can imagine that education's symbolism was similar to the symbolism of computers in the 21st century.

The profits from the coffee boom made a number of other material improvements possible, and these improvements signified to the Costa Ricans that they were moving into the modern world. If modern amenities were seen only in San José, and to some extent for the other towns in the Central Valley, they still marked an important change in the country. Life in rural and urban areas became more distinctly different than it had ever been before. In San José, for instance, water tanks and iron pipes were installed in 1867, and by 1892, a sewer system was in place. The telegraph arrived in 1869, and in 1884, San José was the first city in Central America to have electric lights. In 1899, a trolley car provided public transportation in San José, crossing the city both north to south and east to west. In 1910, the construction of the rail line to the Pacific was finished. The first theater opened in 1850. In 1897, the much larger and more elegant National Theater was inaugurated so that Costa Rica would have an appropriate venue in which to host visiting European actors and opera singers. Other institutions such as the National Archive (1881), the National Museum (1887), and the National Library (1888) were also felt by Costa Ricans to be important signs of their advancement.

The masses also enjoyed new, more modern pastimes. Visitors to San José in the 1850s had complained that there was nothing to do, but by the 1880s, gymnasiums, billiards halls, skating rinks, circuses, and bullfights all offered diversion. Residents had also established an assortment of hotels, restaurants, and clubs. Pastimes like cockfighting that had been very popular in the 1850s seemed uncouth by the 1880s; at the turn of the 20th century, soccer, imported from the United Kingdom, was much more popular. By 1912, a national soccer league was already established, with eight teams and two divisions. Musical societies and municipal bands also enjoyed great popularity. By the beginning of the 20th century, 36 "municipal philharmonics" were performing (Fumero Vargas 2002, 339, 342).

Since the colonial period, the upper classes had always lived near the central plaza, but beginning in the 1890s, with their new money, the coffee elites began to build houses for themselves outside of the city center. These suburbs were still within what might be considered walking distance now, but their style was completely new. They were not the traditional Spanish style with interior courtyards. Instead, the

A wonderful example of the public architecture made possible by the coffee boom, the Old Post Office is one of the few remaining 19th-century buildings in downtown San José. (Photo by Meg Mitchell)

upper classes copied new architectural trends from Europe and the United States, and their neoclassical, Victorian, or even Arab-style houses were filled with imported furniture and china in the latest fashion (Cuevas Molina 2002, 422). This wealth was all very new for Costa Rica. Only a hundred years before this country had such a scarcity of currency that the citizens had resorted to using cacao beans as money.

As the country entered the 20th century, some Costa Ricans came to see that if rapid change brought many benefits, it also led to new and intense social problems. The population of the country had increased from around 100,000 in 1850 to 250,000 at the turn of the century. It would almost double again by 1927, and by then the population of San José alone reached 50,000 (Hall 1985, 99, 131). In 1902, one newspaper commentator noted that the city of San José was the first to feel the effects of "progress in the modification of customs, for both the better and the worse. And thus [the citizens] began to complain there about pool halls and night clubs that encouraged vagrancy; of prostitution that sickened youth; of alcohol that turned the people into brutes . . . of the theft of coffee and counterfeit money. . . . But on the other hand they also spoke of the paving of the streets, the beauty of the city, [and] the construction of public buildings" (*Revista de Costa Rica en el siglo XIX,* 1902, cited in Vega Carballo 1981, 64–65). Calls were made for new laws to control new social problems like prostitution and heroin addiction, and much hand-wringing took place over where all this might lead Costa Rican society (see Marín Hernandez 2005; Palmer 2005). In 1849 and again in 1906, new rules were written governing the police force. A vagrancy law went into effect in 1878, and a new penal code was written in 1880. In 1909, a new jail of the most modern sort was opened in San José (Fumero Vargas 2002, 349–350).

ECONOMIC CRISIS AND CHALLENGES TO THE LIBERAL ORDER

In 1914, however, it became painfully clear how much this material progress depended on foreign markets. Germany and the United Kingdom were two of the principal markets for coffee and sources of imports and investment, and when they went to war, along with the United States, the biggest buyer of Costa Rican bananas, the Costa Rican government's finances immediately collapsed. The coffee oligarchy had imposed a system of government finance that depended almost exclusively on import taxes. Between 1913 and 1915 imports fell 50 percent. This decrease cut the government's tax base in half and left President Alfredo González Flores looking for a way to fill the gap (Salazar 1995, 37–38).

The solutions at hand were representative of a changing attitude toward liberalism in the developed countries of Europe and North America, and also in Latin America. In some cases by accident, in many cases because of the immediate challenges of World War I, and increasingly by design, the role of government in economic affairs was increasing. The growth of labor unions, the concern expressed by many political actors and by the Catholic Church about the social problems that came along with modernization, as well as historic upheavals like the Mexican Revolution (1910–1920) indicated that the age of classical liberalism was coming to a close. No longer would the supposedly benign and impartial laws of the marketplace be trusted to resolve all problems.

Costa Rica's president González focused his efforts on credit and taxes to try to more equally distribute the cost of pulling the economy out of crisis and of sustaining a more activist government. After several failed attempts, González's government managed to create a state bank, the Banco Internacional, which attempted to channel credit to small producers and give them an alternative to the more onerous conditions imposed by private banks. What created more resistance, however, were González's decrees creating new direct taxes on property and a progressive income tax (Salazar 1995, 47–52).

In attempting to shift the tax burden away from consumers of imports and toward producers while promoting the idea of a more activist state, González was testing the limits of Costa Rican liberalism. In January 1917, the minister of war, General Federico Tinoco, led a revolt that removed González under the dubious pretext that he planned to impose himself for a second consecutive term in 1918. Tinoco established himself as a transitional head of state while elections were held for a new president and a constituent assembly to write a new constitution. Since González had created many powerful enemies through his attempted reforms without ever creating an enthusiastic base of working-class allies, Tinoco's election to the presidency in April of the same year was probably a fair reflection of the public mood (Salazar 1995, 68).

Regardless of Costa Rican public sentiment, the U.S. government refused to recognize the Tinoco administration. This lack of recognition, together with other sanctions, worsened the economic climate and undermined Tinoco's brief popularity. The dictatorial practices of Tinoco and his brother Joaquín (the new minister of war) also contributed to the growth of a strong opposition movement. By 1919, an armed movement of Costa Ricans had organized in Nicaragua. Under the leadership of Julio Acosta García, the "Revolution of Sapoá" invaded Costa Rica on May 5, 1919, and took positions along the northern frontier. Meanwhile in San José, several strikes broke out, most notably one by teachers and students of the Liceo de Costa Rica and the women's Colegio Superior de Señoritas. In mid-June 1919, teachers and students together braved the threats and aggressions of the police and demonstrated in the heart of the capital. By July, the U.S. government was coming under pressure to expel the Tinoco brothers and actually sent a Navy ship to Limón Harbor to signal its impatience. In August, the Tinocos were clearly preparing to leave, but not soon enough. Joaquín Tinoco was assassinated on the street near his home. His brother Federico, the president, resigned and fled the country the next day (Salazar 1995, 80–86).

In new elections demanded both by the United States and elements of the domestic opposition, the leader of the Revolution of Sapoá, Julio Acosta García, was elected president at the end of 1919. Yet very little was "revolutionary" about Acosta's government. Once again, the coffee oligarchy regained control of the situation and steered the country back onto a relatively normal liberal path. The Constitution of 1871 was restored, and González Flores's attempted tax reforms were forgotten, or so it was hoped. To the disappointment of the coffee elite, though, the early 1920s seemed to

Julio Acosta García led a rebellion that helped bring about the end of the Tinoco dictatorship in 1919. He was president from 1920 to 1924. (Library of Congress)

shift the momentum gained in the expulsion of the Tinocos toward efforts to reform the liberal economic order. Workers in San José successfully struck for the eight-hour day and pressed for other reforms in 1920 (Salazar 1995, 106). Even in Guanacaste, a frontier region with scant government presence, the early 1920s brought a significant upsurge of social conflict between cattle ranchers and squatters. And in Limón Province, the banana workers went on strike in 1921, continuing a growing trend toward conflict with UFCo that began in 1910.

Despite these conflicts in Limón and Guanacaste, politics was still very much an affair of San José, and social or political change would necessarily originate in the Central Valley. It was one of President Acosta's comrades in the Revolution of Sapoá, Jorge Volio Jiménez, who emerged there as a popular advocate of reform. Jorge Volio was one of the more interesting figures in 20th-century Costa Rican history. An ex-priest from Cartago, he had studied in a Belgian seminary and, later in his life, fought briefly alongside the Nicaraguan rebel leader Augusto César Sandino in his efforts to expel U.S. Marines from that country. After the departure of Tinoco, Volio was elected to the legislature, and in 1923, he was chosen by the country's principal workers' confederation to lead the new Costa Rican National Reformist Party.

The Reformist Party took an ambitious platform into the 1924 election. Volio's Catholicism impelled him to fight for social reform, but it did not translate into any preference for a greater influence of the church in politics. The Reformist Party called for a new constitution that would respect the country's democratic aspirations but put the state in charge of mediating relations between capital and labor, rich and poor, in pursuit of the common good. Among a long list of specific demands in the party program were freedom of religion; municipal autonomy; agrarian reform; the formation of cooperatives; programs to fight illiteracy, poor health, and malnutrition; and the foundation of a university and system of vocational schools. More pointedly, Volio and the Reformists insisted on revisiting the question of a more just system of direct taxation—precisely the issue that led to the overthrow of President González Flores.

Volio's candidacy was a truly popular one, and the Reformist program was in step with similar demands being made in other Latin American countries at the time. But it did not prosper at the polls in 1924: Volio and his party came in third place, behind two more traditionally liberal parties. However, because no candidate got a majority of the votes, the victor would be determined in the legislature, where the reformers had won a strategic bloc of seats and decided to throw their support to ex-President Ricardo Jiménez Oreamuno. The decision was made with the understanding that Volio and other Reformists would participate in the government and that their program would be adopted by Jiménez.

Jiménez named Volio and other Reformist leaders to important government positions and, with Reformist support in the legislature, passed two important measures. In 1924, the insurance industry became a government monopoly, creating the forerunner of today's Instituto Nacional de Seguros (National Insurance Institute). In 1925, Costa Rica took another step toward free and fair elections. During Jiménez's first administration, in 1913, an electoral college system had been eliminated, opening the way for direct election of the president. Now, in his second administration, Jiménez and the Reformists pushed for the adoption of a secret ballot, eliminating in 1925 one of the most obvious sources of electoral manipulation. Despite a spirited suffragist campaign in the 1920s, women would not gain the right to vote until 1949.

Perhaps inevitably, some felt Volio had erred in his alliance with the liberal Jiménez, regardless of the incremental reforms made possible by the relationship. Indeed, the

Reformist Party never again attained the support and influence it enjoyed in 1924. Volio continued to accept subordinate alliances with liberal candidates in the 1928 and 1932 elections. By 1936, both Volio and the Reformist Party had disappeared from Costa Rican politics (Salazar 1995, 123).

However, the movement for social reform was not long without a leader. In 1931, the Workers and Peasants Bloc (as the Costa Rican Communist Party was known) was founded under the leadership of Manuel Mora Valverde. Mora had been frustrated with Volio's decision to ally with the liberals in the 1920s, and he was convinced that only a revolutionary government of workers and peasants could eliminate private property and bring social justice to Costa Rica. Yet this commitment to the idea of an eventual revolution, expressed as it often was with fiery rhetoric, did not prevent the communists from playing the democratic game for the foreseeable future. The party's "minimum program," proclaimed in 1931, acknowledged that Costa Rica's underdeveloped economy and dependence on the United States and other imperialist powers made an immediate social revolution impossible. Instead, the party would participate in the political system to demand far-reaching reforms. These reforms included practical measures like a social security system, labor regulations to protect children and guarantee women equal pay for equal work, the right to organize unions and to strike, the suppression of the state-owned liquor factory, agrarian reform, civil-service legislation, and improvements in education and infrastructure (Edelman and Kenen 1989, 74–76). Many of these demands would actually be fulfilled beginning in the 1940s, which indicates that the communists were not too far ahead of more mainstream reformers.

Yet the communists' first big achievement came in 1934, when they helped to organize the largest strike of banana workers (nearly 10,000) ever attempted in Central America. Although the Communist Party had been founded in San

José, it quickly became involved with the situation of the banana workers of the Caribbean. This involvement was a result of a decision by the national government to exile for a year one Carlos Luis Fallas ("Calufa") to the banana zone in punishment for a seditious May Day speech in 1933. Fallas was the son of a shoemaker in Alajuela who began to work at a very young age. At 16 he was working in Limón, first as a dockworker and then at the various grueling tasks involved in hacking banana farms out of the tropical forest. After six years in the banana kingdom, Fallas returned to Alajuela to become a shoemaker himself and eventually an activist in the workers' movement. By the time the government exiled him to Limón in 1933 he was well acquainted with the conditions there, and he was able to use his skills as an organizer to convince the workers to resist (Paige 1997, 135–136).

Conditions had deteriorated markedly since Calufa's first tour in Limón, as the Great Depression and a banana disease, "Panama disease," had together decimated the banana industry. The United Fruit Company, taking advantage of its control of transportation and marketing, responded to the Depression by buying fruit at low prices or simply refusing to buy it all, regardless of contracts signed with independent farmers. The contracts were full of loopholes that allowed the company to reject fruit for any reason whatsoever. The independent farmers, in turn, tried to deflect costs onto workers, who would be paid for picking and hauling only the bananas that were ultimately bought by the company. The situation was untenable, even for workers accustomed to horrible conditions, and fueled the month-long strike in August 1934.

The United Fruit Company used every lever at its disposal to break the strike, including the promotion of racial conflict between Hispanic and Afro-Caribbean workers. In the end, the strike was broken by police intervention, and no one was killed. The absence of fatalities is notable, as only two years earlier roughly 30,000 peasants had been massacred in nearby El Salvador following a failed communist insurrection there. The banana strike was not much of a success in terms of the workers' demands; the strike seems to have driven UFCo to make the final decision to shut down the Atlantic coast banana industry and move to the Pacific side of the country, where Panama disease did not affect the crops. Even worse for Afro-Caribbean workers (who had not even always supported the strike), UFCo and its jobs were moving to a zone where they were forbidden to follow: a 1934 law forbade UFCo from hiring "noncitizen" workers in its new Pacific plantations. This was a measure obviously intended to confine English-speaking Afro-Caribbean immigrants to Limón Province. Only one legislator, the Communist Party general secretary, Manuel Mora, who had been elected in 1934, voted against it (Chomsky 1996, 254). The strike was a success in other ways, however. It demonstrated the organizing skills of the communists, and it inspired Carlos Luis Fallas's realist novel about life in the banana zone, *Mamita Yunai*. Published in 1941, this became one of the single most important and controversial works of Costa Rican literature in the 20th century.

THE CRISIS OF THE EXPORT MODEL

While the 1934 banana strike had indicated that the export economy of the Atlantic coast was plagued with problems, other economic problems were becoming evident in the Central Valley. The effects of the stock market crash of 1929 and the world depression that followed were immediate and harsh in tiny dependent Costa Rica. Coffee prices and export volumes fell drastically. Adopting a strategy similar to that of UFCo in Limón, the coffee processors in the Central Valley attempted to take advantage of their control of purchasing, processing, and exporting to shift as much of the burden of the crisis as possible onto small independent producers. The political context was different with coffee than with bananas, however, because the aggrieved party occupied an exalted place in Costa Rica's national mythology. Small coffee growers were considered, at least rhetorically, to constitute the bedrock of Costa Rican society, while banana workers (often black and English-speaking) were still thought of as strange "foreigners." Coffee growers used their image to their advantage and successfully pressed the government to create the Costa Rican Institute for the Defense of Coffee in 1933. The Institute was intended to regulate the potentially exploitative relationship between processors and small growers by setting a legal limit on the profit that the processors could make buying cheap and selling dear. Although the more powerful processors managed to gain control of the Institute and its policies, thus limiting the benefits to small growers, the principle of government intervention in the coffee industry had been established and would become extremely important in the 1950s.

Even more importantly, in 1936 another institution was founded that would later become crucial to Costa Rica's distinctive path of economic development in the second half of the 20th century. The National Bank of Costa Rica came into existence as part of a broad package of banking reforms intended to better regulate the financial sector and to increase access to credit for small producers of important food crops. At the time of its creation, the Banco Nacional was simply one of several banks in Costa Rica, most of them private. Following the Civil War of 1948, the Banco Nacional would become a powerful monopoly, strategically manipulating savings and credit in a successful effort to diversify and democratize the Costa Rican economy.

Such institutions became increasingly necessary because the age of extensive growth (simply expanding the frontier to plant more coffee or bananas) was coming to an end. Much of the land suitable for coffee was already occupied, and the yields per acre were dropping. In the banana industry, monoculture had opened the way for disease, and the infection of much of the banana land on the Atlantic with Panama disease caused UFCo to move most of its operations to the Pacific coast. Export agriculture had been a very effective and profitable way to use Costa Rica's natural resources and geographical setting—the rich volcanic soils and the cool climate of the highlands and the hot tropical lowlands of the coastal regions—to the best advantage. Yet as Costa Ricans continued to migrate to other regions of the country, they found the land was not always so fertile once the forest cover was removed. To continue to grow crops for export, farmers would need more capital and technological inputs like fertilizer and pesticide. How would the export model continue to be feasible for Costa Rica in the second half of the 20th century?

MACHINE POLITICS, REFORM, AND THE CIVIL WAR OF 1948

While modest economic reforms, such as the establishment of the National Insurance Institute, the Costa Rican Institute for the Defense of Coffee, and the National Bank, helped create the framework for the country's later successful economic development, the chronic troubles of the first decades of the 20th century pointed to the fact that *political* reform was still urgently needed. The 1871 Constitution had invested the presidency with great power to manipulate elections. The president could control who won elections and, thus, who would have access to government jobs and who would face marginalization, even persecution. Those who lost elections could either accept the results and fight another day or reject them and fight immediately. Given the high stakes of presidentialism, the temptation for the president to use his political machine and for the opposition to consider violent insurrection was wholly logical.

In order to reduce the chances of insurrection and political instability, in the first years of the 20th century the ruling faction had been forced to accept certain changes that reduced presidential prerogatives. After 1910, the president was no longer able to rule by decree without the approval of the full legislature. Under these conditions, it became more important for opposition parties to hold a significant number of seats in the legislature in order to defend themselves from an authoritarian president. And if opposition parties lost the presidency but were permitted to gain seats in the legislature, the chance of insurrection was also greatly reduced. Other incremental changes, such as the direct election of members of the legislature (1913) and the introduction of the secret ballot (1925), went a long way toward cleaning up the electoral process, but they did not resolve the central problem: the presidential temptation to use the considerable tools that remained to him to shut the opposition completely out of power (Lehoucq 1998, 36–50).

In 1932, this problem and the suspicion it created in opposition circles led to a dramatic attempt to prevent the election of the ruling party's favorite candidate, two-time ex-President Ricardo Jiménez Oreamuno. The election to succeed President Cleto González Víquez (himself a two-time president) was slated to be sent into the legislature after no candidate received a clear majority. Before the legislature could decide, however, Manuel Castro Quesada determined that, short of violence, his opponent, Jiménez, could not be stopped from taking office for a third term. On the morning of February 15, a week after the inconclusive election and 10 weeks before the legislature was scheduled to pick a winner, Castro Quesada (accompanied by Jorge Volio, the fading leader of the Reformist Party) took over the Bellavista barracks in downtown San José (today's National Museum). The "Bellavistazo," as it came to be known, was a violent episode. San José residents fled to the countryside while the rebels and the official forces skirmished and negotiated an end to the failed revolt. Fifteen people died and thirty-six were wounded before the besieged rebels surrendered and were allowed to go free, with their lives and continued liberty guaranteed (Salazar 1995, 157).

The 1936 and 1940 elections were uneventfully won by the representatives of the coffee oligarchy. However, in the 1940s perennial electoral suspicions, a highly charged international ideological climate, and a controversial push forward on social reform combined to shatter the old rules of Costa Rican liberalism. The story of this decisive decade begins with the landslide election of Dr. Rafael Ángel Calderón Guardia as president in 1940. Calderón was a member in good standing of the coffee oligarchy and great-grandson of Tomás Guardia. He was the chosen candidate of his predecessor, President León Cortés, who planned to continue exercising influence behind the scenes and to run for office again in 1944.

Calderón, however, was full of surprises. Like Jorge Volio, Calderón had studied at the Catholic University of Louvain in Belgium and adopted the Catholic social reform ideology prevalent there. Based on the papal encyclicals that began in the 1890s, this philosophy rejected the Marxist notion of class struggle but called for harmony to be established between capital and labor through government intervention to address the problems of workers. Calderón was particularly impressed with Pope Pius XI's encyclical *Quadragessimo Ano* that had been published in 1931 to mark 40 years of Catholic social teaching. Calderón and the National Republican Party ran on a reformist program and roundly defeated the communist candidate, Manuel Mora, who came in second with nearly 10 percent of the vote. Yet when he began to aggressively implement his campaign promises, Calderón quickly created enemies in the party that had carried him to power.

Calderón's first move was to create the University of Costa Rica in October 1940. A university not only fulfilled the hopes of earlier generations of reformists but it also provided the training ground for future generations of Costa Rica's burgeoning middle class. Calderón's next reform was directed toward the working classes. In November 1941, Calderón and the congress approved the legislation founding the Caja Costarricense de Seguro Social (Costa Rican Social Security Fund)—the obligatory social security fund that to this day provides the vast majority of social security and health services to Costa Ricans. The system grew slowly after its initial passage and was heavily influenced in its design by experts from the International Labor Organization and by the example of a similar system in Chile. But by 1944, it insured nearly 40,000 urban workers (Salazar 1995, 213).

In October 1942, Calderón made a much bolder move, announcing to the legislature that it was time to amend the Constitution of 1871 to include "social guarantees" among the rights of citizens. Very much in the spirit of U.S. President Franklin Roosevelt and the Atlantic Charter, Calderón proclaimed that "A people that face problems of misery, abandoned children, and hopeless elderly cannot be politically free" (quoted in Salazar 1995, 207). This modern chapter in Costa Rica's constitution, approved in June 1943, proclaimed a long list of new rights, including the right to a minimum wage, an eight-hour workday, the right to form unions and to strike, the right to minimum conditions of workplace safety and hygiene, and the right to dignified housing. Once these principles were included in the constitution, the legislature went on to formalize the details in the Labor Code passed in September 1943.

By this time, Calderón had thoroughly alienated the coffee oligarchy, whose liberal ideology and financial interests were threatened by the new rights and institutions for workers. Calderón had to look urgently for a new political base if his presidency, and his reforms, were to survive. Mass demonstrations of workers and farmers had come out in support of the new institutions and the constitutional reforms in 1942 and 1943. And yet, to effectively consolidate this base, Calderón needed to reach out to Manuel Mora and the Communist Party and to Archbishop Victor Sanabria and the Catholic Church.

Fortunately for Calderón, conditions in 1943 were just right for an alliance with these traditionally antagonistic groups. Communist parties around the world had been given permission from Moscow since the 1930s to form alliances with just about any antifascist political force. Mora's party had successfully taken the electoral route from its foundation, and in Calderón's reforms they saw rapid progress toward many of the demands they had made in their minimum program in 1931. They were eager to defend those reforms as legitimate achievements of the workers' movement and were ready to support Calderón regardless of his oligarchic background. Archbishop Sanabria was not only aligned ideologically with Calderón's Catholic reformism but he was also indebted to him for abolishing the 19th-century laws that had restricted the church's participation in education and prohibited the establishment of religious orders. He genuinely wanted to support Calderón and also to defend the new rights of workers. The only stumbling block was that to do so he would have to ally with communists and permit Catholics to cooperate with communists in unions and other organizations. As it happened, a largely semantic compromise was reached. In exchange for Manuel Mora renouncing revolution and a formal relationship with the Communist International in Moscow and changing the party's name to the Popular Vanguard Party, Archbishop Sanabria released a letter stating it was permissible for Catholics in good conscience to cooperate with party members. In a famous photograph from 1943, the archbishop, the communist, and the reformist president stand together as strange but powerful allies.

Calderón put this alliance—the "Victory Bloc"—at the service of his chosen successor in the 1944 elections,

José Figueres Ferrer was the most important political figure of the 20th century: he led a successful revolt in 1948, was elected president twice, and founded the Partido de Liberación Nacional. (Organization of American States)

Teodoro Picado Michalsky. The opposition gathered around ex-President León Cortés. Cortés's followers were quite a mixed group. Naturally, members of the coffee and commercial oligarchy felt betrayed and were eager to defeat Calderón. But there were also two more modern groups in the opposition. José Figueres Ferrer, the son of Spanish immigrants and a largely self-made and self-educated man, was a virulent opponent of Calderón and led a segment of Cortés's party known as Democratic Action. Figueres considered Calderón a dictator and was also offended by his alliance with the communists. Figueres had been sent into exile in Mexico in 1942 after vehemently denouncing on the radio Calderón's decision to expropriate the property of German immigrants following a U-boat attack in Limón Harbor. During his exile he helped found a group called the Caribbean Legion dedicated to overthrowing dictators in Venezuela, Nicaragua, the Dominican Republic, and Costa Rica. Regardless of his status as an elected leader, Calderón was eventually marked as the first "dictator" to be removed by the Legion, and Figueres was to lead the effort. Thus, when he returned from Mexico in 1944, Figueres was able to add international support to his growing local network of anti-Calderonistas.

Figueres's desire for military action and his animosity toward Calderón and communism did not mean, however, that he was opposed to reform. Indeed, the key to understanding the events of the 1940s is to recognize that *both* sides in impending civil war were largely in agreement about the need for reform, but disagreed about how and by whom it should be implemented. A group of young law students gave a more elaborate and intellectually considered expression to this point of view than the more political Figueres. In 1940, a group of law students, professors, secondary school students, and middle-class professionals had formed the Center for the Study of National Problems. The center published a magazine and a series of studies on the opportunities and impediments to modernization in Costa Rica. Its most visible leader was 23-year-old Rodrigo Facio Brenes (for whom the main campus of the University of Costa Rica is now named). Facio and his colleagues agreed with Calderón that it was time for the state to step in, but not only to provide social services. They argued that though the fundamentals of a capitalist economy should not be abolished, the state *should* take measures to free Costa Rica from its excessive dependence on coffee, bananas, and foreign capital. Where they disagreed strongly with Calderón was in his willingness to work with the Communist Party and with what they saw as the disorderly and even corrupt way he had implemented the reform agenda. In their anticommunism and their faith in administration and technical solutions to problems, the *centristas* epitomized the rising middle class.

Amidst accusations of fraud, Picado and the Victory Bloc defeated Cortés in the 1944 elections. The opposition, including Democratic Action and the Center for the Study of National Problems, immediately turned their attention to the 1948 elections, when everyone assumed Calderón would seek reelection. Figueres was determined that this would not occur, and neither he nor anyone else in the opposition was appeased by Picado's much more cautious approach to the reform agenda. In 1945 Figueres's Democratic Action formally joined the Center for the Study of National Problems in the new Social Democratic Party. This modernizing party, however, was a minority in the opposition to Calderón. Hence, they chose to join with more traditional liberals who were tied to the coffee oligarchy and other business interests and led by newspaper publisher Otilio Ulate.

This charged political atmosphere found its lightning rod in the imperfect electoral system the political class had been tinkering with since 1871. An estimated 40,000 to 60,000 false voter identification cards were in circulation in the 1940s. This segment represented between one-third and one-fourth of the total electorate (Lehoucq 1998, 51). Whether or not Calderón used his presidential prerogatives to help Picado win the 1944 election, the opposition was convinced that he did. This belief was behind the demand for a further reform of the electoral system. In 1946, a new electoral code was passed that greatly reduced the ability of the president to manipulate the elections or control the officials charged with supervising them. Yet by then, the political climate had become so polarized that neither side trusted the new rules to prevent a fraud. The most dramatic evidence of this lack of confidence was the "strike of fallen arms" called to demand the integrity of the upcoming elections. For five days beginning July 27, 1947, opponents of Picado refused to open stores, factories, and banks throughout the Central Valley. The government fought the strike with various punitive and ameliorative measures, and "shock brigades" of communists and Calderonistas looted businesses without being stopped by the police (Salazar 1995, 249). The strike ended after negotiations produced further commitments from Picado that the voters' will would be respected.

When the day of the election arrived in February 1948, the opposition forces led by Otilio Ulate defeated the National Republican Party, led once again by Rafael Ángel Calderón Guardia, by 10 percent of the vote. But Calderón would not accept the results and made use of the Calderonista majority in the legislature to annul the presidential elections on March 1, 1948. This sort of situation was, of course, nothing new in the troubled history of Costa Rican democracy. Under more normal conditions the issue might have been solved by negotiations between Ulate and Calderón, or by a more controlled show of force. Figueres, however, was prepared to fight and had established a strong position in the mountains of Talamanca to the south of San José, with weapons and foreign fighters sent from allies in the Caribbean Legion.

The civil war began on March 8, near the southern town of San Isidro del General. Figueres quickly defeated the poorly armed and trained Costa Rican army and, from a stronghold near San Isidro, proceeded to take Puerto Limón by air on April 11. The next day he took Cartago, infiltrating the city by foot from the surrounding mountains under cover of fog (Ameringer 1978, 57). After fairly heavy fighting in Cartago, the stage was set for a bloodier battle for San José between Figueres's army and the communist militias known as "mariachis." At this point, Figueres and Manuel Mora met on Ochomogo, the high ground dividing the Atlantic from the Pacific slope, and Cartago from San José. These talks, where Figueres reportedly guaranteed Mora that no reprisals would be taken against the Communist Party, were the beginning of negotiations that would be completed on April 19 at the Mexican Embassy.

According to the pact reached there, Picado would resign in favor of an interim president. Officials of the Picado government were guaranteed safe conduct out of the country and, should they choose to stay, respect for their lives and property (Salazar 1995, 265). The Pact of the Mexican Embassy ended the war and prevented an ugly battle for control of the capital. Figueres and Ulate had agreed separately that once the rebel forces took control of San José, Figueres and the Founding Junta of the Second Republic would be allowed to govern unchecked for 18 months, with an option to extend for 6 more months. During that time, the Junta would convoke elections in December 1948 for a constituent assembly, which would write a new constitution. When the Junta's term expired, Ulate would assume the presidency for the four-year term he had won in the contested elections of 1948.

On May 8 the interim president turned power over to the Junta led by Figueres, and the process of building the institutions that govern Costa Rica to this day was begun.

Figueres's proclamation of a new republic certainly overstated the revolutionary implications of the civil war. The violence did not break the continuity of Costa Rica's liberal political and economic traditions, nor was it intended to. What it did was break an impasse that had developed in Costa Rican politics, which would have made addressing the problems that had accumulated in the country's first phase of extensive export-led growth more difficult.

The 1949 Constitution greatly reduced the power of the Costa Rican president. As a result, the electoral system and the government agencies responsible for social and economic development gained some autonomy from the political machinery that had been functioning (and malfunctioning) since 1871. Orderly transfers of power and an increasingly educated and professional public bureaucracy would help Costa Rica develop innovative solutions to the problems it shared with its Central American neighbors: economic dependence on a few exports, poverty and inequality, and potential for social conflict. Costa Rica's relative success in addressing these problems elevated the former colonial backwater to the status of a model for other developing countries. We will examine that model in the next chapters.

References

Alvarado Induni, Guillermo E. 2000. *Los volcanes de Costa Rica: Geología, historia, y riqueza natural.* 2nd ed. San José: Editorial Universidad Estatal a Distancia.

Ameringer, Charles D. 1978. *Don Pepe: A Political Biography of José Figueres of Costa Rica.* Albuquerque: University of New Mexico Press.

Augelli, John P. 1987. "Costa Rica's Frontier Legacy." *The Geographic Review* 77 (1): 1–16.

Blake, Beatrice, and Anne Becher. 2002. *The New Key to Costa Rica.* Berkeley, CA: Ulysses Press.

Bray, Warwick. 1981. "Goldwork." In *Between Continents/Between Seas: Pre-Columbian Art of Costa Rica.* New York: Henry Abrams, 153–166.

Bulmer-Thomas, Victor. 1987. *The Political Economy of Central America since 1920.* Cambridge: Cambridge University Press.

Cardoso, Ciro F. S. 1986. "Central America: The Liberal Era, c. 1870–1930." In Leslie Bethell, ed., *The Cambridge History of Latin America, vol. V: c. 1870 to 1930.* Cambridge: Cambridge University Press, 197–228.

Carmack, Robert M. 1994. "Perspectivas sobre la historia antigua de Centroamérica." In Robert M. Carmack, ed., *Historia general de Centroamérica, vol. I: Historia antigua.* San José: Facultad Latinamericana de Ciencias Sociales (FLACSO), 283–319.

Chomsky, Aviva. 1996. *West Indian Workers and the United Fruit Company in Costa Rica, 1870–1940.* Baton Rouge, LA: Louisiana State University Press.

Coates, Anthony G. 1997. "The Forging of Central America." In Anthony G. Coates, ed., *Central America: A Natural and Cultural History.* New Haven, CT: Yale University Press, 1–37.

Coe, Michael. 1962. "Costa Rican Archeology and Mesoamerica." *Southwestern Journal of Anthropology* 18 (2): 170–183.

Colón, Hernando. 1947. *Vida del almirante Don Cristobal Colón, escrito por su hijo Hernando Colón.* Ramon Iglesia, ed. Mexico City: Fondo de Cultura Económica.

Cooke, Richard. 1997. "The Native Peoples of Central America during Pre-Columbian and Colonial Times." In Anthony G. Coates, ed., *Central America: A Natural and Cultural History.* New Haven, CT: Yale University Press, 137–176.

Corrales Ulloa, Francisco. 2002. "Más de diez mil años de historia precolombina." In Ana Maria Botey Sobrado, ed., *Costa Rica: Desde las sociedades autóctonas hasta 1914.* San José: Editorial de la Universidad de Costa Rica, 25–66.

Cuevas Molina, Rafael. 2002. "Cambio cultural en Costa Rica, 1821–1914." In Ana Maria Botey, ed., *Costa Rica: de las sociedades autóctonas a 1914.* San José: Editorial de la Universidad de Costa Rica, 409–436.

Day, Jane Stevenson. 1988. "Iconos y símbolos: cerámica pintada de la región de Nicoya." *Mesoamérica* 15 (June): 137–161.

Dillehay, Thomas. 2000. *The Settlement of America: a New Prehistory.* New York: Basic Books.

Edelman, Marc. 1992. *The Logic of the Latifundio: The Large Estates of Northwestern Costa Rica since the Late Nineteenth Century.* Stanford, CA: Stanford University Press.

Edelman, Marc, and Joanne Kenen, eds. 1989. *The Costa Rica Reader.* New York: Grove Weindenfeld.

Ferrero, Luis. 1987. *Costa Rica Precolombina.* San José: Editorial Costa Rica.

Fonseca Corrales, Elizabeth. 1994. "Economía y sociedad en Centroamérica (1540–1680)." In Julio Pinto Soria, ed., *Historia general de Centroamérica, vol. 2: El régimen colonial.* San José:

Facultad Latinoamericana de Ciencias Sociales (FLACSO), 95–150.

Fonseca Zamora, Oscar. 1981. "Guayabo de Turrialba and Its Significance." In *Between Continents/Between Seas: Pre-Columbian Art of Costa Rica.* New York: Henry Abrams, 104–112.

Fonseca Zamora, Oscar. 1992. *Historia Antigua de Costa Rica.* San José: Editorial de la Universidad de Costa Rica.

Food and Agriculture Organization of the United Nations (FAO). 2007. "State of the World's Forests." www.fao.org/docrep/009/a0773e/a0773e00.htm/.

Fumero Vargas, Patricia. 2002. "Vida cotidiana en el Valle Central 1850–1914. Los cambios asociados con la expansión del café." In Ana Maria Botey, ed., *Costa Rica: de las sociedades autóctonas a 1914.* San José: Editorial de la Universidad de Costa Rica, 327–365.

González Chaves, Alfredo, and Fernando González Vásquez. 1989. *La casa cósmica talmanqueña y sus simbolismos.* San José: Editorial Universidad Estatal a Distancia.

González V., Gerado. 2007. "Mapas digitales ayudarán a conservar áreas protegidas." *La Nacíon*, March 14, sec. "Aldea Global."

Graham, Mark M. 1992. "Art-Tools and the Language of Power in the Early Art of the Atlantic Watershed in Costa Rica." In Frederick W. Lange, ed., *Wealth and Hierarchy in the Intermediate Area.* Washington, D.C.: Dunbarton Oaks, Research Library and Collection, 165–206.

Graham, Mark M. 1993. "Displacing the Center: Constructing Prehistory in Central America." In Mark Miller, ed., *Reinterpreting Prehistory of Central America.* Niwot, CO: University Press of Colorado.

Gudmundson, Lowell. 1995. "Peasant, Farmer, Proletarian: Class Formation in a Smallholder Coffee Economy, 1850–1950." In William Roseberry, Lowell Gudmundson, and Mario Samper Kutschbach, eds., *Coffee, Society, and Power in Latin America.* Baltimore: Johns Hopkins University Press, 112–150.

Hall, Carolyn. 1985. *Costa Rica: A Geographic Interpretation in Historical Perspective.* Boulder, CO: Westview Press.

Hall, Carolyn, and Hector Pérez Brignoli. 2003. *Historical Atlas of Central America.* Norman, OK: University of Oklahoma Press.

Holden, Robert H. 2004. *Armies without Nations: Public Violence and State Formation in Central America, 1821–1960.* Oxford: Oxford University Press.

Jackson, Jeremy B. C., and Luís D'Croz. 1997. "The Ocean Divided." In Anthony G. Coates, ed., *Central America: A Natural and Cultural History.* New Haven, CT: Yale University Press, 38–71.

Kramer, Wendy, W. George Lovell, and Christopher Lutz. 1994. "La conquista española de Centroamérica." In Julio Pinto Sora, ed., *Historia general de Centroamérica, vol. 2: El régimen colonial.* San

José: Facultad Latinoamricana de Ciencias Sociales (FLACSO), 21–93.

Lange, Frederick W. 1993. "The Conceptual Structure in Lower Central American Studies: A Central American View." In Mark Miller Graham, ed., *Reinterpreting Prehistory of Central America*. Niwot, CO: University Press of Colorado, 277–324.

Lange, Frederick W. 1996. "Summary: Gaps in Our Databases and Blanks in Our Syntheses: The Potential for Central American Archeology in the 21st Century." In Frederick W. Lange, ed., *Paths to Central American Prehistory*. Niwot, CO: University Press of Colorado, 305–326.

Lehoucq, Fabrice Edouard. 1998. *Instituciones democráticas y conflictos públicos en Costa Rica*. Heredia, Costa Rica: Editorial Universidad Nacional (EUNA).

MacLeod, Murdo J. 1985. *Spanish Central America: A Socioeconomic History, 1520–1720*. Berkeley, CA: University of California Press.

Marín Hernandez, Juan José. 2005. "Prostitución y pecado en la bella y próspera ciudad de San José (1850–1930)." In Ivan Molina and Steven Palmer, eds., *El paso del cometa: Estado, política social, y culturas populares en Costa Rica (1800–1950)*. San José: Editorial Universidad Estatal a Distancia, 51–107.

Molina, Iván and Steven Palmer, eds. 2004. *The Costa Rica Reader: History, Culture, Politics*. Durham, NC: Duke University Press.

Molina, Iván and Steven Palmer. 2006. *The History of Costa Rica: Brief, Up-to-Date and Illustrated*. San José: Editorial de la Universidad de Costa Rica.

Molina Jiménez, Iván. 1991. *Costa Rica (1800–1850): El legado colonial y la génesis del capitalismo*. San José: Editorial de la Universidad de Costa Rica.

Molina Jiménez, Iván. 2000. "Clase, género y étnia van a la escuela. El alfabetismo en Costa Rica y Nicaragua (1880–1950)." In Iván Molina and Steven Palmer, eds., *Educando a Costa Rica: Alfabetización, formación docente y género (1880–1950)*. San José: Editorial Porvenir, 19–56.

Molina Jiménez, Iván. 2002. "Del legado colonial al modelo agroexportador." In Ana Maria Botey, ed., *Costa Rica: de las sociedades autóctonas a 1914*. San José: Editorial de la Universidad de Costa Rica, 437–494.

Moya Gutiérrez, Arnaldo. 2002. "Cultura material y vida cotidiana: El entorno doméstico de los vecinos principales de Cartago (1750–1820). In Iván Molina Jiménez and Steven Palmer, eds., *Héroes al gusto y libros de moda: Sociedad y cambio cultural en Costa Rica (1750–1900)*. San José: Editorial Universidad Estatal a Distancia, 1–60.

National Institute of Biodiversity (INBio). 2007a. "Ecomapas: Metodología." www.inbio.ac.cr/ecomapas/metodologia.htm/.

National Institute of Biodiversity (INBio). 2007b. "Estado de la biodiversidad en Costa Rica: diversidad de especies y genes." www.inbio.ac.cr/es/biod/estrategia/estudio.html

National Institute of Biodiversity (INBio). 2007c. "Estado de la biodiversidad en Costa Rica: diversidad de ecosistemas." www.inbio.ac.cr/es/biod/estrategia/Paginas/frame_estudio.htm/.

Oliva Medina, Mario. 1991. *Movimientos sociales en Costa Rica (1825–1930)*. Serie Nuestra Historia, no. 13. San José: Editorial Universidad Estatal a Distancia.

Paige, Jeffery M. 1997. *Coffee and Power: Revolution and the Rise of Democracy in Central America*. Cambridge, MA: Harvard University Press.

Palmer, Steven. 2005. "Pánico en San José. El consumo de heroína, la cultura plebeya y la política social en 1929." In Iván Molina Jiménez and Steven Palmer, eds. *El paso del cometa: Estado, política social y culturas populares en Costa Rica (1800–1850)*. San José: Editorial Universidad Estatal a Distancia, 281–345.

Picado, Miguel. 1989. *La iglesia costarricense entre Dios y el césar*. 2nd ed. San José: Editorial Departmento Ecuménico de Investigaciones (DEI).

Pinto Soria, Julio. 1994. "Nota preliminar." In Julio Pinto Soria, ed., *Historia general de Centroamerica, vol 2: El régimen Colonial*. San José: Facultad Latinoamericana de Ciencias Sociales (FLACSO): 9–20.

Programa Estado de la Nación. 2006. *Estado de la Nación en Desarrollo Humano Sostenible: Un análisis amplio y objetivo sobre la Costa Rica que tenemos y a partir de los indicadores más actuales (2005)*. San José: Programa Estado de la Nación. www.estadonacion.or.cr/.

Quesada Camacho, Juan Rafael. 1991. *Educación en Costa Rica, 1821–1940*. Serie Nuestra Historia, no. 15. San José: Editorial Universidad Estatal a Distancia.

Quilter, Jeffrey. 2004. *Cobble Circles and Standing Stones: Archeology at the Rivas Site, Costa Rica*. Iowa City, Iowa: University of Iowa Press.

Quiros, Claudia. 1990. *La era de la ecomienda*. San José: Universidad de Costa Rica.

Salazar, Jorge Mario. 1995. *Crisis liberal y estado reformista: Análisis político-electoral 1914–1949*. San José: Editorial de la Universidad de Costa Rica.

Salazar Mora, Orlando. 1990. *El apogeo de la república liberal en Costa Rica, 1870–1914*. San José: Editorial de la Universidad de Costa Rica.

Sheets, Payson. 1992. "The Pervasive Pejorative in Intermediate Area Studies." In Frederick W. Lange, ed., *Wealth and Hierarchy in the Intermediate Area*. Washington D.C.: Dunbarton Oaks, Research Library and Collection, 15–42.

Snarskis, Michael. 1981. "The Archeology of Costa Rica." In *Between Continents/Between Seas: The Pre-Columbian Art of Costa Rica*. New York: Henry Abrams, 15–84.

Solorzano Fonseca, Juan Carlos. 1992. "La búsqueda de oro y la resistencia indígena: campañas y exploración en Costa Rica, 1502–1610." *Mesoamérica* 24 (December): 313–363.

Solorzano Fonseca, Juan Carlos. 2002. "La sociedad colonial. 1575–1821." In Ana Maria Botey Sobrado, ed., *Costa Rica: Desde las sociedades autóctonas hasta 1914*. San José: Editorial de la Universidad de Costa Rica, 115–172.

Stone, Doris. 1977. *Pre-Columbian Man in Costa Rica*. Cambridge, MA: Peabody Museum Press, Harvard University.

Vargas Arias, Claudio. 2002. "Historia política, militar, y jurídica de Costa Rica entre 1870 y 1914." In Ana Maria Botey Sobrado, ed., *Costa Rica: Desde las sociedades autóctonas hasta 1914*. San José: Editorial de la Universidad de Costa Rica, 295–326.

Vega Carballo, José Luís. 1981. *Orden y progreso: la formación del estado nacional en Costa Rica*. San José: Instituto Centroamericano de Administración Pública.

Webb, David S. 1997. "The Great American Faunal Interchange." In Anthony G. Coates, ed., *Central America: A Natural and Cultural History*. New Haven, CT: Yale University Press, 97–122.

Williams, Robert G. 1994. *States and Social Evolution: Coffee and the Rise of National Governments in Central America*. Chapel Hill, NC: University of North Carolina Press.

Winson, Anthony. 1989. *Coffee and Democracy in Modern Costa Rica*. Toronto: Between the Lines.

CHAPTER TWO
The Costa Rican Economy

Civil wars have a way of becoming "revolutions" in the memories of the victors. It is important to emphasize that the conflict that dominated the tropical summer of 1948 was not the beginning of a Costa Rican revolution. The reforms undertaken by José Figueres and his successors had a definite continuity with the work begun as far back as the aborted presidency of Alfredo González Flores in 1917. Yet the civil war itself—the violence and the heroism and the rupture in the usual modes of Costa Rican life and politics— does seem to have been decisive in putting reform onto a different and faster track. Political reform, in turn, opened the door to new opportunities for economic development. For that reason, key political decisions shaping the economy will be discussed here; a more detailed analysis of Costa Rican political institutions is discussed in chapter 3.

As the dictatorship of Tomás Guardia did in the 1870s, the civil war and governing junta of 1948–1949 marked an interruption in democratic politics that, in retrospect, served to improve conditions for the next round of political, economic, and social reform. Guardia's legacy was the Constitution of 1871, a modernized and disciplined military, and the "Olympus Generation" of liberals who carried out the legal and educational reforms that made Costa Rica's relative prosperity and stability notable in Central America. The legacy of José Figueres and the Founding Junta of the Second Republic was a reformed constitution, the abolition of the military, a new approach to public administration and finance for development, and the National Liberation Party (PLN), which would pursue that new approach with great success for three decades. During that time Costa Rica was held up as an example of the way in which electoral democracy and social and economic progress could be mutually reinforcing, even in a small, poor country. Since 1982, Costa Rica has been unwilling to abandon the institutions and achievements of the generation of 1948, but also unable to match that nostalgia with the resources and reforms required to pursue ecologically sustainable, socially democratic development in the 21st century.

THE EXHAUSTION OF THE CLASSICAL EXPORT MODEL AND THE BIRTH OF THE MIXED ECONOMY

As mentioned in Chapter 1, Costa Rica's political crisis in the 1940s coincided with an accumulating crisis in the country's model of export-led development. Dependence on foreign markets for tropical products was fine as long as those markets grew, or at least remained open. Two world wars and an intervening economic depression demonstrated the risks of dependence. By the 1940s, the coffee exporters were reeling from these adverse shocks. In 1938, 193 coffee export firms were operating in Costa Rica; by 1941, that number had been reduced by nearly 50 percent, and by 1944, only 19 export firms remained. Six of the remaining exporters were American owned, and they controlled nearly 80 percent of coffee exports (Winson 1989, 41).

Economic systems do not change easily, however, even when experience suggests that they no longer work as well as they once did. Coffee producers were weakened, but managed to carry on in the 1930s by opening up more land to cultivation and keeping wages under control. The United Fruit Company (UFCo) had weathered a major strike in 1934, which was called as a reaction to the measures it took to cope with the world economic crisis, and it moved operations to the Pacific coast to escape labor problems and "Panama disease," a banana contagion that plagued the banana industry on the Atlantic coast. Both producers of coffee and bananas were comfortable with Costa Rica continuing as a free-trading agricultural society where they would have inexpensive access to the imports they required and would not need to compete with new industries for scarce labor. Local bankers and merchants had also built their businesses on the known quantities of coffee harvest cycles and markets for imported goods (Winson 1989, 30–40). Together, these interest groups made for a powerful force of inertia that José Figueres and the Social Democrats would find difficult, but not impossible, to overcome.

It is possible that if the Calderonistas simply accepted the victory of Otilio Ulate in the 1948 elections, Costa Rica would have never distinguished itself so sharply from the rest of its neighbors in Central America. Figureres and his supporters were a tiny minority in the coalition that opposed Calderón. Ulate was a respected newspaper owner, and the Union Nacional Oppositora (UNO), which he led, was much more conservative than Social Democratic Party founded by Figueres and the intellectuals of the Center for the Study of National Problems. Included within the UNO were traditional business interests that felt betrayed by Calderón's turn toward social reform and by his alliance with the Communist Party and the progressive archbishop of San José. Had the electoral rules of the game held in 1948, it is possible that the Social Democrats would have been pushed aside by the more conservative elements in the coalition and reform would have progressed much more slowly than it did (Winson 1989, 52). This outcome appears even more probable when one considers the rude shock received by Figueres and the Social Democrats in the 1948 elections for the constituent assembly. They only won 4 of the 45 seats in the body that would draw up a new constitution (Edelman and Kenen 1989, 125).

Clearly, Costa Ricans were not yet ready to choose profound reform at the ballot box. The peace agreement, however, had given Figueres and the Founding Junta of the

Second Republic 18 months to rule the country more or less as they pleased. The Junta made excellent use of this opportunity to shift momentum decisively toward social reform and state-led economic development. One month into the Junta's rule, it decreed a 10 percent wealth tax on all assets over $10,000 and nationalized the banking system (Mesa-Lago 2000, 406). Of the two decrees, the second was by far the most important. With the stroke of a pen, the Costa Rican state took control of all savings deposits and of the priorities that would determine where those savings would be invested in the national economy.

Both of these decrees, along with more aggressive efforts at taxation of both the coffee and banana sectors, were designed to address the principle dilemma that had faced Latin American reformist governments in the 20th century: finding the money to attack poverty, improve education, provide for social security, improve health care, and finance the infrastructure to diversify dependent economies. Without access to domestic savings and taxes, progressive governments were tempted to rely on foreign lenders and on the state's ability to simply print money to pay its bills. Excessive debt put the nation at the mercy of lenders domestic and foreign, while printing money led to inflation.

NATIONALIZATION OF THE BANKS

The only way to avoid these dangers was to find ways to channel local resources into development. Figueres later recalled the bank nationalization as "by far the most important measure for social and economic development taken by the National Liberation Movement" (Figueres Ferrer 1956, 128). Other analysts would also conclude that the nationalization of the banking system was one of the most important reasons why the post–World War II economic development of Costa Rica differed so sharply from its fellow "coffee and banana republics" in Central America (Bulmer-Thomas

1987, 154). Public control of the banking system meant that profits earned in export agriculture would not simply be reinvested in those same sectors (and benefit the same privileged social groups), as tended to be the case in the rest of Central America. In Costa Rica, bank lending was carried out within a system of lending targets and controlled interest rates established by government policy makers. The goal of the national banks was to support the traditionally profitable export activities and at the same time to support small farmers, promote new industries, and thus diversify the country's base of producers and products.

The nationalization of the banks and the tax on wealth were only the first in a series of measures that post-1948 governments would take to increase the resources at their disposal for economic and social development. Astute political maneuvering by the Ulate government, which took over when the Junta relinquished power, led to the establishment of a tax on the processors and exporters of coffee in January 1952 (Winson 1989, 86). In 1953, José Figueres returned to office, this time as an elected president, and managed to increase domestic income taxes, and even the tax levied on the UFCo for each box of exported bananas (Mesa-Lago 2000, 410). Borrowing and economic aid from the United States and other foreign sources were also important elements of Costa Rican public finance.

AUTONOMOUS INSTITUTIONS AND THE MANAGER STATE

Equally important, however, were the measures taken by the Junta and succeeding governments to establish efficient channels for spending these funds. Even before the events of 1948, the Center for the Study of National Problems had promoted the notion of "autonomous institutions" as the best vehicles for state intervention in economic development. These institutions were conceived as public institutions where independent boards of directors would make policy and appointments, and career advancement would be determined by academic training and civil service regulations, rather than by political affiliation. Rodrigo Facio, José Figueres, and the middle-class reformers who would come to dominate the PLN believed that development problems should be solved pragmatically through the application of technology and enlightened administration. Political criteria, which in their estimation led inevitably to corruption, which they associated with Calderonismo, were to be filtered out of development policy to the extent possible.

In 1949, the first institution the Junta established was the Costa Rican Electricity Institute (ICE), which was to be responsible for the development of the country's electrical and telecommunications infrastructure. It is still one of the most highly respected institutions in Costa Rica, perhaps because of its great success in bringing power to many remote corners of the country. From 1950 to 1965, the ICE succeeded in expanding electrical capacity 10-fold (Winson 1989, 63). Indeed, it is difficult to find a town in Costa Rica without access to electricity and at least one public telephone. Tour guides have been known to point with pride to an electricity meter as a humble sign of a great achievement for a small country with no fossil fuel reserves and a very complicated geography.

The National Production Council (CNP) was also given new life as an autonomous institution in 1949. The mission of the CNP was to "stabilize agricultural prices in the domestic market, stimulate production through price subsidies, and act as an intermediary between farmers and consumers" (Mesa-Lago 2000, 406). Working together with the national banking system, the CNP provided credit to farmers while guaranteeing them a market and a fair price for their crops. Furthermore, the CNP invested in warehouses and transportation to protect producers and consumers from the dangers of private monopolies on food distribution. The CNP's operations were complicated. They were also expensive, as the government had to absorb the costs associated with ensuring stable prices for farmers' produce. The CNP also ensured that urban consumers paid low prices for the basic ingredients of the Costa Rican diet. Nonetheless, when it worked well it helped small farmers doing the humble work of putting food on Costa Rican tables (rather than coffee and bananas on the breakfast tables of the developed world). It also helped keep groceries affordable for the growing urban middle class. Thus, the CNP also became a highly valued institution.

Between 1948 and 1977, 119 new autonomous institutions were created to deal with matters ranging from urban housing to the development of water and sewage systems to land colonization and reform to the development and management of the port of Limón. The public sector workforce grew along with this approach to development—from 23,023 workers in 1954 to 162,600 in 1985 (Clark 2001, 34). However, it is important to point out that until the 1970s, the overall objective of this increasingly complicated bureaucracy was simply to regulate, facilitate, and channel the efforts of private property owners to grow and diversify the economy. The Costa Rican state saw itself as a "manager state," with the autonomous institutions as its tools (Edelman 1999, 56). At a time when the world was being rigidly divided into capitalist and communist systems, Figueres liked to refer to Costa Rica's as a "mixed" economy, a "combination of the two systems . . . that tries to pull together the benefits of both, and reduce the disadvantages of each" (Figueres Ferrer 1956, 114).

The manager state, helped by favorable prices for coffee and other exports in the postwar decades and by the efforts of the private sector it worked to encourage, had considerable success in stimulating and diversifying the Costa Rican economy. From 1951 to 1979, the economy sustained an average annual growth rate of 6.1 percent (Clark 2001, 40). However, this growth translated only into a 2.3 percent per capita growth rate, because the Costa Rican population grew at one of the highest rates in the world, particularly during the 1960s (Mesa-Lago 2000, 421). Economic growth resulted in a sustained reduction in poverty and income inequality, particularly because of a focus on improving conditions in rural areas. (A strong urban bias characterized post–World War II development in much of the rest of Latin America.) The proportion of Costa Ricans in poverty dropped from 50 percent in 1961 to between 20 and 25 percent in the mid-1970s. The Gini coefficient, a statistical measure of income inequality that moves downward as inequality is reduced, moved from 0.52 in 1961 to 0.44 in the mid-1970s (Clark 2001, 40).

Social progress was steady throughout the three postwar decades but accelerated markedly in the 1970s, when aggressive investments were made in health care, water, sanitation, and education. From 1972 to 1982, infant mortality rates dropped from 56.5 per thousand births to 18.9. Over this same period life expectancy increased from 67.6 to 73.5 years, and Costa Rica's disease profile had changed by the end of this period from "diseases of underdevelopment" caused by malnutrition and lack of access to clean water and preventive health care to "diseases of development" like cancer and cardiovascular illness. Already a leader in primary education and regional literacy rates, the Costa Rican educational system grew even more dramatically in the 1970s, as more than 600 elementary schools and 100 new secondary schools were added to the system, along with three new public universities (Mesa-Lago 2000, 459–460). By the end of the 1970s, Costa Rica's state-managed economic growth had been effectively, although perhaps not durably, linked to the creation of what has been called a "tropical welfare state" (Edelman 1992, 44). This accomplishment was an impressive feat for a country that, prior to World War II, had "ranked below nine Latin American countries in three per capita consumption indicators: total calories, grams of daily protein, and annual consumption of milk" (Mesa-Lago 2000, 399).

The generation of 1948 was well aware that social progress depended on the growth, diversification, and productivity of the Costa Rican economy. Rodrigo Facio, the most important intellectual of that generation, explained the situation this way:

> In a country such as ours, social justice can only be achieved by the double path of social legislation that guarantees juridically to the less-fortunate classes their right to life, and by economic organization which guarantees, materially, in terms of an augmented and diversified production, that the lower classes will be able to effectively exercise that right. (quoted in Winson 1989, 89)

While this might seem a bland statement, it pointed to a common situation in 20th-century Latin American development. Almost every country in the region adopted socially progressive laws after the Great Depression; some, like Mexico and Chile, had moved to the progressive vanguard even sooner. Yet very few Latin American countries had succeeded in making good on ambitious declarations of their citizens' rights to a dignified standard of living. The large gap between the theory and practice of social reform was the result of political and administrative failures, but perhaps even more so it was due to the financial limitations imposed by dependent export economies. It is for this reason that social democrats in Costa Rica (represented primarily, but not exclusively, by the PLN) were so adamant about the need to increase and diversify the productive capacity of their tiny economy.

Coffee and Cooperatives

The reformers first attended to the situation of the "golden bean." For over a century, Costa Ricans had been able to increase production extensively by simply increasing the amounts of land and labor devoted to coffee. The story of the expanding Costa Rican frontier, of the displacement of basic grain and cattle producers to the margins of the country, and of the increased wages and bargaining power of agricultural workers is essentially a story about an extensive approach to economic development. Extensive growth, however, has its limits. By the mid-20th century, land and labor available for coffee production had become scarce relative to the golden years of the 19th century. One agronomist analyzing the situation in 1952 concluded, "Coffee production in Costa Rica is in a state of complete exploitation. There is no technology. The agriculturalists are not concerned with conservation. They cultivate coffee like a mine, taking out and never returning anything to the land" (quoted in Winson 1989, 97).

The stagnation of coffee productivity became a principal target of the state banking system and of other government agencies funded in part by the new tax imposed on the coffee processors in 1952. The formula for success consisted in replanting coffee farms with more productive hybrid varieties of the bush and in financing the purchase of fertilizers and herbicides to increase the productivity of the new plants and to economize on labor. The government also invested in agricultural research to improve farming practices and to develop coffee trees short enough to be easily harvested by women and children. These efforts were wildly successful. Between 1950 and 1970, the average yield per hectare of Costa Rican coffee increased 170 percent. By the late 1970s, Costa Rica had become the third most productive coffee exporter in the world, and the most productive in Latin America (Winson 1989, 106–110). This "green revolution" in coffee, however, had mixed effects, both environmentally and socially. The new varieties of coffee required sun rather than shade, leading to rapid deforestation of the highland zones where coffee was produced. Birds and other wildlife dependent on the tree cover of the shade-grown varieties of coffee lost habitat in the process. Intense use of chemical

The volcanic soils and temperate climate of the Central Valley make it perfect for growing coffee, but rapid urbanization has pushed coffee fields further and further from San José. (Corel)

fertilizers and herbicides also had negative effects on the workers who applied them and on the watersheds into which their residues inevitably found their way.

There were also clear winners and losers on the social scale. The winners were those growers with enough land and capital to benefit from the government's replanting programs. These programs were designed to make it easy for farmers to convert their farms to more productive varieties and practices. Loans, for example, were designed so that interest payments would not come due until farmers had the chance to reap the gains of their more productive farms (around three years). Yet the replanting program was limited to producers with more than two *manzanas* (roughly 3.5 acres) of coffee, and the loan programs would only cover 75 percent of the cost of the new investments. In 1940, three-fourths of Costa Rican coffee growers had less than the required number of coffee bushes to participate in the replanting program, and others who cleared that obstacle were still unable to come up with their share of the costs of conversion (Winson 1989, 102–103).

Small farmers were not the only ones hurt by changes in coffee cultivation. Increased herbicide use reduced employment in the coffee fields, or *cafetales,* by 50 to 60 percent. This meant that many rural workers lost their close, year-round relationship with the boss and became instead seasonal harvesters. Not only did temporary workers have looser bonds with the coffee farmer but they also did not benefit much from a government safety net designed to serve full-time workers (Winson 1989, 123). By undercutting the economic position of the rural workers, these changes also weakened one of the important elements of the country's founding myths of rural democracy.

The government did try, however, to level the playing field somewhat by aggressively promoting cooperatives. Indeed, enthusiasm for cooperatives (co-ops) was another notable characteristic of the generation of 1948 as it sought a middle road between unrestrained capitalism and much-feared communism. Cooperativism speaks to the recurrent Costa Rican concern with the relationship between farmers and merchants, between those who produce and those who process and export the final product. Chapter 1 discussed how the real profits in both coffee and banana production accrued to the coffee processors and exporters and to UFCo because they controlled credit, processing, transport, and overseas marketing. It also showed how conflicts between independent farmers and the middlemen they depended on pushed the Costa Rican government into the role of mediator, particularly in the coffee sector, where the government set limits on the processors' ability to "buy cheap and sell dear."

Co-ops address this same problem by giving small farmers an alternative to dependence on the processor. With various forms of government credit and assistance, small farmers

Coffee processing plants, known as beneficios, *are profitable enterprises.* Beneficios *produce lots of waste water and are under pressure to lessen their environmental impact. (Photo by Meg Mitchell)*

are able to pool their efforts, purchase processing equipment, and even undertake marketing efforts at home and abroad. These forward steps in the chain of production and marketing are taken at cost, rather than at whatever price the market (and government regulation) will bear, thus allowing co-op members to keep more of the profits from the final sale of coffee for themselves. In 1962, the government established the Cooperative Federation to organize the efforts of cooperatives in coffee and other sectors of the Costa Rican economy. By 1975, one-third of the annual coffee crop was processed by cooperatives (Clark 2001, 36). This shift diluted the power of the processors, but only slightly. By 1978, the 13 largest private firms controlled 55 percent of the harvest; the top 6 alone controlled 37 percent of the harvest (Winson 1989, 130).

With coffee, then, the manager state took effective, although not cost-free, measures to increase the productivity of the primary engine of the Costa Rican economy. Yet increasing the productivity of coffee did nothing to reduce the country's dependence on that crop and on foreign markets that were entirely beyond its control. In fact, the new coffee varieties' need for imported fertilizers and herbicides to thrive meant that dependence was actually increased somewhat. Conscious of this implication, the state took measures to diversify the country's exports and even to reduce its imports.

Cotton, a very successful export product in the rest of Central America in the 1950s and 1960s, made a modest contribution to export diversification in Costa Rica. Sugar had more success, particularly after the United States ceased to import it from socialist Cuba and turned Cuba's share of the U.S. sugar market over to several Latin American countries in the 1960s (Bulmer-Thomas 1987, 156–160). (The sugar industry developed in the 1950s is positioned to benefit handsomely from the free trade agreement with the United States, if it is approved.)

Cattle Ranching and Deforestation in Guanacaste

Export diversification was most notably successful in Guanacaste. The *guanacasteco* hero is the *sabanero*, or cowboy, whose image has been romanticized much like that of the North American variety. Yet in Costa Rica, he is more likely to encounter a monkey than a coyote as he tends his cattle. After 1950, however, as vast amounts of credit were channeled into the cattle industry, the northern Pacific rangeland became less romantic as it became more modern. This transformation was intricately tied to conditions in the North American beef market. After World War II, the United States was consuming much more beef than it produced. In the

1970s, for example, the United States accounted for 6 percent of the world's population, 9 percent of the world's cattle herd, and 28 percent of the world's beef consumption (Edelman 1992, 189). Under these conditions, the tendency in the United States was for beef prices to rise and for consumers and food processors (like fast food chains) to look for cheaper sources of beef. Specialization occurred as U.S. cattlemen sought the highest grades awarded by the U.S. Department of Agriculture (USDA) for the corn-fed beef they produced, while overseas cattlemen supplied the market for "industrial grade" beef (i.e., hamburger) with grass-fed cattle. As the fast food industry took off in the 1950s and 1960s, the market for industrial-grade beef expanded, and the ranchers of Guanacaste were able to find a niche in the market. Costa Rica actually became the fourth largest exporter of beef to the United States by the end of the 1970s (Edelman 1992, 195–196).

However, it has been argued that the growth of the cattle industry in Guanacaste was far from a case of the "invisible hand" of the market responding to Americans' increasing infatuation with the hamburger. Politics, policy, and, most importantly, subsidized credit made cattle ranching in Guanacaste much more profitable than it otherwise would have been. As a new potential export, the cattle industry was an early and natural favorite of José Figueres and subsequent PLN leaders. Cattle ranchers had privileged access to the PLN leadership from the early 1950s and astutely used that access to secure privileged treatment from the state banking system and from the CNP, which regulated domestic beef prices and export quotas. Cattlemen pushed successfully for more credit at lower interest rates and for permission to export as much beef as possible, rather than being forced to supply the domestic market at controlled prices (Edelman 1992, 202–207). The World Bank, Inter-American Development Bank (IDB), and other important players in the international development field became strong proponents of cattle ranching in Costa Rica (and elsewhere in the developing world), thus lending

Much of the tropical dry forest of Guanacaste has been destroyed, primarily for cattle raising. Deforestation has led not only to loss of wildlife habitat, but also to serious erosion. (Gary Braasch/Corbis)

considerable international weight to the local cattlemen's arguments. In the 1960s, World Bank loans to Costa Rica required the government to create an extension service for cattle ranchers at the Central Bank. The IDB also conditioned its lending on the establishment of an institutional support network for the cattle sector. As foreign and domestic credit flowed rapidly through those channels, the Guanacastecan landscape changed dramatically. Between 1950 and 1973, the area devoted to pasture in Guanacaste more than doubled, making that province the most seriously deforested region in the country. By the 1970s, a boom atmosphere had set in; the cattle industry received as much credit as crop agriculture, and beef became Costa Rica's third most important export after coffee and bananas (Edelman 1992, 196–198, 200, 246).

As with the changes made in the coffee sector, the cattle boom created winners and losers. Probably the biggest losers were the tropical dry forest and those that depend on it for habitat, erosion control, and rainfall. While the trade balance benefited from this destruction, the Costa Rican consumer did not. Ironically, as Costa Ricans produced more beef, they failed to consume more. Because prices were higher in the North American market, cattlemen preferred to export what they produced, and they would even inflate the size of the herds they reported to the CNP to secure larger export quotas. What could not be exported, or what could not pass USDA inspection in the United States, was sold in the domestic market. Thus, domestic supply did not increase, and quality probably declined (Edelman 1992, 213).

Nor did the rural workforce benefit from the cattle boom. The Costa Rican cattle sector, like the coffee sector before its conversion after 1950, had grown extensively—by adding more land to pasture. The process begun in the 1920s of fencing in land and pushing off *campesinos* with uncertain or nonexistent claims intensified, as large stretches of pasture were needed to gain access to easy credit and lucrative export markets. The scarcity of land for crop agriculture and the low demand for labor on the cattle ranches led to significant exodus of young men from Guanacaste to other regions of Costa Rica (particularly the southern Pacific banana zone) in search of other opportunities (Edelman 1992, 260–263).

Whether or not the overall economy benefited from the cattle boom is also open to question. Overseas market demand fueled the growth of the cattle sector, but so did easy credit. This fact makes it hard to determine if cattle ranching really produced better returns than other alternative investments might have. Furthermore, there was very little oversight by the state banks to ensure the loans were used to improve the ranches. Cheap bank loans given for ranching often found their way not into ranch improvements but into higher-yielding investments like bank certificates of deposit. Regardless of where loan capital was ultimately invested, the delinquency rate on loans made to cattle operations was nearly double (32 percent) that of loans made to agriculture and industry (Edelman 1992, 250). The costs of subsidized loans and loans that went unpaid were absorbed by the Costa Rican government and by other sectors of the economy that might have made more profitable use of those scarce funds.

INDUSTRIALIZATION AND THE CENTRAL AMERICAN COMMON MARKET

The cattle industry was perhaps the most spectacular example of the costs and benefits of diversifying the country's exports. However, the grandest dream of modernizers in Costa Rica, and throughout the developing world, was industrialization. Power plants and factories producing goods that once had to be imported from the United States or Europe symbolized independence for countries tired of depending on the whims of the international marketplace. Building local industry was a nationalistic enterprise that was both inspiring and costly. To do it, most countries in Latin America adopted policies grouped under the rubric of import substitution industrialization (ISI). As the name suggests, the objective of ISI policies was to industrialize by progressively substituting locally manufactured goods for those previously imported. However, local producers could not hope to compete with foreign suppliers without government help. Such policies were heavily promoted by the United Nations Economic Commission for Latin America, founded in 1948.

In line with this philosophy, governments throughout Latin America took steps to close their markets to certain manufactured imports (usually by raising import tariffs) and to give special privileges to local entrepreneurs willing to try their hand at the substitution of imports. These privileges typically included tax-free importation of machinery from abroad; subsidized credit; special access to foreign currency to import machinery and other essential components in the manufacturing process; help in keeping labor unions and wages under control; and technical assistance. With these policies in place, many Latin American countries began the process of industrialization, usually with simple products like clothing and processed food. The long-term goal, particularly in larger countries like Mexico and Brazil, was to develop in this way a complete industrial economy where everything from steel to electricity, from industrial machinery to automobiles and high-tech equipment, was produced domestically. The country that achieved this goal would take its place alongside the world's industrial powers and would no longer suffer the dependence and indignity of being a coffee or banana republic. The overall approach of ISI was riddled with flaws, as will be seen in the Costa Rican case, but the dream of industrialization was a potent one. Similar protectionist policies allowed the United States, Germany, and other countries to successfully industrialize in the 19th century. Latin Americans simply wished to follow the same path that had been marked out by the countries they depended on for imports and exports.

A fundamental obstacle to Costa Rica's participation in the nationalistic drive to industrialize Latin America was the tiny size of its market. Even with high tariffs on imports and generous incentives to local industry, a very small market would not attract many investors. Fortunately, Costa Rica shared this problem with her sister republics in Central America, which led to the formation of the Central American Common Market (CACM) to expand the market for regional manufacturing. As with today's Dominican Republic–Central America Free Trade Agreement (DR-CAFTA), Costa Rica was the last country to join the regional organization. It finally went into effect in 1963 as all five countries took steps to eliminate most tariffs on internal trade and to agree to a common external tariff on goods imported from outside of Central America.

As expected, the larger market proved a good stimulus to industrial investment. The share of manufacturing in Costa Rica's gross domestic product (GDP) went from 15 percent

This is the opening session of the Central American Common Market (CACM) in San José in 1963. Costa Rica was the last to join CACM and will be the last to join DR-CAFTA, if it is approved. (John Dominis/Time Life Pictures/Getty Images)

in 1960 to 20.5 percent in 1970. Costa Rica's industrial exports grew from $2.2 million in 1961 to $53.5 million in 1970. Unexpected effects also appeared, however. While Central American workers manufactured goods in Central American locations, a majority of the investment came from overseas, often from U.S.-based transnational corporations. In Costa Rica, transnational corporations invested $281 million over the course of the 1960s, while domestic investors provided $218 million (Mesa-Lago 2000, 425–426). Central American investors, in general, found the returns to be had from export agriculture more attractive and left for foreign investors most of the opportunities created by the newly protected regional market (Bulmer-Thomas 1987, 176). By

1978, three-fourths of the manufactured goods exported from Costa Rica to other markets within the CACM came from factories owned by foreign investors or by joint ventures between foreigners and Costa Ricans (Clark 2001, 38).

Contrary to the initial hopes of ISI enthusiasts, a second, and unexpected, effect of the CACM was that industrialization actually increased imports rather than reducing them. From 1964 to 1970 Costa Rican exports (some of them manufactured exports to the CACM) increased by 13.9 percent per year, but imports increased even more, at a rate of 14.8 percent per year (Mesa-Lago 2000, 426). Furthermore, as the economy industrialized, the imports it depended on were even more crucial than the finished products that came from overseas when Costa Rica was devoted entirely to agriculture. Jobs, not just the availability of consumer goods, now depended on the country's ability to pay for imported machinery, inputs, and, most crucially, petroleum. According to one calculation, Costa Rica had to import $80 worth of intermediate inputs to produce $100 of manufactured exports (Edelman 1999, 74). Industrialization did not magically eliminate the problem of how to balance imports and exports; it simply increased the scale and complexity of the problem.

Another problem industrialization could not solve, and that the CACM actually exacerbated, was how to pay for the government policies and services that supported import substitution industrialization and the tropical welfare state. Costa Rican opponents to participation in the CACM had foreseen this problem. While the Costa Rican government was considerably more advanced than other Central American countries in the use of direct taxes (like income taxes and profit taxes on coffee and bananas) to finance its operations, it still depended greatly on import taxes. Membership in the CACM required elimination of most of those taxes, even before finding a substitute for them. As it is always easier to eliminate taxes than to create them, the country began to borrow money instead, and Costa Rica's foreign debt slowly began to increase even as it industrialized at an impressive pace. In 1960, the country's foreign debt stood at $158 million, equivalent to 8.6 percent of GDP and 40.3 percent of annual exports. By 1970, the debt had grown to $354 million, or 13.6 percent of GDP and 48.2 percent of the annual value of exports (Mesa-Lago 2000, 427).

The CACM began to fall apart by the end of the 1960s. Disputes arose over the division of the costs and benefits of increased trade, and increasingly violent conflicts consumed Costa Rica's northern neighbors and complicated regional trade relations. Most tragically, a brief but bitter border war broke out between El Salvador and Honduras in 1969. This became known as the "Soccer War," because the tensions between the two countries had become evident in a pair of particularly heated soccer matches between the two national teams immediately prior to the outbreak of the war. That war signaled the beginning of the end of the CACM. It did not, however, end the zeal for rapid development in Costa Rica, a country that, even in the best of circumstances, was uncomfortable with linking its destiny with that of its poorer neighbors.

CODESA AND THE ENTREPRENEUR STATE

While the 1970s were years of dramatic progress in health and education, they were also a time of heady, and even reckless, efforts to increase the state's involvement in the development of the economy. In 1970, José Figueres was elected to his second term as president, and the PLN that he founded took control of the Legislative Assembly. In 1974, Daniel Oduber, a representative of a younger generation of Liberationists who also enjoyed a PLN majority in the legislative branch, followed him into office. This was the first time since its foundation in 1951 that the PLN had succeeded itself in the presidency. The failure of the CACM did not dilute the nationalistic impulses of the PLN leadership. Indeed, they used their political capital in an attempt to transform Costa Rica's manager state into what analysts concur was a much more aggressive "entrepreneur state." This new approach to development led the government to invest directly in enterprises deemed necessary to the progress of import substitution industrialization.

The change of policy was a reflection, no doubt, of impatience with the pace of industrial development and with the seeming willingness of Costa Rican investors to concede many of the opportunities created by ISI to foreign investors. In 1972, the Costa Rican Development Corporation (CODESA) was founded as a government holding company. The plan was for CODESA to enter into joint ventures with the private sector to develop crucial parts of the economy, with the government as majority shareholder. Once the businesses became profitable and no longer required government assistance, they were supposed to be sold to private investors. In 1976, under President Oduber, CODESA went into operation, focusing on investments in cement, sugar, and cotton (Mesa-Lago 2000, 431). It soon became apparent that nearly all of the funds invested in these enterprises would be public money, and no enterprises would be sold off until CODESA itself went bankrupt in the 1980s (Clark 2001, 40).

As might be expected when politics, public funds, and business overlap, CODESA quickly became the target of accusations of corruption. CODESA employees had some obvious advantages, such as "lavish salaries, expense accounts, and free use of company vehicles, as well as insider knowledge and connections that frequently enhanced the performance of their private holdings" (Edelman 1999, 63). As it began to monopolize access to public-sector credit, CODESA also quickly came into conflict with the private sector. By 1983, CODESA absorbed 18 percent of the capital available in the national banking system (in addition to other lines of public financing). Yet it only contributed 1.8 percent of GDP and only employed 0.3 percent of the labor force in the enterprises it held (Mesa-Lago 2000, 452). The suspicion, later borne out when CODESA was liquidated, was that most of CODESA's enterprises operated at a loss, and those operations were far from transparent (Clark 2001, 53). The Costa Rican Development Corporation would have been a costly affair even under the best of circumstances. Unfortunately, international market and financial conditions in the 1970s were such that profligacy on that scale—particularly when added to the more laudable and successful efforts to improve the population's health, education, and general living standards—could not be sustained.

The Debt Crisis and Neoliberal Reforms

Perhaps the most important global economic development in the 1970s was the creation of the Organization of Petroleum Exporting Countries (OPEC). An interesting example of how the industrialized world could be effectively held hostage by oil-exporting countries on the periphery of the global economy, this cartel of oil producers succeeded in controlling the world's oil supply and effecting dramatic price increases in 1973 and 1979. The first "oil shock" produced a bulge of sorts in the international banking system when the OPEC countries deposited their profits in European and North American banks. This influx of cash was problematic for the banks because they had to find ways to invest the money in order to earn the interest they would need to pay on the OPEC countries' deposits. Banks turned to the developing world, where countries like Costa Rica were thirsty for foreign loans, both to pay their increased oil import bills and to engage in the sort of aggressive state-led development programs that were typical at the time.

Costa Rica was particularly eager to borrow in the 1970s, as the prices of coffee and bananas were not favorable, and efforts to raise taxes were stalled in the Legislative Assembly

(Clark 2001, 45). During the 1970s, government spending increased by a factor of 10, to the point where it represented 22 percent of the gross national product (GNP), while domestic tax revenues remained stagnant at 13 percent of GNP (Bulmer-Thomas 1987, 315; Edelman 1999, 74). With bankers eager to lend and Costa Rica driven to borrow, the country's foreign debt exploded in the 1970s. By 1978, the country's total debt was a little more than a billion dollars (Molina and Palmer 2006, 117). The amount of money the country required simply to pay interest on the debt quickly became overwhelming, particularly after the second oil shock of 1979 and a sharp increase in international interest rates in 1981.

Rodrigo Carazo Odio was the president from the opposition party who took office in 1978. Despite his pledge to get CODESA and other government spending under control, he proved ineffective at convincing the Legislative Assembly of the need for radical tax and spending reforms. Nor could he manage the relationship with the International Monetary Fund (IMF) as the country found it increasingly difficult to repay its foreign debt (Clark 2001, 43–44). In July 1981, Costa Rica was the first country in Latin America to declare a moratorium on the payment of interest on its foreign debt—an unpleasant distinction for a country that had prided itself on so many positive accomplishments over the previous three decades (Edelman 1999, 74).

Costa Rica was only the first of several countries in Latin America to encounter serious problems with debt repayment. Like individual consumers defaulting on their credit cards, country after country entered into a situation similar to a "credit counseling" relationship with the IMF, the institution all of the international banks and other lending institutions looked to for leadership in resolving the debt crisis. The goal of these negotiations was to make it possible for governments to properly service their debts and thus to restore their access to international financial markets. To achieve that goal, the IMF called on countries to make radical reforms in their spending habits and to push their economies to export more to earn the dollars (and other foreign currencies) needed to repay their debts. Both the "austerity measures" (as the spending cuts were called) and the "structural adjustments" (as the economic reforms were called) were painful and generated a good deal of public hostility toward the IMF and the government officials who cooperated with it. Throughout Latin America, typical austerity measures included cuts in government spending on social programs; strict control of the growth of public-sector employment and wages; and increases in the rates paid for utilities, public transportation, and other subsidized goods like gasoline and certain basic foods. Structural adjustment usually meant dismantling the ISI policies that had been in place for some 30 years in most places. The IMF and other lenders applied pressure to lower tariffs, devalue national currencies, and cut subsidies and other privileges to domestic producers to force them to compete in an open world market. These policies came to be deemed "neoliberal" by their opponents, to highlight their similarity to the laissez faire policies adopted in the 19th century and subsequently abandoned after the Great Depression. The objective of these neoliberal policies was to turn Latin American economies away from import substitution and toward export promotion, and to lower domestic inflation by opening markets to cheaper foreign goods.

USAID AND THE PARALLEL STATE

Special circumstances made Costa Rica's passage through the trials of austerity and structural adjustment somewhat more rapid than elsewhere in Latin America, where the 1980s were commonly referred to as "the lost decade." On July 17, 1979, a national insurrection led by the Sandinista National Liberation

President Luis Alberto Monge (shown here with President Reagan in 1982) had to court U.S. economic support while preserving Costa Rica's commitment to unarmed neutrality. (Ronald Reagan Presidential Library)

Front (FSLN) ousted the dictator Anastasio Somoza Debayle in Nicaragua. The Somoza family had ruled Nicaragua since 1936 and kept itself closely allied with the United States during the Cold War. The FSLN included Nicaraguans of different ideological backgrounds, but the top leaders were sympathetic with Cuba and the Soviet bloc and were interested in building a mixed economy decidedly more socialist than the version pursued by the Costa Ricans. The victory of the FSLN corresponded to the election of Ronald Reagan in the United States in 1980 and a sharp turn to the right in U.S. foreign policy. The U.S. government perceived Nicaragua's revolution as a threat to national security and as a dangerous example to El Salvador and Guatemala, where civil wars were raging at the time. Against this backdrop, tiny Costa Rica was a "showcase" for democracy in Central America and a potential staging ground for efforts to subvert the Nicaraguan government.

Suddenly Costa Rica's economic crisis became a great concern for the United States government. The crisis was the worst Costa Rica had experienced since the Great Depression. As access to foreign financial markets became restricted and the dollars needed to finance imports and repay debt became scarce, the Costa Rican economy went into a deep plunge. From 1979 to 1982, per capita GDP declined by 10 percent. Inflation reached 90 percent by 1982, eroding the value of real wages, which dropped by 18 percent during the three years of the crisis. Relative to the U.S. dollar, the value of the national currency, the *colón,* fell abruptly—from about 8 colones to the dollar to 21 colones to the dollar in 1981 alone. By the end of the decade, a dollar would be worth a little more than 91 colones (Mesa-Lago 2000, 485, 508). Devaluation of the currency would eventually make Costa Rican goods cheaper and thus more competitive in the international market. More immediately, however, it made all products and goods from overseas much more expensive, driving up the cost of living.

Costa Rica's presidents Luis Alberto Monge (1982–1986) and Óscar Arias Sánchez (1986–1990), astutely manipulated U.S. concerns to gain the aid so needed by their country. Monge accentuated his rhetoric about the dangers of "Marxism-Leninism" in Central America to increase the Reagan administration's concern for the future of Costa Rica (Clark 2001, 45). While running for the presidency in 1986, Óscar Arias baldly stated that "as long as there are nine *comandantes* in Nicaragua, we'll be able to get $200 million [a year from Washington], more or less, in aid" (quoted in Clark 2001, 46).

The United States, however, also used Costa Rica's dire economic circumstances as an opportunity to push the radical free-market policies preferred by the Reagan administration. The United States gave Costa Rica $1.2 billion in aid during the 1980s, which was more than the combined assistance given by the World Bank, IMF, and IDB (Clark 2001,

49). During the crucial years of 1983–1985, U.S. assistance accounted for 35.7 percent of the Costa Rican government budget, 20 percent of exports, and 10 percent of GNP (Edelman 1999, 78). The principle channel for American assistance was the United States Agency for International Development (USAID). The United States was already very influential at the IMF and World Bank, which were prodding Costa Rica toward the goals of austerity and structural adjustment. USAID, however, took a much more direct approach to pushing free-market reforms and in supporting, and even creating, domestic interest groups to fight for reforms that would promote exports and benefit the private sector.

The U.S. Agency for International Development focused its efforts in the 1980s on opening Costa Rica's banking monopoly, privatizing the bankrupt CODESA, and promoting new exports. The nationalized banking system was considered perhaps the single most effective tool for government intervention in the economy. The national banks were highly valued institutions; outright privatization was politically out of the question. Instead, USAID and domestic financial interests pushed for and achieved changes in the banking laws that allowed private banks to compete on equal footing with the national banks. Banking reform was so important to officials at USAID that in 1983–1984, they conditioned the continuation of financial aid to the Costa Rican government on the passage of bank reform legislation (Clark 2001, 61). In 1984, the Legislative Assembly yielded to this pressure and began the process of effectively rolling back what José Figueres had called the "most important measure taken for social and economic development by the National Liberation Movement" (Figueres Ferrer 1956, 22). Between 1984 and 1990, the Costa Rican Central Bank dismantled the system of lending targets, subsidies, and differential interest rates that had permitted the national banks to operate differently from private-sector institutions. By 1996, private banks enjoyed nearly all of the same privileges as the national banks; the latter were forced to compete with the private-sector institutions by lending according to strict criteria of collateral and profitability and by working to increase efficiency (Clark 2001, 62–63; Honey 1994, 90–96).

In 1984, USAID began to work closely with the Costa Ricans to liquidate CODESA. This step not only accorded well with the neoliberal tone of the 1980s; it was also a financial necessity. Nonetheless, it was a politically delicate operation, and one that ultimately took 13 years to complete. The Costa Rican Development Corporation was closely identified with the PLN, which meant that fully exposing its business failures and financial irregularities was acutely embarrassing to powerful people. The solution found by USAID was to establish a new holding company with a Costa Rican board of directors drawn from the private sector and to endow it with a $140 million budget to buy all of CODESA's holdings and cancel its debts. That holding company subsequently took on the longer-term, but now less bureaucratic and politically charged, task of selling off the individual subsidiaries to private-sector buyers, including some cooperatives (Clark 2001, 53–55).

The U.S. Agency for International Development and the World Bank also pushed for another step in the same direction—dismantling the CNP and its complicated system of price supports and protections for the basic grains sectors of Costa Rican agriculture: corn, beans, rice, and sorghum (Edelman 1999, 80). The objective was to shift emphasis away from basic grains that might be imported more cheaply from abroad and toward new agricultural exports that could earn scarce foreign currency. Ending support to small farmers of basic grains was also considered a financial necessity at the time because "USAID estimated that by 1980 CNP losses equaled 40 percent of the national budget deficit" (Clark 2001, 65). Taking this step, of course, was politically very difficult. Farmers protested these reforms fiercely, but the executive branch, which controlled price support policies, was firm in its resolve to phase them out, and by 1994, the CNP ceased to function as it once did (Edelman 1999; Clark 2001, 65).

The constructive part of the neoliberal agenda had to do with realizing the vision of Costa Rica as a vibrant export economy. Various countries were held up as models of export success—the East Asian "tigers" (Taiwan, South Korea, Singapore) in the 1980s and 1990s; the "Celtic tiger," Ireland, is more often cited in the 21st century. Costa Rica's experience with new exports will be examined in the next section. However, it is important to point out here the role played by USAID in creating the conditions for new export industries to grow. Ironically, for an institution that held that the free market was the solution to most economic problems, USAID acted aggressively in Costa Rica to create organizations that lobbied to gain government assistance for the export sector.

The best example of this kind of organization was the Costa Rican Coalition for Development Initiatives (CINDE), founded in 1982. Its board of directors was Costa Rican, representative of various political parties, and very well connected. Its budget, however, was directly supported by USAID. The foreign agency provided CINDE with $47 million between 1983 and 1989. The Coalition for Development Initiatives was responsible for drawing up legislation favorable to new export initiatives and pushing it through the Legislative Assembly. Nearly all the tax and other incentives created to stimulate exports in the 1980s and 1990s trace their origins to CINDE (Clark 2001, 57, 58). And CINDE was not the only player to benefit from U.S. government largesse. New private banks also enjoyed direct financial assistance from USAID as they began operations and entered into competition with the Costa Rican national banks (Honey 1994, 79–80; Robinson 2003, 239).

For many observers, USAID's creation of CINDE and other organizations amounted to the creation of a "parallel state." Rather than helping or challenging the Costa Ricans to reform the state institutions they had built for themselves over the previous 30 years, USAID chose to create new institutions and staff them with like-minded people dependent on USAID for their funding (Edelman 1999, 78; Honey 1994, 97–132). This approach allowed USAID to avoid direct conflict with government institutions that were still attached to policies of import substitution industrialization. It also allowed USAID to claim that it was merely promoting open competition between private-sector and state institutions, rather than outright privatization of state functions. However, mandated austerity policies had starved government agencies of funds, and thus it was not difficult for USAID-funded competitors to gain decisive advantages.

The combination of austerity measures and structural adjustment policies under pressure from the United States and international financial institutions began to work in 1983. Positive economic growth rates resumed in that year and averaged 4.4 percent between 1983 and 1994. Given the depths of the crisis, this compared well with the 4.9 percent average growth rate sustained between 1971 and 1982. Inflation, which reached 90 percent in 1982, had dropped down to an average rate of 18.2 percent from 1983 to 1994 (Mesa-Lago 2000, 485, 487). As the crisis passed both in the Costa Rican economy and in the Central American isthmus in the 1990s, USAID radically reduced its assistance levels. In 1985, with deep U.S. involvement in civil conflicts in Nicaragua, El Salvador, and Guatemala, aid to Costa Rica's showcase democracy reached $219 million. In 1995, with the Berlin Wall gone, U.S. concern focused on Eastern Europe and the Middle East, and, with many of USAID's goals for Costa Rica achieved, aid dropped to a mere $6.1 million. The USAID office in San José was closed the following year, leaving behind some political hard feelings and a new landscape upon which Costa Rica would build a new export economy (Clark 2001, 69).

FROM 1990 TO THE PRESENT: A NEW ECONOMIC MODEL WITH SOME FAMILIAR WEAKNESSES

In response to incentives designed by CINDE and other actors, nontraditional exports grew rapidly in the 1990s. By the start of the 21st century, it was difficult to find any vestiges of ISI, as the economy had been reoriented toward new agricultural crops and manufacturing for export, as well as toward the service industries, especially the "export" of tourism. By 1993, tourism earned more foreign exchange than coffee or bananas, Costa Rica's traditional exports, and it has only continued to grow since (Honey 2003, 39). By that same year, manufactured goods for export (such as textiles, electronics, and pharmaceuticals) along with nontraditional agricultural products (fruits, vegetables, ornamental plants, flowers, spices, etc.) already made up 53.3 percent of all export earnings. They have since become only more important (Robinson 2003, 161, 174).

What impact did these changes have on society, the economy, and the environment? Will this new model of development prove any more sustainable over the long term than the model it replaced? In trying to answer these questions, we take as an organizing point the one used by the Costa Rican report *El Estado de la Nación* (the State of the Nation), which, in the past decade has become one of the country's most respected authorities on development. This report is not simply a compilation of statistics; it is an analysis of the economy that "has as its objective to evaluate the national efforts in this area from the point of view of human development" (Programa Estado de la Nación 2005, 135).

Statistics certainly point to economic success in the 1990s and early 2000s. Economic growth since 2000 has been constant, but fluctuating, increasing to 4.1 percent in 2005 (PROCOMER 2005, 11). Costa Rica has long had a higher per capita income than its Central American neighbors have:

Costa Rican Traffic

One result of increased economic development in Costa Rica has been that more and more people can afford to own their own cars. The number of cars doubled from 1995 to 2006, and now a little more than a million cars are in circulation (Programa Estado de la Nación 2006, 414). Over the same period of time, the network of roads in the country has not expanded accordingly, and this has caused increasing numbers of traffic jams and delays. Unfortunately, many Costa Ricans seem somehow not to have noticed the changes that have taken place and drive as if theirs were the only car on the road.

According to the 2006 edition of the annual statistical compilation put together by the magazine *The Economist,* Costa Rica has among the world's worst records for traffic accidents, injuries, and deaths on the road. Figures from 2002 and later place Costa Rica at number four in the world (after Malawi, Rwanda, and South Korea) in number of people injured in traffic accidents. In the number of deaths over the same period of time, Costa Rica ranked number 16 in the world, and number 3 in Latin America, behind only Colombia and Honduras (*The Economist* 2005, 71). In 2006, more than 700 people died in car accidents in Costa Rica. And 2007 did not start off well: in only the first two months of that year, 78 people were killed on the roads and highways (Loaiza 2006a, 2007).

These poor ratings are due in some part to the difficult geography of the country, the dangerous weather conditions in the rainy season, and the very poorly maintained roads throughout the country. Only an estimated 32.4 percent of the national network of roads is in good condition (Programa Estado de la Nación 2006, 307). But it must be attributed in equal measure to lack of driver education programs, aggressive driving, drunk driving, and lack of enforcement of traffic laws. Very few transit police patrol Costa Rica's highways or its cities and towns, and they often lack reliable transportation—patrol cars and motorcycles—as well as the tow trucks needed to respond to accidents and to prevent them (Loaiza and Mora 2006). Fines for violations have not been increased in years and, as a result of inflation, are now ridiculously low. In early

2007, a proposed transit law before the legislature would attempt to remedy this problem. Among other goals, the new law would increase fines for drunk or reckless driving from about $50 to around $700; the fine for driving with an expired license would increase from about $5 to around $200, and the fine for driving with children not in seatbelts or carseats would increase from about $25 to $500. This proposed law has found much support from many political parties and other segments of the population alarmed about the rising numbers of traffic fatalities (Mora 2007). A speedy passage is hoped for, which would help turn around some very dangerous trends.

Sources: The Economist. 2006. *Pocket World in Figures: 2006 Edition.* London: Profile Books.

Loaiza, Vanessa. 2006. "Muertes en vías durante 2006 superan las de últimos dos años." *La Nación* December 31, sec. "Nacionales."

Loaiza, Vanessa. 2007. "Accidentes viales cobran 78 vidas en primeros dos meses." *La Nación* March 6, sec. "Nacionales."

Loaiza, Vanessa and Zoyla Rita Mora. 2006. "Policía de transito trabaja a pie." *La Nación* October 21, sec. "Nacionales."

Mora, Ana Lupita. 2007. "PAC y Liberación apoyan elevar multas de transito." *La Nación,* March 6, sec. "Nacionales."

Programa Estado de la Nación. 2006. *Estado de la Nación en Desarrollo Humano Sostenible: Un análisis amplio y objetivo sobre la Costa Rica que tenemos y a partir de los indicadores más actuales (2005).* San José: Programa Estado de la Nación.

$4,628 in 2005, in a population of 4,325,808 (Programa Estado de la Nación 2006, 394, 409). The total value of Costa Rican exports increased from $1.08 billion in 1985 to $3.4 billion in 1995, then to $7 billion in 2005 (Observatorio del Desarrollo 2005, 31; PROCOMER 2005, 3). During the 1990s, Costa Rica experienced annual economic growth of nearly 5 percent. Yet in the World Bank's Index of Human Development, which takes into account measures of poverty, literacy, school enrollment, and GNP per capita in 177 countries, Costa Rica fell from 28th place in 1990 to 47th in 2005 (World Bank 2003, 2; Programa Estado de la Nación 2006, 70). In 2005, the *Estado de la Nación* declared that Costa Rican society in general over the last 15 years "has been characterized by an inability to achieve a connection between the development of human capabilities and the construction of a more equitable society" (Programa Estado de la Nación 2005, 77). To understand why this might be the case despite much economic growth, we must look in more detail at what has taken place over the last 15 years.

Manufacturing

Since Costa Rica began exporting coffee in the first half of the 19th century, it has relied on international markets for its products. As we have seen, in the 1960s and 1970s, attempts at industrialization focused on manufacturing for domestic and regional markets. Yet since the 1980s, prodded by U.S. and international lenders, Costa Rica has again turned outward, participating in "global capitalism," with its particular emphasis on the liberalization of markets for goods and services and the globalization of processes of production (offshore assembly, etc.). A decisive door to the hemisphere's largest market was opened in 1987 with the passage by the U.S. Congress of the Caribbean Basin Initiative (CBI). This initiative was a trade measure that gave all Central American countries (except Nicaragua, which was at that time controlled by the anticapitalist, anti-U.S. Sandinistas) duty-free access to U.S. markets for most of their products (although several promising export sectors like sugar and textiles were subject to restrictions to protect U.S. interest groups).

One way in which the Costa Rican government encouraged manufacturing for export to the United States and other markets was by providing incentives for the establishment of free trade zones. Manufacturing companies pay no

Costa Ricans are hoping for more high-tech jobs like these done by workers at the Intel Corporation silicon chip factory near San José in 2000. (Gilles Mingasson/Liaison/Getty Images)

taxes on materials imported or on manufactured products exported from these enclaves. Interestingly, these are some of the same sorts of incentives earlier offered to companies participating in import-substituting industrialization. These offshore assembly operations, typically called *maquiladoras,* increased exports greatly, but it was mainly large companies that were able to take advantage of the incentives offered. In 2002, a new program was established to offer incentives and training to small- and medium-size companies—that is, the majority of Costa Rican enterprises (Programa Estado de la Nación 2005, 167). The effects of this effort are not yet clear, and large-scale enterprises are still the most important. Although large companies make up only 20 percent of the total number of manufacturers, in 2005 their exports accounted for 84 percent of the value of all goods exported (PROCOMER 2005, 200). It is also interesting to note that while the most high-value exports are manufactured in free trade zones, the majority of manufacturing has never taken place in maquiladoras. In fact, it was the growth in manufacturing taking place *outside* of free trade zones that contributed most to total manufacturing growth in 2004 (Programa Estado de la Nación 2005, 53).

What products does Costa Rica now manufacture for export that it did not in the past? It makes goods like medical equipment, medicine, hair dryers, textiles, and electronics. By 2004, Costa Rica's most valuable export was computer microchips from two Intel factories near San José. The value of all integrated circuits exported was $803.3 million in 2005 and $1.211 billion in 2006. The next most valuable manufactured exports were other parts for modular circuits, textiles, medical equipment, and pharmaceuticals (Programa Estado de la Nación 2005 138; PROCOMER 2005, 201; PROCOMER 2006, 48). Although the range of exports has grown, just a few products, including manufactured and agricultural products, account for the majority of export value. Yet producing a wide range of goods remains necessary if Costa Rica is to be able to weather fluctuations in a world market over which it has little control.

Vulnerability to world markets is not new to Costa Rica; exported coffee was for many years the basis of its entire economy. Yet the globalization of its economy has recently made the country more vulnerable in new ways as well. Similar to what happened with ISI, as the complexity of the economy and of consumer tastes has increased, Costa Rica has become more dependent on the international market for imports, as well as for selling its exports. For example, Costa Rica has been hit particularly hard by rising oil prices. All oil is imported, and it cost 60 percent more in 2004 than in 2000. Also, many exported products are manufactured using imported raw materials, and many agricultural products rely on imported inputs. Not surprisingly, then, throughout the 1990s and early 2000s, while exports were increasing, imports were increasing even more. In 1995, for instance,

Costa Rica imported $4.08 billion worth of goods (and exported $3.4 billion); in 2005, it imported $9.7 billion (and exported $7 billion) (Observatorio del Desarrollo 2005, 3; PROCOMER 2005, 3).

To cover this stubborn gap between exports and imports, Costa Rica must work hard to attract dollars to the country in the form of direct foreign investment. One very important point that Costa Rica has in its favor is that its location—only a few hours by plane south of the United States—makes it very attractive to large U.S. and international corporations looking to outsource their operations. A 2005 report ranked it as the third most competitive offshore destination after India and China. Large multinational manufacturers of surgical tools, medical products, and medicines, to name a few, have set up factories in Costa Rica, and the country now exports the most computer software per capita in Latin America. High literacy rates and peaceful political conditions have been a strong lure for high-tech manufacturing; yet over time, the small number of skilled workers and higher labor costs (as compared with India or China) may limit possibilities for further expansion (Dickerson 2006).

Agriculture

Manufacturing is not the only engine of the new export economy. Although they have lost ground to manufacturing and to new nontraditional agricultural exports, the traditional Costa Rican exports of bananas and coffee are still important. The banana industry, after nearly doubling the land under cultivation between 1988 and 1995—opening new areas on the Atlantic coast and returning to some areas that had been abandoned in the 1940s when most operations were moved to the Pacific—has seen its business decline. This decline is due to factors such as the decrease in world prices, conflict with European countries over tariffs, and a series of devastating floods on the Atlantic coast in late 2004 and early

2005 (Programa Estado de la Nación 2005, 138). It is, however, still the second leading producer of bananas in the world, after Ecuador (ACAN-IFE 2006). Yet, the industry has not been completely passive in the face of these challenges. For many years, banana companies were accused of contributing to deforestation and loss of biodiversity by clear-cutting large tracts of land, and of threatening the environment and their employees' health by using large amounts of dangerous pesticides and fungicides (Vandermeer and Perfecto 2005, 7–8). A few companies—in Costa Rica the most notable is Chiquita (formerly the United Fruit Company)—have responded by changing their practices and appealing to a new market by becoming certified by nongovernmental agencies like the Rainforest Alliance. Such groups inspect the conditions under which the bananas (among other crops) are grown and harvested, certify that they meet certain criteria for environmental safety and sustainability, and certify that they offer their employees fair wages and safe working conditions.

Coffee producers also have tried to counter years of falling international prices and falling production with new practices and new marketing. Although in the harvest of 2003–2004, 7.4 percent less coffee was produced than the year before, a much larger proportion of it was of much higher quality. Almost half of the harvest of 2004–2005 was of very high quality beans, which earn much more on the international market than beans of lesser quality. Value has also been increased in some cases by certification processes similar to those for bananas (Programa Estado de la Nación 2005, 140–142). This increase in value was evident in the production and export figures from 2005: although the volume of coffee exported (in metric tons) fell, the value of the exports rose (Programa Estado de la Nación 2006, 146). Some Costa Rican coffee processors have taken advantage of the growing world market in gourmet coffees by not simply selling their beans to foreign companies to be marketed, but by becoming involved in the marketing and sales of their own products abroad.

Despite changes in production and marketing, these traditional exports are now far out-earned by nontraditional agricultural exports. In 2005, traditional products were only worth $757 million, while nontraditional exports earned more than $6.2 billion (Programa Estado de la Nación 2006, 410). These nontraditional exports include crops such as pineapple, melons, vegetables, ornamental plants, flowers, and palm oil. The production of all these exports has increased greatly in the last few years, but pineapple exports have shown probably the most startling growth.

From 2000 to 2004, exports of pineapple more than doubled, from $121 million to $256 million. And by 2006, they were valued at $430.4 million. The number of companies producing pineapple increased from 35 in 2002 to 118 in 2006 (PROCOMER 2004, 61; PROCOMER 2005, 141; PROCOMER 2006, 48, 54). But this rapid growth has come at a price. Critics have pointed out that, particularly in the Atlantic region, increased production of pineapple has contributed to deforestation (it requires the removal of almost all trees) and that its highly mechanized processes have caused soil erosion and increased pesticide runoff into streams and rivers (Programa Estado de la Nación 2005, 201).

Although these new agricultural exports may prove very profitable, their production is not without risk. These crops require more financing than traditional crops. Farmers need capital to obtain inputs like new seeds, fertilizers, and pesticides (almost all of which must be imported), and new technical skills. This capital may be readily available to large companies, but it is harder to come by for small producers. As we saw with coffee and bananas in earlier eras, large (often international) companies frequently make contracts with many small producers. The small producers tend to assume more of the risks and costs of production, while not always having a guarantee that the large exporters will buy

A farm worker carries a basket of pineapples at a plantation in Pital de San Carlos, 150 kilometers north of San José. Costa Rica has become one of the world's top pineapple exporters, devoting more and more cultivated—and even previously forested—land to the fruit. (Juan Carlos Ulate/Reuters/Corbis)

what they produce. If small farmers fail to sell their crops, they may be left with debts that cannot be paid and be in danger of losing their land (Robinson 2003, 179–181). Just as with bananas and coffee in the past, much of the profit is not made in the production of the crop, but in its financing, export, and marketing.

Globalized production of fresh fruits and vegetables can be a tricky business. In 2006, producers of melons and mangoes suffered thousands of dollars of losses because of lack of containers and ships to take their produce to foreign markets. Shipping lines, for various reasons, cut back that year on the number of ships sent to transport the fruit; changes in ownership of the companies may have affected their service to Costa Rica. Shipping companies may also be less interested in crops like melons and mangoes that are harvested only a few months of the year and are more likely to be damaged during shipment than the more durable pineapple, which can be harvested year-round (Barquero 2006b). Such problems highlight the fact that merely producing more does not always guarantee selling more when local farmers find themselves at the very end of a supply chain they do not control.

Even when products do find their way safely to overseas markets, the profits accruing to farmers can be disappointing. A recent study by researchers in Costa Rica and by universities in the Netherlands and Sweden determined that only 8 percent of the final profit from the export of coffee and only 6 percent from the export of melon are received by Costa Rican farmers. In March 2006, the value of a kilo of coffee on the New York Stock Exchange was only $2.29—about the price American consumers pay for a single cup of coffee at their corner café. All that value was added *after* the coffee left Costa Rica. Although some of the methods of production and some of the products may be new, this situation is not: Costa Rica is still exporting raw agricultural products, not the finished product (Barquero 2006a).

Several other factors must also be taken into account when evaluating the recent agricultural changes in Costa Rica. Although nontraditional agricultural exports increased greatly in the last few years, the amount of land under cultivation has not. In December 2005, the *Contralaría General de la República* (Comptroller General of the Republic) reported that 450,000 hectares of vegetables, fruits, ornamental plants, tubers, and sugarcane were under production in Costa Rica in 2002. This is the same number of hectares as in 1990 (Leitón 2006a). As we have seen, Costa Rica has a varied and often very difficult geography in which only a finite amount of land is suitable for cultivation. If more of what is produced on this land is for export, then less land is available to produce crops for domestic consumption.

Changes in agricultural production may also have important environmental and health impacts. The same report from the Controlaría General (2005) noted that the amount of land under cultivation remained more or less the same from 1990 to 2002 and indicated that over the same period of time, the amount of imported chemicals (pesticides and fungicides) applied to that land increased from 4,000 tons (1990) to 10,000 tons (2002), an increase of 150 percent (Loaiza N. 2006). The Controlaría has been very critical of the Ministry of Agriculture for failing to monitor the use of chemicals in agriculture. Reports in 2005 and 2006 from the Controlaría noted that Costa Ricans eat cucumbers, celery, cilantro, lettuce, tomatoes, cabbage, carrots, and red peppers that contain levels of pesticides that have been determined to be unsafe for human consumption. Costa Rica also continues to import and use chemicals that many other countries have banned as too hazardous to human health and to the environment. Farmers tend to choose the chemicals that are the cheapest, not those that are the least toxic or most effective; and they often apply the chemicals without using protective equipment. Improper use of these chemicals has led not only to many poisonings but also to the contamination of surface water through agricultural runoff (Leitón 2005, 2006a). Thus, although export numbers may increase and the economy may expand overall, risks and side effects arise that must be considered when evaluating whether or not economic changes are beneficial over the long term.

Problems of degradation of natural resources and pollution have caused some producers to change their methods. In 2004, 10,800 hectares of land were certified in Costa Rica for organic production. This number appears to be growing as the worldwide market for organic produce grows. The amount of land under various international certification programs is also increasing. As in the case of coffee and bananas, numerous nongovernmental organizations from around the world also certify crops such as melons, pineapples, oranges, and ornamental plants. This certification may or may not mean that the produce is organic, but it does mean that the crops are produced using sustainable, environmentally friendly practices in terms of soil, irrigation, fertilizers, and pesticides. Certification may also encompass regulation of working conditions and just salaries for workers. These certifying agencies include organizations such as the Rainforest Alliance, EurepGap, and ISO 14100, among others. Their number of projects increases as world demand for certified produce increases (Programa Estado de la Nación 2005, 204).

Service Industries

It is neither manufacturing nor agriculture, however, that brings the most money into Costa Rica; it is the service industry, two of the most important elements of which are tourism and customer service call centers. Although tourism "imports" people from other countries to Costa Rica rather than exporting Costa Rican products abroad, it technically has the same impact on the economy as an export. Tourists bring foreign currency with them to spend while on vacation; some of this currency is never exchanged for colones because many tourist businesses accept, and even prefer to receive, dollars. Although call centers do not export a product, the service they provide is usually for foreign customers and financed by foreign investment, so it is also considered an export.

U.S. companies run most of the call centers found in Costa Rica and provide services like data processing, customer service, medical attention, software services, and sports wagering. These businesses are attracted to Costa Rica because it is relatively close to the markets they serve, and many workers have the level of education, and particularly of English skills, necessary for these jobs. Some firms moved their operations from countries such as Pakistan after 9/11 because they felt that Costa Rica offered more political and economic stability. In 1998, only two call centers were operating in the country, and they employed around 200 people. In 2006, Costa Rica had 39 international and national call center companies, with more than 8,000 employees (Lara 2006).

It is tourism, though, that has seen the greatest economic growth in recent years. The Costa Rican Tourism Institute (ICT), a government agency, has a very broad view of the benefits tourism will bring to the country. On its Web site it says "the development of tourism ought to effectively and constructively work against any form of social deterioration, generating economic benefits, protecting the environment and respecting the culture and values of our people" (ICT 2007). In many parts of the world, tourism has been praised as a clean industry that brings in money and development without the environmental destruction and health hazards that may accompany the growth of other industries. This optimistic attitude permeates much of the publicity generated by the Costa Rican tourist industry, but tourism may turn out to be more of a mixed blessing.

Costa Rica first gained worldwide attention as a tourist destination when President Óscar Arias received the Nobel Peace Prize in 1987 for his role in ending the armed conflicts that were so damaging to Costa Rica's Central American neighbors in the 1980s. Costa Rica was in a particularly good position to promote itself because it already had in place a successful system of national parks, which made it very attractive to nature tourists. The first national park was created in 1969, and by 1990, 230 areas were under various degrees of protection. By 2004, about 25 percent of the country was protected area; about half of this is under strict protection (Honey 2003, 40). (For a discussion of the creation and administration of the National Park System, see chapter 3.) In 2005, 611,334 foreigners visited Costa Rica's national parks; this figure does not include those who visited the many private nature reserves (Programa Estado de la

Nación 2006, 411). Tourists travel to Costa Rica to experience the great biodiversity of its protected areas, but they also visit because the country has the reputation of being peaceful, socially and environmentally progressive, and welcoming to foreigners.

Tourist arrivals had been increasing for decades—an average of 9 percent a year from 1969 to 1982. From 1986 to 1994, this average was 14 percent a year (Inman 2001, 1). In 2005, Costa Rica received 1,679,051 tourists, a 15.6 percent increase over 2004. The income provided by tourism increased from $22 million in 1970 to $659.6 million in 1995, then to $1.57 billion in 2005 (ICT 2003; Programa Estado de la Nación 2006, 410–411). Tourism gives direct employment to about 85,000 people and indirect employment to 400,000, and these numbers are expected to grow (LANAMME-UCR 2005, 9). Although the profitability and scale of the tourism industry is relatively new, it is interesting to place it in the context of the country's historical economic development. From this perspective, tourism is not very different from the cultivation and export of coffee, bananas, or pineapple, for instance. These are all products whose production is facilitated by a tropical climate and has the possibility of disturbing that same delicate natural environment, just like tourism.

Costa Rica's climate, geography, and biodiversity give it a comparative advantage in the tourism industry, especially in the development of what has come to be called ecotourism (Inman 2001, 1). A broad definition of ecotourism given by the International Ecotourism Society is "responsible travel to natural areas that conserves the environment and sustains the well-being of local people" (quoted in Stern et al. 2003, 323). As it makes clear on its Web site, the ICT takes pains to promote the country as a "green" destination. This makes sense considering the resources the country possesses in its national parks and private nature reserves. Yet no strict rules have been established for determining just

There has been a great deal of investment in ecotourism options, like this tram ride through the rainforest. But Costa Rica must also take care to regulate tourism's impact on delicate tropical ecosystems. (AP/Wide World Photos)

what "eco" means, and different tourists arrive with different expectations. Some visitors to Costa Rica are willing to rough it in order to see untouched wilderness areas. Others, however, are more interested in "adventure" tourism—outdoor activities like whitewater rafting, mountain climbing, and sailing through the forest canopy on zip lines. Students and researchers with plans to study the biology of the area constitute another group of foreign visitors. But most people participate in "soft" or "general" ecotourism. They are "tourists who want to observe wildlife, a natural environment or a culture, but casually" (Inman 2001, 7–8).

Considering Costa Rica's progressive reputation, all of these visitors might be led to expect that the places where they spend their vacations strive to protect the natural environment from which they are profiting. This is not always the case. Many tourist businesses are guilty of "greenwashing": they promote themselves as environmentally friendly while never taking any pains to be so. Examples of this phenomenon can be found all over the country, but developments in coastal areas have been some of the most notorious offenders. On the Pacific coast, especially in the booming northwestern region of Guanacaste, hotel and condominium projects, while billing themselves as "eco-developments," have built hundreds of rooms and sprawling golf courses, often in areas where water is scarce. Although the country's image abroad is one of "small eco-lodges and beach cabinas," the Costa Rican government has, in fact, often been friendlier to large projects than to small ones (Honey 2003, 43–44). Beginning in the 1980s, the government gave to hotels, transportation companies, car rental companies, and tour operators incentives and tax breaks that favored foreign investors and hotels of more than 20 rooms (Robinson 2003, 195).

Both large- and small-scale developers have taken advantage of the fact that the municipalities (under whose jurisdiction much of the permitting falls) have lacked the personnel, the resources, and sometimes the political will to prevent unlawful constructions in coastal areas. The law states that no construction should take place in the first 50 meters from the shoreline, and special concessions are required in order to build within the next 150 meters. Nevertheless, a 2007 survey found many examples in many beach areas of hotels, restaurants, and other businesses established within these zones and without appropriate permission (Loaiza 2007). Municipalities often lack even the most basic zoning plans (which are theoretically necessary before handing out any coastal concessions), and some have been implicated in apparent corruption in the process of awarding concessions (Sherwood 2007). In one recent scandal, an investor apparently received an illegal concession, which was later rescinded, to build an extremely inappropriate million-dollar commercial plaza directly in front of the entrance to the Manuel Antonio National Park, one of the most visited in the country (Feigenblatt 2007).

In 1995, the government created the Secretaria Técnica Nacional Ambiental (SETENA) to study the environmental impact of and approve all new construction projects. Despite this well-intentioned attempt at regulation, by 2007 even the secretary general of the SETENA herself admitted that the institution was in a state of almost complete administrative collapse. It lacked both the funds and the personnel to monitor and approve the ever-increasing number of construction projects in the country. The demand for permits rose from 1,030 in 2003 to 3,511 in 2006, and the organization has simply been unable to keep up (Fallas 2007). Difficulty and delays in obtaining municipal or federal permits have led to many complaints by businesspeople and developers that the process has become too slow and burdensome. Some entrepreneurs have apparently resorted to bribery, while others work under the assumption that it is better to ask forgiveness than to ask permission and have simply begun construction without any type of permit. They figure into their costs a fine that they may have to pay in the future, when their business will be already up and running. A study released in 2007 by the Federated Association of Engineers and Architects of construction projects in Guanacaste found that of 217 hotels, condominium, and other residential developments, 45 had no kind of government permit at all for their work (Sherwood 2007).

In this same study, it was also determined that the *kind* of coastal development in Costa Rica is changing. Of these same 217 projects, 80 percent were not hotels or cabins, but rather condominiums and other residential units. These developments are aimed primarily at foreign retirees who purchase a home as an investment or with the intention of remaining in the country for longer periods of time. This sort of real estate market may bring new regulatory and environmental challenges (Sherwood 2007). Such challenges are becoming clear as the real estate boom moves south down the Pacific coast. In the central Pacific area near Dominical Beach (a popular surfing area) and Ballena National Marine Park, hundreds of hectares of mountain land with ocean views have been stripped of their plant cover to build new vacation homes, usually for foreigners. The local municipal governments are proving incapable of regulating this process, and university researchers have only in the last three years seen severe erosion problems caused by the new clearing and construction. Sediments have been carried down to the sea and are killing coral reefs inside the protected marine park (Baxter-Neal 2007).

The construction of vacation homes and resort areas and the inability of the municipal or federal government to control illegal constructions are bound to have a significant impact on the surrounding environment, but tourists themselves have an impact as well. While park fees and tourist interest may contribute to the maintenance, and even to the creation of national protected areas and the establishment of more private reserves, the presence of tourists can also cause environmental problems. More people in any area means more generation of solid wastes, more habitat destruction, more disturbance of local wildlife, and more trail erosion. It is not clear that ecotourism always has a positive effect on conservation efforts. As one observer put it, "Ironically . . . ecotourism's success may actually lead to its demise" (Stern et al. 2003, 324). If the impact of tourist development is such that it permanently disrupts or changes the natural environment that the tourists have paid to travel to Costa Rica to see, it is ultimately defeating its own purpose.

Tourism may produce other negative externalities, or unintended consequences, that must be taken into account when evaluating its impact on the economy, the local communities, and the environment. For instance, not all the money that tourists bring into the country stays there. Some "leaks out" in the form of the purchase of a variety of

Tourism: A New Enclave Economy

At the beginning of the 20th century, North American investors created a vast enclave economy devoted to the production of bananas on Costa Rica's Atlantic coast. The United Fruit Company imported most of what it and its workers needed to operate, exported all of its products, and was largely left alone to run things the "American way." At the beginning of the 21st century, a new sort of enclave appears to be developing on the Pacific coast, in Guanacaste Province.

This enclave is devoted to tourism, the single most important "export" as Costa Rica entered the new century. Beachfront property is being monopolized by foreign—mostly American—investors. This monopolization became much easier with the arrival of international flights to the airport in the Guanacaste town of Liberia. When direct flights from the United States began arriving there in 2003, only about 50,000 tourists a year visited the area. By 2007, more than 300,000 people were visiting. The airport in Liberia, only about an hour's drive from the closest Pacific beaches, is hardly luxurious (it still lacks air conditioning). Slowdowns in Costa Rican customs and immigration there can cause huge delays for travelers, but they just keep coming. And beachfront construction keeps increasing.

As the *New York Times* reported in its travel section in 2006, "All up and down the coast, bulldozers are at work. Three major developments, including a project anchored by a Four Seasons hotel, are already selling luxury condominiums for $500,000 and up, and hundreds of smaller, more speculative endeavors are also breaking ground." Americans see this boom in oceanfront properties as a great real estate opportunity. Some of the houses purchased only a few years ago have already doubled in price: "The new homesteaders envision a beach, golf, and spa destination equal to the Puerto Vallarta corridor in Mexico or Wailea Beach on Maui—without, so far at least, the high-rise blight."

But this is a region of great contrasts. As the *Times* reported, "Roads must be shared with herds of ambling cattle and are often so potholed that local people drive on the ground along the side. Yet strung all along them are signs, all in English, advertising million-dollar villas." Public services like roads, electricity, and water have not always been able to keep up with increasing demands, so developers have often taken these tasks upon themselves. Some of the larger developments have not only paid for their own roads and electricity but have even established services like paramedics and firefighters to protect their visitors and their investments. The virtue of these practices is that, as a sales agent for the large Papagayo project put it, "We sell 'Costa Rica Lite': all of the upside and none of the downside. We're our own municipality."

The essence of an enclave economy is that it attempts to be self-sufficient and to remain unaffected by any problems in the society or the economy that surround it. While the new luxury developments have been able to do this to some extent, it may not be possible forever. There are many problems—problems that promotional tourism articles for the U.S. market and Costa Rican developers might prefer not to mention. The booming town of Tamarindo, for instance, is quickly depleting its aquifer in order to provide for the needs of more and more tourists. There is also a lack of treatment facilities for all the wastewater that these new arrivals produce in their condominiums, hotels, and restaurants. A lack of urban planning has meant over-building, traffic jams, and lack of public space. The impact of ever-increasing construction on the beautiful tropical environment (which is what people come to see) must be taken into account. How long can an enclave hold out, and at what price?

Sources: Brown, Janelle. 2006. "In a Corner of Costa Rica, a Beachhead for Luxury." *New York Times,* February 3. http://travel.nyt.com/2006/02/03/realestate/03costarica.html/

Gutiérrez, Javiera. 2007. "Tamarindo clama por ayuda." *La Nación,* June 16, sec. "M Supplement: Zona Pacífico Norte."

imported goods needed to maintain and entertain the tourists (Inman 2001, 6). Although tourism creates many jobs for local residents, it may also increase tensions within communities: economic change always creates some "winners" and some "losers." Some people are simply in a better position to profit from an influx of tourists than others are (Eadington and Smith 1992, 9). Although it may provide use value for rural land that is considerably higher than for farming, tourism may also fluctuate seasonally and not always consistently provide enough jobs or widespread economic benefits to local communities (Stern et al. 2003, 324). Tourism may also take resources out of the hands of local people altogether. By the early 1990s, foreigners owned 80 percent of beachfront property in Costa Rica, and many new luxury hotels are part of foreign chains (Honey 2003, 43).

One promising, yet small-scale, possibility for avoiding at least some of the direst consequences is the growth of rural tourism cooperatives. These tours and lodgings, developed by local farmers, fishermen, and indigenous communities, represent probably the lowest-impact type of eco-development. They allow rural people to stay on their lands and to protect the surrounding natural environment while gaining a small share of tourist income. These are never luxury developments, but many tourists have found that local people who are intimately familiar with their area can be the very best guides. Such cooperatives protect an estimated 25,000 hectares of forestland (Programa Estado de la Nación 2005, 190).

It is also possible that changing conditions and markets for tourism and real estate will change the expectation that Costa Rica *be* an eco-destination. An article published in the *New York Times* in February 2006 and frequently circulated on Costa Rican real estate Web sites extols the virtues of new developments on the northern Pacific coast in the Guanacaste region (Brown 2006). As discussed earlier, Guanacaste took on importance within the Costa Rican economy as a cattle export zone, particularly during the 1970s. The debt crisis and the austerity measures it forced on the heavily subsidized cattle industry pushed Guanacaste into the background in the 1980s and 1990s, as the area's relatively dry climate and miles of Pacific beaches became the region's principal selling point. These beaches became even more attractive with the opening of a new international airport in the old cattle town of Liberia. Resorts that used to be a five-hour drive from the San José airport are less than an hour from Liberia.

Direct flights from cities like Atlanta, Miami, and Houston make Guanacaste a place where, more and more frequently, foreigners not only vacation but also buy property. The ever-increasing number of Guanacaste's hotel and real estate developments has proven very appealing to affluent Americans. Although the foreigners participating in this real estate boom may appreciate the natural beauty of the area, neither they nor the real estate promoters can make any claim that much of this development is environmentally friendly. No mention is made in promotional materials that the bulldozers, the million-dollar condominiums, or the water-consuming golf courses might have any environmental impact at all. This is not Costa Rica as eco-paradise, but, as one developer quoted in the *New York Times* article put it, "a high-end happening" (Brown 2006). Costa Rica may thus sell itself differently to different kinds of tourists. It may ultimately become not an eco-destination but merely a destination with a great deal of tourism, some of which in some vague way is related to nature (Robinson 2003, 200). The possibility of offering different experiences to different kinds of tourists could certainly broaden Costa Rica's appeal to foreign visitors, but it could also irreparably change the natural environment that made it an appealing destination in the first place.

In 1998, the ICT, conscious of the confusion and environmental hazards inherent in much of the tourist development up to that point, launched a new project to certify and

Several of Costa Rica's lush golf resorts are located in dry Guanacaste Province, prompting debates over the best use of scarce water. (Bob Wragg)

regulate hotels (but not other types of developments) claiming to be eco-friendly. Under the program for Certification in Sustainable Tourism (CST), hotels are given a ranking of sustainable certification based on a questionnaire of 153 yes/no questions about the actions the establishment has taken to preserve the environment and minimize the dangerous impacts tourism might have. Although the program is voluntary, several hundred hotels applied to be certified. Unfortunately, the certification processes has proven very slow; as of 2005, only 59 hotels had been certified. Plans are being made to use the CST as a model to develop a certification program for all of Central America, but critics have accused the program of being poorly marketed and poorly executed and say that it has so far added little benefit to the continuing tourist development of Costa Rica (Honey 2003, 45; Programa Estado de la Nación 2006, 62). Others have complained that the system is geared toward larger hotels and that small community-based businesses find it difficult to participate (Silva 2003, 113).

To understand tourism's real consequences, just as with any economic development, it must be seen in the context of the development of its host society, not as somehow separate or insulated from that society. As a Costa Rican researcher has pointed out, "We ought to understand that in the long run the tourism on offer is related to the quality of life that as a country, we provide for our own people; that is to say, that the sustainability of our natural resources, our capacity to live in peace and democracy, the possibilities our citizens have for education and for health are a virtuous circle that motivates and cooperates with the expectations of the tourists who visit us" (Vargas Alfaro 2005). The impacts and benefits of tourism will vary greatly according to how it is developed and regulated and whether it is seen as a boom industry or a long-term project that must be carefully planned and executed in order to obtain the maximum benefit for the most people (Butler 1992, 34).

Social Development

One of the most interesting aspects of economics is that alluded to in the quote in the previous paragraph, and it applies as well to other industries as to tourism: the impact that economic change has on the quality of life of the inhabitants of any given country, region, city, or even neighborhood. Who has benefited from this most recent period of sustained economic growth in Costa Rica, and who has not? And how reliable is this growth model in terms of producing jobs and an acceptable standard of living?

At least by macroeconomic measures, the turn toward export-oriented development provided a great boost to the Costa Rican economy beginning in the 1990s. Yearly growth rates were high, many jobs were created, and economic stability was greater. More Costa Ricans have had access to

While Costa Rican poverty levels are still very low by Central American standards, stark disparities between wealth and poverty are not hard to find in San José. (Mary Thorman/morgueFile)

more of the material benefits of development. While in 1988 only 29 percent of the population had a telephone, in 2004, 72 percent had access to a phone, either a fixed line or a cell phone. In 1988, 35 percent of homes had a color television, while in 2004, this number was 90 percent, and a larger percentage of Costa Ricans now own their own home, rather than renting (Leitón 2006c).

By 2004, however, signs were pointing to a growth slowdown. In that year, only 13,000 new jobs were created; in the previous 10 years, the average annual growth had been 48,000 jobs. Although the rate of unemployment remains low, considering four-year periods, its average has increased over the last 10 years: from 4.5 percent (1990–1994) to 5.7 percent (1995–1999) to 6.2 percent (2000–2004). The unemployment rate for women and for young people from age

This slum, or precario, *is located in a ravine along a river directly behind the packed parking lot of a luxury shopping mall in San José. (Photo by Meg Mitchell)*

16 to 25 and for Costa Ricans living in certain rural areas was much higher than the overall average for 2004. Inflation has been increasing, and in 2005, it stood at 14 percent. This percentage is one of the highest rates in Latin America (Programa Estado de la Nación 2005, 131–133; Sauma 2005, 52; PROCOMER 2005, 5).

As measured by insufficient income, in 2004 the poverty rate increased to 21.7 percent from 18.5 percent in 2003. Another way to imagine this is that the number of poor households in the country increased from 168,659 to 208,680, the highest number since 1990. If we measure poverty both by insufficient income and by unsatisfied basic needs—for housing, potable water, basic sanitation, education, and health care—the 2004 poverty rate looks even higher: 36.2 percent. This rate is lower than in 2000 (37.7 percent) and much lower than in the early 1960s (50 percent), which would seem to argue for a positive direction of the economy over the last 40 years (Sauma 2005, 50–51). Over the last few years, however, the *rate* of poverty reduction has greatly slowed (World Bank 2003, 2). This trend would seem to raise the question of whether the current sort of economic development is sufficient to maintain the successful social development that the country has experienced since the 1960s.

Also being considered is the question of whether or not economic development benefits all sectors of the population. Income inequality as measured by the Gini coefficient, after decreasing for many years, began to rise in the late 1990s. After 1997, when this statistical measure was .380, it began to increase, reaching .433 in 2001 and falling slightly to .418 in 2004. This is almost the same level of inequality as in the 1970s, which suggests that the economic growth of the last 15 years has not benefited all equally (Programa Estado de la Nación 2005, 368). Other statistics make this even clearer. The National Survey of Income and Expenses published in 2006 determined that in the wealthiest households, the income per person nearly doubled between 1988 and 2004; in the poorest households, income per person increased only 7 percent. In 1988, income per person in the wealthiest households was 11 times greater than the income in the poorest households. In 2004, it was 20 times greater (Leitón 2006b). These numbers would seem to indicate that Costa Ricans with more money, and more and better education were much better prepared to participate in and take advantage of the economic expansion than those with fewer resources and less preparation. A rising tide may lift all boats, but it seems to lift some higher than others.

As mentioned earlier, at least since the 1950s the Costa Rican state has tried to remedy these types of inequalities by investing in public services and developing a mixed-type economy with the government playing a managerial role. Through the 1970s, investments by the autonomous state institutions in projects for electrification and potable water, public schools, and national health care obtained very positive results. By 2004, literacy rates were extremely high: 90.5 percent for women and 89.7 percent for men (Programa Estado de la Nación 2005, 386). Almost universal health coverage had resulted in high indicators of general health. Infant mortality per 1,000 live births decreased from 13.25 in 1995 to 9.78 in 2005. Life expectancy rose over this same period: from 73.96 to 76.91 years for men and from 78.6 to 81.42 years for women (Programa Estado de la Nación 2006, 393).

Yet despite these successes, the state overreached itself in the 1960s and 1970s, promoting import substitution industrialization and active (rather than simply managerial) involvement in the economy. As discussed earlier, the resulting debt crisis was resolved through assistance from the United States and international organizations like the World Bank. The solution that these powers mandated was neoliberal reform. However, given the United States' heightened concern for Costa Rica's political and social stability during the years of the Central American crisis, and the understanding that stability depended in part on the value placed on the country's mixed economy, Costa Rica was allowed some leeway to implement these reforms gradually. It complied with the prescription for opening the economy to more foreign investment and the promotion of more agriculture and manufacturing for export. Costa Rica did not, however, immediately open all public services to competition. Although the government opened up the banking system and liquidated CODESA at the insistence of USAID, it did not do away with highly respected autonomous institutions such as the ICE or the National Insurance Institute (INS).

The question of whether or not to force these institutions to compete with private providers is still the stickiest point in the fight over the approval of the DR-CAFTA. Voters will decide whether or not to ratify the treaty in Costa Rica's first-ever binding referendum on October 7, 2007 (see chapter 3). In many ways, DR-CAFTA merely ratifies and extends trends in the economy that are already long-standing: export-led development focused on the U.S. market and a domestic market open to imports. But it is the demand to open more public agencies to competition, and the suspicion that the real objective is to do away with them altogether, that hardens many Costa Ricans' opposition to the trade treaty.

Costa Rica has, up to this point, "embraced neo-liberalism in a piecemeal and selective fashion" (Seligson and Martínez, 2005, 10). For political reasons—as well as for the reason that for a long time they worked rather well—public institutions have not been entirely abandoned, but these programs do not work as well as they once did. Their lessened effectiveness can be explained in part by the fact that despite overall economic growth, state institutions have become progressively underfunded. They lack funding not because investment in them has ceased to grow at all—public investment in social programs increased from 14.5 percent of gross domestic product in 1990 to 18.2 percent in 2002. Rather, at the same time the Costa Rican population was increasing, per capita amounts of social spending have never regained the levels of the 1970s (Seligson and Martínez 2005, 11). Thus, without ever having to take the politically difficult step of opening the ICE or the public health care system to private investment, the government has been able to diminish the power of these institutions.

Deteriorating public services and decreasing per capita spending despite overall economic growth go a long way in explaining Costa Rica's precipitous fall in the rankings of human development. The health care and education systems as well as the national infrastructure have many problems. Recently, the average time on waiting lists at public hospitals has increased, and some patients have been unable to receive needed treatments for lack of drugs or medical equipment. Although health coverage is nearly universal, the number of nurses and doctors per inhabitant varies greatly in different parts of the country. This variance would seem to indicate that not all patients receive the same level of care (Barquero 2006c; Varela 2006). This is certainly true in indigenous communities, where the infant mortality rate is often twice that of the rest of Costa Rica; in the first years of the 21st century, children in these areas are still dying of diseases that have not done much damage in the rest of the country since the 1980s (Cantera 2007).

This sort of inequality is also seen in the public schools. Although almost all school-age children are enrolled in elementary school, the schools themselves are often dilapidated and overcrowded. In 2004, 33 percent of the classrooms in public schools were found to be in a poor state. The rate of private schools in a state of disrepair was only 1 percent (Programa Estado de la Nación 2005, 89; Villegas S. 2006). Some elementary schools, particularly in poor neighborhoods, are so crowded that they operate three different sessions a day in the same buildings; each group of children attends class for only a few hours. Ironically, because of poor planning, other schools, especially in downtown areas, had so few students at the start of the school year in 2006 that they were forced to close. Costa Rican parents may choose the public school that their children attend, but if the school is outside the neighborhood, the family must pay for transportation. If it cannot, the children have no option but to attend the more crowded, but more convenient, local school.

The rise and decline of the systems of health and education will be discussed in more detail in chapter 3, but here one more example will serve to illustrate the sort of contradictions inherent in the current developmental path and the results of lack of funding for public services. One of the public services most essential to continued economic growth, but in dire need of reform, is the national transportation infrastructure. A study released in 2006 found that around two-thirds of Costa Rica's road network was in fair or poor shape. In the province of Guanacaste, one of the provinces that receives the greatest number of tourists, around 90 percent of the roads are in bad shape (Programa Estado de la Nación 2006, 307). Every tourist who has ever traveled around the country has experienced these bad roads. But can tourism be expected to increase when the roads visitors use to see the country continue to deteriorate? How can exports continue to increase if the roads needed to get goods to port continue to fall apart? A study investigating the impact of bad roads on commerce looked at the highway that connects San José to the Caribbean ports of Moín and Limón; three-quarters of all national commerce must pass along this stretch of road. The study determined that taking into account only the superficial state of the pavement, 20 percent of the transportation costs to businesses was due to poor highway conditions (LANAMME-UCR 2005, 4). In the short run, lack of investment in infrastructure and social services may be unavoidable (or even desirable, for those who would rather turn these public services over to private providers). But in the long run, this state of underfunding threatens to slow economic growth by changing many of the very conditions that made Costa Rica so appealing to foreign investment in the first place: its social stability, healthy population, and high level of education.

The more public services decline, the harder it becomes to ever improve them, much less to bring them back to the levels of success they enjoyed in the past. Investment in education, public health, or infrastructure is particularly difficult because Costa Rica has become one of the most poorly funded countries in Latin America as regards tax revenue. Unlike the generation of 1948, which succeeded in taxing the coffee industry in order to invest in its improvement, the neoliberal generation of lawmakers has been unable to build a similar consensus around the need to tax the new export industries in order to reinvest the money in the foundations of growth and human development.

In 2005, taxes amounted to only 13 percent of the gross domestic product; this rate places Costa Rica near the very bottom of a ranking of all Latin American countries in terms of taxes collected (Agosin et al. 2005). Taxes that are collected must go not only to public programs but also to service an ever-increasing public debt; in 2003, debt service accounted for one-quarter of the national budget. It is not only individuals in Costa Rica who pay very little in taxes, it is also large private corporations. The government used huge tax breaks as one of its primary lures to attract businesses like Intel and other manufacturers. In this way, multinational companies today operate under the same low-tax conditions as did the banana enclaves in an earlier era. The result has been that despite a booming economy during the last 15 years, "the most dynamic sectors were exonerated from the fiscal effort" (Seligson and Martínez 2005, 12).

Even though they might produce computer chips rather than bananas, today's large corporations may still be considered "enclaves" because of the special deals they made with the government, including not only tax breaks but also benefits like special utilities rates and special road construction for their plants. These businesses are also delinked from the broader national economy because their production is based almost entirely on imported raw materials and exported finished products. From 2000 to 2003, foreign businesses purchased only about 3.2 percent of their needs in Costa Rica; the other inputs were imported (Seligson and Martínez 2005, 16). Just as was the case with certain agricultural exports, little of the final value of a product may actually be added in Costa Rica. The value added by the Intel plant, for example, is estimated to be only about 7 percent (Villasuso 2003, 313). The World Bank, among other institutions, has suggested that the slowing of the rate of poverty reduction may be explained in part by economic growth associated almost exclusively with export industries that do not have strong links with the rest of the economy, and by levels of education and training among the poorest segments of the population that do not prepare them sufficiently to take advantage of the new economic opportunities (World Bank 2003, 14). Other critics have suggested that, in general, the jobs generated by export-oriented development have been mostly low skilled and low paying and have not created a particularly inclusive dynamic of development over the last years (Raventós Vorst 2003, 51).

Less money collected in taxes and less emphasis on public services makes it more difficult to resolve certain problems generated or complicated by the process of economic growth itself. As Costa Rica has changed over the last 15 years, a notable lack of planning and regulation has been seen both in rural areas that have suddenly experienced rapid growth as a result of tourist development, as well as in the metropolitan area of the Central Valley, where half of the country's population lives. Lack of planning and public services might eventually affect tourism, but it already has a pronounced impact on the lives of Costa Ricans, who must daily confront problems of traffic, air and water pollution, and overcrowding.

One 2006 article in Costa Rica's most important newspaper, *La Nación,* was frank about one of the biggest problems, trash and how to dispose of it: "In spite of the fact that Costa Rica promotes itself as a country committed to the natural environment, its treatment of its solid wastes reflects a different reality." From 1984 to 2004, the amount of trash produced per person in the Central Valley increased from 600 grams to 1,150 grams. The entire country now generates 9,000 tons a day, and there is a serious lack of sanitary landfills to receive this. The Ministry of Health has ordered many existing dumps closed for sanitary reasons, but has provided few alternatives (Ventaja 2006). The mayor of one small town announced in 2006 after the closing of the local landfill that the municipal government would no longer be picking up the trash, and the residents of the town should find some way to bury or burn their own garbage. Luckily for the town, it received at least a brief reprieve when the dump was temporarily reopened (Iglesias 2006a, 2006b). In the Central Valley, much trash finds its way into the rivers. *La Nación* reported in 2005 that the national electric company pulls items like "old tires, electric appliances, furniture, plastic bottles, and dead animals" from the Virilla River at the rate of 375 tons a month. This garbage clogs the five hydroelectric plants that operate on that river (Loaiza 2005). Unfortunately, all the rivers in the metropolitan area are polluted not only with solid waste but also with untreated sewage (for more information on this problem, see chapter 3).

Without unduly exaggerating the negative aspects of recent economic growth (after all, many of these problems had their beginnings in earlier phases of Costa Rica's development), it is evident that social and structural problems, in both urban areas and in tourist areas, must be weighed in the balance when evaluating the impact of economic change since the 1990s. This is a difficult evaluation to make, not in the least because a great variety of opinions are held regarding the success or failure of neoliberal reforms and export-oriented development. Different commentators have taken exactly the same data and reached diametrically opposed conclusions. One social scientist has examined the results of 15 years of economic policy and concluded that "the findings are overwhelmingly positive." The new sectors of tourism, nontraditional exports, and finance have boomed; the poor have generally benefited; and "the only dark spots on the economic ledger are the 'procrastination costs' that unfinished reforms may levy on growth" (Clark 2001, 138). Another social scientist believes that the problem is that *only* these new sectors have benefited from economic change: traditional agriculture and manufacturing for the domestic market have not shared in the boom, and meanwhile the gap between rich and poor has increased dramatically (Villasuso 2003, 325). Another author has even stronger criticism, asserting that this process of economic change has caused the increase "of social inequality and poverty, has diminished the institutional capacity of the State, and has not generated processes of sustained economic growth, and has increased political corruption" (Raventós Vorst 2003, 51). There is no disagreement among these authors about the accuracy of the economic statistics; they disagree over the direction in which economic development ought to be heading—who should benefit, how, and when. They cannot agree on the success or failure or the process because they do not agree on what Costa Rica should want.

Predictably, this dissension and indecision has come to focus on the question of whether or not the free trade agreement with the United States and the Dominican Republic, the DR-CAFTA, should be ratified. Costa Rica's representatives signed the agreement in August 2004; but the Costa Rican president did not submit it to the Legislative Assembly until September 2005, after an unsuccessful attempt to delay doing so until the legislators had passed a tax reform bill (Storrs 2005, 5, 21). The Legislative Assembly, in turn, proved unable to reach a decision about the agreement. In March of 2007, under pressure from groups opposed to the DR-CAFTA, President Óscar Arias made the decision to put the question of ratification to the voters in a referendum, to be held on October 7, 2007. Unlike the Caribbean Basin Initiative, the DR-CAFTA would be permanent. The U.S. Congress must periodically renew the CBI, always an uncertain process. If ratified by Costa Rican voters, the new trade agreement would eliminate this uncertainty, creating a more stable climate for investment. Furthermore, the death of the CBI is now certain, as the DR-CAFTA was explicitly intended to replace it. That means that if Costa Rica does not ratify the new agreement, it cannot simply continue with the status quo. The U.S.

market would not be closed to Costa Rica; it would simply no longer have a privileged trade relationship.

In exchange for this permanence, the United States would gain reciprocal access to Costa Rican markets in a way that it did not have before. The CBI, put into place in the waning years of the Cold War, was presented as a way for Costa Rica and other countries to pull themselves out of the debt crisis and away from interest in alternative development strategies (like communism). The DR-CAFTA, on the other hand, was sold to U.S. interest groups and legislators as a bilateral trade agreement from which they could benefit (despite the minuscule size of the Central American market) and which would build momentum toward a much larger free trade area of the Americas.

For Costa Rica, this demand of reciprocity would mean further lowering of already low tariffs on many goods it imports from the United States. Within 10 years, according to the terms of the treaty, 100 percent of U.S. consumer and industrial products will enter the trade area duty free (Storrs 2005, 6). The treaty would also require Costa Rica eventually to open up certain segments of the ICE's telecommunications monopoly (cellular telephony and Internet) and all of the INS insurance business to competition. This move, of course, is very controversial. Costa Rican negotiators briefly withdrew from the treaty discussions when ICE and INS were put on the table, and the U.S. trade representative, Robert Zoellick, responded by saying that the agreement would go forward without Costa Rica if they refused to negotiate access to these monopolies (Storrs 2005, 16). Not wanting to be left out entirely, Costa Rica returned to the table and agreed to open the monopolies to competition.

Another area of concern for Costa Rica in the trade negotiations was agriculture. The United States refused to discuss its own huge agricultural subsidy program, indicating that the proper place to negotiate its eventual abolition was at a higher, multinational level. Costa Rica was allowed to protect its market for fresh potatoes and onions, but nearly all other Costa Rican agricultural tariffs are slated to disappear over the next 20 years (Storrs 2005, 19). In exchange for these concessions, Costa Rica would gain increased access to U.S. markets for a few crucial products. Import quotas have long protected U.S. producers of textiles, sugar, and beef. Under the CBI, U.S. interests managed to limit the impact of Central American textile imports by demanding that a certain proportion of garments imported from abroad be manufactured with U.S. yarn or cloth. Under DR-CAFTA, the quotas for sugar and beef will be steadily increased, and the rules of origin in the clothing industry are loosened (Storrs 2005, 19).

With the exception of popular concern for the ICE and the INS, debate over the trade agreement rarely enters into the details sketched out above. Promoters of the agreement have taken the Spanish acronym for it (TLC) and used it to announce that the initiative will bring Trabajo para Los Costarricences (Jobs for Costa Ricans). For them, the agreement means more foreign investment, and thus more jobs. As the country lags farther and farther behind in the process of ratification, dire warnings can be heard that investors will abandon Costa Rica for neighboring countries that have accepted the pact with the United States.

From opponents of the agreement, one hears concern about the ICE and the INS, about farmers, and about the prospect of Costa Rica lowering its environmental and labor standards to compete with its poorer regional trade partners for investment. What one does not hear, but suspects, is that people are opposed to DR-CAFTA because it gives permanence to the reforms that were made gradually over the last two decades. With the treaty now before the voters, Costa Ricans can no longer entertain the notion that these neoliberal reforms were temporary or perhaps reversible, and that they do not together constitute a very different economic model than the one established by the generation of 1948.

It is unfortunate that debate over the trade agreement seems to distract attention from the more mundane, but perhaps more important, measures that could be taken to reverse the deterioration of human development indicators in Costa Rica. Nothing in the trade agreement prevents Costa Rica's legislators from raising the taxes needed to fix the roads, improve the schools, collect the garbage, protect the environment, and police the streets. Furthermore, the trade agreement does nothing to prevent Costa Ricans from working together to find ways to better enforce the environmental, labor, and tax laws that are already on the books. For the moment, these issues are of secondary interest as Costa Ricans take sides over the trade agreement. However, it is interesting to recall that the tropical welfare state built on the ideas of Rodrigo Facio, José Figueres, and the generation of 1948 was never hostile to trade. The country's infrastructure, schools, and health clinics were built with the aid of taxes the government collected from the successful export of coffee, bananas, and other products. José Figueres once defined the modern, democratic state he had in mind for Costa Rica as "a sort of cooperative; everyone keeps what's theirs, but everyone contributes so that nobody lacks for anything." He concluded, "Within the imperfections of human affairs, I don't think there is a system better-suited to Costa Rican ways than a system of private property in which every citizen pays voluntarily and honorably the taxes established by law" (Figueres Ferrer 1956, 177, 179).

References

ACAN-IFE. 2006. "Crecen exportaciones de banano y piña, pero caen las de café." *La Nación,* March 8, sec. "Sala de Redacción."

Agosin, Manuel R., Alberto Barreix, Juan Carlos Gómez Sabini, and Roberto Machado. 2005. "Tax Reform for Human Development." *CEPAL Review* 87 (December). www.eclac.cl/publicaciones/xml/8/25578/G2287iAgosin.pdf/.

Barquero S., Marvin. 2006a. "Menos del 10% de ingresos por café y melón llegan al productor." *La Nación,* March 29, sec. "Economía."

Barquero S., Marvin. 2006b. "Melón y mango se pierden por escasez de transporte." *La Nación,* March 30, sec. "Economía."

Barquero S., Marvin. 2006c. "Enfermos asumen espera como parte del padecimiento." *La Nación,* April 9, sec. "Nacionales."

Baxter-Neal, Leland. 2007. "Southern Ecosystems at Risk." *Tico Times,* March 16, 1.

Brown, Janelle. 2006. "In a Corner of Costa Rica, a Beachhead for Luxury." *New York Times,* February 3, sec. "Real Estate."

Bulmer-Thomas, Victor. 1987. *The Political Economy of Central America since 1920.* Cambridge: Cambridge University Press.

Butler, Richard. 1992. "Alternative Tourism: The Thin End of the Wedge." In Valene L. Smith and William R. Eadington, eds., *Tourism Alternatives: Potentials and Problems in the Development of Tourism.* Philadelphia: University of Pennsylvania Press, 31–46.

Cantero, Marcela. 2007. "Salud de niños indígenas ticos tiene 25 años de rezago." *La Nación,* March 15, sec. "Aldea Global."

Clark, Mary. 2001. *Gradual Economic Reform in Latin America: The Costa Rican Experience.* Albany, NY: State University of New York Press.

Costa Rican Tourism Institute (ICT). 2004. "Anuario Estadístico de Turismo." www.visitcostarica.com/ict/paginas/estadistica.asp/.

Costa Rican Tourism Institute (ICT). 2007. Home page. www.visitcosta rica.com/.

Dickerson, Marla. 2006. "Costa Rica Rides High-Tech Wave." *Los Angeles Times,* March 18, Home edition, sec. C1 (Business).

Eadington, William, and Valene L. Smith. 1992. "Introduction: The Emergence of Alternative Forms of Tourism." In William Eadington and Valene L. Smith, eds., *Tourism Alternatives: Potentials and Problems in the Development of Tourism.* Philadelphia, PA: University of Pennsylvania Press, 1–12.

Edelman, Marc. 1992. *The Logic of the Latifundio: The Large Estates of Northwestern Costa Rica since the Late Nineteenth Century.* Stanford, CA: Stanford University Press.

Edelman, Marc. 1999. *Peasants against Globalization: Rural Social Movements in Costa Rica.* Stanford, CA: Stanford University Press.

Edelman, Marc, and Joanne Kenen, eds. 1989. *The Costa Rica Reader.* New York: Grove Weidenfeld.

Fallas, Hassel. 2007. "País carece de adecuado control ambiental de obras." *La Nación,* March 12, sec. "Nacionales."

Feigenblatt, Hazel. 2007. "Municipio negará concesión a español." *La Nación,* March 5, sec. "Nacionales."

Figueres Ferrer, José. 1956. *Cartas a un ciudadano.* San José: Imprenta Nacional.

Honey, Martha. 1994. *Hostile Acts: US Policy in Costa Rica in the 1980s.* Gainesville, FL: University of Florida Press.

Honey, Martha. 2003. "Giving a Grade to Costa Rica's Green Tourism." *NACLA Report on the Americas* 36 (6): 39–47.

Iglesias, Laura. 2006a. "Siquirreños están sin servicio de recolección de basura." *La Nación,* March 29, sec. "Nacionales."

Iglesias, Laura. 2006b. "Siquierres: botadero continuará abierto." *La Nación,* April 4, sec. "Nacionales."

Inman, Crist. 2001. "Impacts on Developing Countries of Changing Production and Consumption Patterns in Developed Countries: The Case of Ecotourism in Costa Rica." United Nations Environment Programme and INCAE. www.iisd.org/susprod/ecotour.pdf/.

Laboratorio Nacional de Materiales y Modelos Estructurales LanammeUCR (LANAMME-UCR). 2005. "La infraestructura: base principal para el desarrollo económico y social." In *Estado de la Nación en Desarrollo Humano Sostenible: Un análisis amplio y objetivo sobre la Costa Rica que tenemos y a partir de los indicadores más actuales (2004).* San José: Programa Estado de la Nación. www.estadonacion.or.cr/Info2005/Paginas/ponencias.html/.

Lara S., Juan Fernando. 2006. "País explota posición geográfica para expandir área de servicios." *La Nación,* March 13, sec. "Economía"

Leitón, Patricia. 2005. "Ticos comen vegetales con exceso de plaguicidas." *La Nación,* February 20, sec. "Nacionales.".

Leitón, Patricia. 2006a. "Controlaría da ultimatum al MAG por débil control de plaguicidas." *La Nación,* February 27, sec. "Nacionales."

Leitón, Patricia. 2006b. "Brecha social aumentó en los últimos 16 años." *La Nación,* March 31, sec. "Economía."

Leitón, Patricia. 2006c. "Hogares mejor equipados." *La Nación,* April 23, sec. "Nacionales."

Loaiza N., Vanesa. 2005. "Joséfinos lanzan por año 4,500 toneladas de basura al río Virilla." *La Nación,* September 9, sec. "Nacionales."

Loaiza N., Vanesa. 2007. "Hoteleros burlan regulaciones a construcciones en playas." *La Nación,* March 18, sec. "Nacionales."

Mesa-Lago, Carmelo. 2000. *Market, Socialist and Mixed Economies: Comparative Policy and Performance—Chile, Cuba, and Costa Rica.* Baltimore: Johns Hopkins University Press.

Molina, Iván, and Steven Palmer. 2006. *The History of Costa Rica: Brief, Up-to-Date and Illustrated.* San José: Editorial de la Universidad de Costa Rica.

Observatorio del Desarrollo. *Costa Rica en Cifras, 1985–2004.* 2005. San José: Observatorio del Desarrollo and Universidad de Costa Rica.

Programa Estado de la Nación. 2005. *Estado de la Nación en Desarrollo Humano Sostenible: Un análisis amplio y objetivo sobre la Costa Rica que tenemos y a partir de los indicadores más actuales (2004).* San José: Programa Estado de la Nación.

Programa Estado de la Nación. 2006. *Estado de la Nación en Desarrollo Humano Sostenible: Un análisis amplio y objetivo sobre la Costa Rica que tenemos y a partir de los indicadores más actuales (2005).* San José: Programa Estado de la Nación.

Promotora del Comercio Exterior de Costa Rica (PROCOMER). 2004. "Costa Rica: Estadísticas de Exportación." www.procomer.com/ est/mercados/libros.cfm/.

Promotora del Comercio Exterior de Costa Rica (PROCOMER). 2005. "Costa Rica: Estadísticas de Exportación." www.procomer.com/ est/mercados/libros.cfm/.

Promotora del Comercio Exterior de Costa Rica (PROCOMER). 2006. "Costa Rica: Estadísticas de Exportación." www.procomer.com/ est/mercados/libros.cfm/.

Rainforest Alliance. 2007. "Sustainable Agriculture." www.rainforest -alliance.org/programs/agriculture/.

Raventós Vorst, Ciska. 2003. "¿Hacía la ruptura de la relación entre legit- imidad política y bienestar social?" In Juan Manuel Villasuso, ed., *Procesos de cambio en Costa Rica: Reflexiones al inicio del siglo XXI.* San José: Fundación Friedrich Ebert, 45–56.

Robinson, William. 2003. *Transnational Conflicts; Central America, So- cial Change, and Globalization.* London: Verso.

Sauma, Pablo. 2005. "Pobreza, desigualdad de ingresos y empleo." In *Es- tado de la Nación.* www.estadonacion.or.cr/Info2005/Paginas/ ponencias.html/.

Seligson, Mitchell, and Juliana Martínez Franzoni. 2005. "Limits to Costa Rican Heterodoxy: What Has Changed in 'Paradise.'" Paper pre- pared for delivery at The Politics of Governability in Latin Amer- ica: Clues and Lessons conference. Kellogg Institute, University of Notre Dame, October 6–8. sitemason.vanderbilt.edu/files/gL22Fa/ 2005%20Conference%20Paper%20Limits%20to%20Costa %20Rican%20Heterodoxy%20What%20Has%20Changed%20in %20the%20Switzerland%20of%20Central%20America%20by% 20Mitchel.pdf.

Sherwood, Dave. 2007. "Coastal Development Rampant." *Tico Times,* March 16, 1.

Silva, Eduardo. 2003. "Selling Sustainable Development and Shortchang- ing Social Ecology in Costa Rican Forest Policy." *Latin American Politics and Society* 45 (3): 93–127.

Stern, Caroline, James P. Lassoie, David R. Lee, and David J. Dessler. 2003. "How 'Eco' is Ecotourism? A Comparative Case Study of Ecotourism in Costa Rica." *Journal of Sustainable Tourism* 11 (4): 322–347.

Storrs, K. Larry, coord. 2005. *Central America and the Dominican Repub- lic in the Context of the Free Trade Agreement (DR-CAFTA) with the United States.* Report prepared by Congressional Research Ser- vice for the U.S. Congress, October 24. www.opencrs.com/ document/RL32322/.

Vandermeer, John, and Ivette Perfecto. 2005. *Breakfast of Biodiversity: The Political Ecology of Rain Forest Destruction.* 2nd ed. Oakland, CA: Food First Books.

Varela, Ivannia Q. 2006. "Serio faltante de médicos y enfermeras en zonas rurales." *La Nación,* April 8, sec. "Nacionales."

Vargas Alfaro, Leiner. 2005. "Informe Final: Balance general de la economía en 2004." In *Undécimo Informe del Estado de la Nación.* www.estadonacion.or.cr/Info2005/Paginas/ponencias.html/

Ventaja C., Cristina. 2006. "9,000 toneladas de basura asfixian al país." *La Nación,* April 2, sec. "Nacionales"

Villasuso, Juan Manuel. 2003. "Balance de la política económica en Costa Rica: ¿Quiénes son los ganadores?" In Juan Manuel Villasuso, ed., *Procesos de cambio en Costa Rica: Reflexiones al inicio del siglo XXI.* San José: Fundación Friedrich Ebert, 311–342.

Villegas S., Jairo. 2006. "Profunda brecha entre educación pública y privada." *La Nación,* February 22, sec. "Nacionales."

Winson, Anthony. 1989. *Coffee and Democracy in Modern Costa Rica.* New York: St. Martin's Press.

World Bank. 2003. "Costa Rica: Social Spending and the Poor." www.worldbank.org/lac/.

CHAPTER THREE

Politics and Institutions

Costa Rica now tends to lack many of the more colorful cultural traditions that we associate with Latin American countries. In the second half of the 20th century, as the country became increasingly urbanized and as its population increased exponentially, the traditions that had been maintained in small communities, as well as in urban areas, were frequently lost. Although in some regions and at some times of the years (particularly Independence Day and Christmas) certain traditions do remain, the modern "traditions" of fast food and malls have become more popular in most urban and suburban areas (Molina Jiménez 2003, 5–7). However, roughly over this same 50-year period, a number of important new institutions of the Costa Rican state were created: inclusive systems of public education and health, as well as institutions providing services like electricity and potable water. In the 1970s, Costa Rica established a system of national parks to preserve its biodiversity and beautiful natural areas. All of these grew alongside and came to rely upon peaceful and democratic political institutions. These social and political institutions have, perhaps, come to play the central role in defining the national identity that is played in some other Latin American countries by more tangible things like costume, folk art, and traditional music and dance. Costa Rican institutions, besides serving (sometimes more and sometimes less well) the practical functions that they were designed to serve, also define and bolster the nation's self-image and the citizens' ideas of themselves as Costa Ricans. Thus, corruption or deterioration of services not only poses moral or technical problems but can also be a painful blow to the country's self-esteem.

EDUCATION

Unlike in the United States, education is not primarily a responsibility of local governments, but rather of the national government. Since 1949, the planning and organization of public education has been a highly centralized process. Costa Rica's 1949 Constitution stated that "public education will be organized as an integral process, linked in its various cycles from preschool to university" (Cordero 1985, 225). Over the last 60 years, although Costa Rica has one of the highest literacy rates in Latin America (96 percent), this goal of interconnection has never been achieved (UNICEF 2004). In June 2006, in her annual address, the rector of the University of Costa Rica, Yamileth González, stated that primary and secondary education were "disconnected" from higher education and as a result, "a great effort must be made because [the education system] ought to function as an interconnected system from preschool to the university" (Miranda 2006). Although the country is known for its well-educated citizenry, at the beginning of the 21st century, financial and structural problems make reforming the education system difficult. Many Costa Ricans believe that education, despite the high aspirations of the country's leaders, has fallen into crisis.

Since shortly after independence from Spain, Costa Ricans have shown an interest in improving education. Yet the system was not consolidated until the late 19th century, when Liberal politicians took control of education away from the Catholic Church and the municipalities. Liberals came to see the formation of citizens through education as an integral part of the project of modernization, and Costa Ricans since then have, at least in theory, placed a high value on education. The illiteracy rate fell from an estimated 90 percent in 1864 to only about 32 percent in 1927. By 1951, only 21 percent of the population was illiterate (Quesada 2003, 9; Dengo 1995, 160). Between 1890 and 1940, the total population grew 310 percent, while the enrollment of school-age children in primary school increased 529 percent. Yet by 1940, only 5 secondary schools had been established in the Central Valley. None had been established in the provinces. And it was only in 1940 that Costa Rica would again have a university; the University of Santo Tomas had been closed since 1888, although some of its departments had continued to function separately (Quesada 2003, 8, 13, 17).

The 1940s were a crucial decade for the expansion and modernization of education. As discussed earlier, the goal of an integrated educational system was incorporated into the new constitution. The new University of Costa Rica (UCR) opened in 1941 with 719 students in eight departments. New secondary schools were opened in the Central Valley and in the provinces, and the number of students enrolled almost tripled from 1942 to 1951 (Dengo 1995, 162). This educational growth meant that more students were better prepared to attend the UCR, whose enrollment grew rapidly. It increased 1,064 percent from 1951 to 1968 (Quesada 2003, 41). By 2005, 46,000 students were enrolled at the various campuses of the UCR (*La Nación* 2005).

Although by the 1940s and 1950s many more opportunities in higher education were available, not all students were prepared to take advantage of them. In 1949, of 926 elementary schools, only 164 (mostly in the Central Valley) went all the way to sixth grade. Complaints were heard of poor physical facilities and lack of necessary equipment, like desks. Many schools were so crowded that two shifts operated per day—some children attended only in the mornings, others only in the afternoons, thus severely limiting the number of hours in the classroom (Quesada 2003, 23). Interestingly, many of these same complaints have resurfaced in the late 20th and early 21st centuries, and the same sorts of disparities between urban and rural schools still exist (Stanley 2006a).

The 1950s, 1960s, and 1970s were the heyday of Costa Rican education. In 1958, education represented 22.96 percent of the national budget; by the early 1970s, it was more than 30 percent (Quesada 2003, 41). In the 1950s, the Costa Rican government began to work with the United Nations Educational, Scientific and Cultural Organization (UNESCO) to expand rural education and vocational education, and the number of elementary schools increased. New schools for teacher training were also established (Dengo 1995, 160, 162). It is the successes of these decades that Costa Ricans remember and that provide them with their enduring self-image as a country that invests in education and relies on it to maintain peace, prosperity, and social integration. This period came to a screeching halt in the 1980s with the debt crisis; by 1985, the government was spending only 17 percent of the national budget on schools (Quesada 2003, 42).

The crisis of the 1980s not only reduced financing for schools but also increased desertion rates, especially in rural and marginal urban areas where young people had to leave school to help support their families (Dengo 1995, 195). Since the 1990s, however, with the turn toward greater economic stability, investment in education has been increasing. Between 1990 and 2004, the number of schools increased by 150 percent, and the number of jobs in education doubled (the majority of these were administrative, rather than teaching, positions). (Programa Estado de la Nación 2005b, 41). Costa Rica now spends an average of $1,300 per elementary school student (as opposed to $4,800 in developed countries and $100 in neighboring Nicaragua). Only $21 of that expenditure, however, is provided to the schools for basic operating funds per student. The rest goes for teachers' salaries and other administrative expenses (Stanley 2006b). Despite increased investment, the administrative structure of the education system was never reorganized or even recreated, as was that of some government ministries in the

Students attending high school in the 1980s. Since then, many ticos *have come to feel that their schools have fallen into crisis, yet they still place a high value on public education. (Owen Franken/Corbis)*

1990s. Its basic "institutional design" is the same as it was in the 1970s (Programa Estado de la Nación 2005a, 47). President Óscar Arias, elected in 2006, has said that a reorganization of the Ministry of Public Education and a general improvement in all levels of education will be one of the priorities of his administration (Stanley 2006a).

The full course of preuniversity education in Costa Rica is 11 years plus kindergarten, which was made mandatory in 1997. Primary school, or *escuela,* consists of six years of classes divided into two cycles—first through third grades, and fourth through sixth grades. Secondary school, or *colegio,* combines what in the United States would be junior high (or middle school) with high school. The last compulsory years of education are seventh through ninth grades, the third cycle. The final or diversified cycle consists of two more years on an academic track or three more years to obtain a vocational certificate. In theory, students are supposed to be able to choose which track they want to pursue; in practice, especially in rural areas, only the vocational track is offered (Biesanz, Biesanz, and Biesanz 1999, 204).

Costa Rican public education is free, at least in theory; in fact, it can cost quite a bit to keep children in public school. Families must pay for transportation if their children do not live within walking distance of school. Uniforms, school-books, and other educational materials are compulsory and must be bought. It was estimated in 2005 that these compulsory materials cost about 40,000 colones (about $76) per child in elementary school and about 45,000 colones (about $86) each for children in the higher grades (Feigenblatt 2005). Vocational classes require the purchase of extra materials. Students may even be charged for the photocopies of exercises they are required to do and of tests they are required to take (Stocker 2005, 95; Stanley 2006a). Private schools are also an option, the number of which has been increasing over the last 20 years. Private schools, however, still enroll only 7 percent of elementary students and 11.8 percent of secondary students; the tuition is unaffordable for most Costa Rican families (Programa Estado de la Nación 2005a, 23).

Many current infrastructure problems were exacerbated by the economic crisis of the 1980s and have proven difficult to overcome since. For example, in primary schools in 2005, there were only 168 school gymnasiums of the 402 needed; there were only 15 science labs, and 139 more were required; and while there were 504 school libraries, there was a need for at least 576 more (Programa Estado de la Nación 2005a, 17). Although the numbers seem to indicate that the system has reached 100 percent coverage for elementary school-age children, for every 100 who enter first grade, only 88 continue into fourth grade. Student retention is not the only difficulty. Many teachers complain that the five-hour school day is not nearly long enough to accomplish their tasks. A few unlucky students, mostly in marginal urban areas, attend schools that are so crowded that two or even three different sessions are held every day, thus each student receives very few hours of instruction. Some students also attend classes on Saturdays; yet even with these extra hours, many schools do not have time to offer classes like English, music, or art (Programa Estado de la Nación 2005a, 22, 41; Stanley 2006b).

Costa Ricans have even more concerns over secondary education. In 2002, only one out of every three students who began secondary school eventually graduated, and it took an average of 9.4 years for a student to complete 5 years of secondary education. Only 20 percent graduated without ever having repeated a year. In 2004, the yearly desertion rate was around 12 percent, but this varied greatly depending on the region of the country. In the central urban areas it might be as low as 7 to 9 percent, while in the rural areas of the north and south the rate was often more than 14 percent. Of those between 12 and 17 years of age who were not in school, 16.3 percent dropped out for economic reasons. However, almost twice as many (27.6 percent) said they stopped studying simply because they were "not interested" (Programa Estado de la Nación 2005a, 25, 15, 37, 39). In 2006, of all 89,000 17-year-olds in the country, only 36,000 were in school. This statistic is particularly disturbing because Costa Ricans have found that changing labor markets now demand a higher level of education (Villegas 2006).

Despite problems in secondary schools, the number of students attending universities has been steadily increasing. Until the 1970s, the UCR was the only institution of higher learning in the country. In that decade, three more public universities were founded: the National University (in Heredia), the Technological Institute of Costa Rica (in Cartago), and the University for Distance Learning (with campuses in various locations). The first private university—the Autonomous University of Central America (in San José)— was also established. More private universities were created

Founded in 1940 as part of a wave of reforms, the University of Costa Rica is a source of national pride and a crucial avenue to the middle-class status to which Costa Ricans aspire. (Photo by Meg Mitchell)

beginning in the late 1980s, and by 2000, there were nearly 50. The National University and the UCR also began to open campuses around the country. At least in part due to this increase in options for study, between 1984 and 2000 it is estimated that the percentage of the population aged 18 to 24 that was enrolled in a university increased from 15.6 to 29.6. In 2004, around 53.8 percent of all students enrolled attended private universities and 45.6 percent attended public institutions (Programa Estado de la Nación 2005a, 98, 97). Comparing the quality of education in public and private universities is difficult because few statistics are available about the programs of study and the student bodies of private schools; as might be imagined, some private universities have good reputations, while others are known as places where anyone who can pay can get in. Unlike in the

United States, the public universities are generally perceived to be superior to the private universities.

The question of how to measure quality is an important one, not only at the university level but at all levels of education. Although many "policies, plans, and education programs" have been implemented over the last 15 years, little attempt has been made to evaluate how the money, time, and effort invested has positively or negatively affected the education offered to young people (World Bank 2003, 11). Costa Rica has not participated in international standardized tests, so it is hard to compare its schools to those of other countries (Programa Estado de la Nación 2005a, 14). In some ways, the very existence of so many plans and programs is a problem. Continuity in planning and execution of programs has been notably lacking between one presidential administration and the next; each new president has tended to put in place new plans and new administrators—sometimes based more on political considerations than on any other criteria (Dengo 1995, 207).

A World Bank study on social spending in Costa Rica asserted that despite increased spending on education, the benefits have not been immediately obvious. The report found the system to be inefficient overall and poorly targeted to reach the people who most need it. The biggest problem is not lack of money to spend on education but rather how this money is allocated and how the system as a whole is managed. This problem is evident, the report concluded, in the fact that Costa Rica has a much lower rate of school completion than other countries with similar per capita gross national product and public education expenditure. Primary and secondary school curricula were also criticized for failing to meet new labor market demands, especially as the country has seen its opportunities in high-tech fields expand (World Bank 2003).

The problems in Costa Rican education are certainly not unique. All over the world, as countries attempt to prepare more and more students to live and work in the 21st century, reformers encounter the same sorts of problems and the same sorts of financial and ideological barriers to resolving them. The interesting aspect of Costa Rica's situation is that because education has become an integral part of its self-image, the problems related to education seem to Costa Ricans to be even more urgent. Since the 19th century, they have boasted that they had more teachers than soldiers, and since the armed forces were abolished in 1949, they have had no soldiers at all. The money that would have been spent on defense was to be available, at least in theory, to invest in education and other social programs.

Costa Ricans came to believe that their schools not only provided an excellent education but also functioned as a means of social integration. This integration is threatened, in the view of some, by the growth of private schools and universities that segregate young people from well-off families from the rest of their peers (Villasuso 2005, 22). Until the 1980s, education could be seen as the surest path to social and economic mobility. Costa Ricans now tend to believe, however, that education "has lost its usefulness as a place of encounter for all economic levels; the gaps between urban and rural populations in terms of equality of opportunity and of access have become notorious." And in urban areas, inequality between the haves and the have-nots is clearly evident (Chavarría Navas et al. 1998, 3). Thus, perhaps more than might be the case in other countries, an educational crisis in Costa Rica not only is composed of various technical, structural, or philosophical problems that must be solved but it also represents a threat to citizens' vision of their country, to their ideals of social integration and political cooperation. As a result, Costa Ricans have come to focus many of their hopes and fears for the future on efforts to improve their schools.

HEALTH CARE

In health care, in contrast to education, Costa Rica spends less than countries of similar levels of income and expenditure, but tends to get better results This does not mean that the system is without problems, yet it has achieved an enormous improvement in the health of the country's citizens since 1950. Health insurance coverage is nearly universal. Other public health programs (such as nearly countrywide provision of potable water) and social insurance (old-age pensions and workers' insurance) have also contributed to maintaining a healthy population (World Bank 2003, 39). According to the World Health Organization, life expectancy in Costa Rica is the longest in Latin America: 75 years for men and 80 years for women, the same as it is in the United States and in Cuba (WHO 2004).

Although attempts were made to establish social security institutions as early as the mid-1920s, it was in the early 1940s under the presidency of Rafael Ángel Calderón that institutions of social protection were finally created. Costa Rica (unlike most of its neighbors in Central America) was part of a wave of social reform in Latin America in the 1940s; it based its first social programs on a Chilean model. The establishment of the social security system—the Caja Costarricense de Seguro Social (CCSS or Caja)—did not result from any agitation or particular demands by workers; rather, it came from the "top down." Calderón saw a program of social security as a way to protect workers against risks such as illness or injury that would make it hard for them to earn a living. He did not see himself, however, as a radical reformer but instead was influenced by Catholic social teachings. The legislature was not at first enthusiastic about creating a large new institution, as the size of the public sector in Costa Rica had always been "consciously checked" (Rosenberg 1981, 286).

Various modifications were made to the president's original plan, and the Caja at first limited its coverage to the lowest-earning workers. Protection was available only for the workers and was not extended to their families until 1956. There was not much popular support for the Caja at first, either; the workers had to be convinced that it was an institution meant to benefit them and not just another government tax. To help win their support, Calderón proposed amendments to the constitution to protect workers' rights. These included the "social guarantees," which established the eight-hour workday, the minimum wage, and the right to unionize, among other rights (Rosenberg 1981, 294; Jaramillo Antillón 1993, 114, 110).

Just as workers may not have realized the possible benefits of insurance provided by the Caja, the Costa Rican elites did not at first realize how the state could be used as an instrument of social reform: how social reform could be a means to consolidate political power. In some ways, the 1948 Civil War was a dispute over who would control state-sponsored reforms. José Figueres, the victor of that conflict, proved better than his predecessors at using the state's power to enact social reform, and he began the period of active intervention by the government in the social arena (Rosenberg 1981, 296). The Caja became the most respected of the Costa Rican public institutions, and the social guarantees that were first proposed by Calderón became the bedrock of many of the social innovations to come.

But the coverage offered by the CCSS expanded slowly. By 1960, its insurance covered only 18 percent of the total population, though it was gradually incorporating higher-earning workers and their families. In 1961, the legislature mandated that coverage be extended universally over the next 10 years, but it would turn out to take a little longer than that. By 1972, the Caja covered half the population but had only two hospitals in San José and two in the provinces. Hospitals that had earlier been run as public charities or by the Ministry of Health gradually were added to the Caja system to allow it to serve more patients. The crisis of the

1980s affected health care, as it did all social services, and participant contributions were increased in order to keep the system solvent. By the 1990s, with the improvement in economic conditions, health coverage again expanded, incorporating the most remote areas of the country and many people who were too poor to contribute (Jaramillo Antillón 1993, 119). By 1996, health costs represented 10 percent of gross domestic product, and by 2003, 89 percent of the population was covered by health insurance from the CCSS (de Bertodano 2003, 626).

There had been calls since the 1960s and 1970s to make the growing system more efficient, but no real reorganization took place until the 1990s. Problems arose with the financing of health care, which were aggravated by frequent evasion of payment by workers and employers. A new model was needed, as well, that focused not only on hospitalization but also on preventive medicine and community health care (World Bank 2003, 98–100). Under the reforms of the mid-1990s, the Ministry of Health came to provide only supervisory and regulatory functions, while the Caja was made responsible for all purchasing and provision of health care.

Perhaps the most important change in the 1990s was the creation of a system of local clinics, or Basic Health Attention Teams (EBAIS) at the community level. The entire system was divided into 29 hospitals and 90 "health zones," each with 10 EBAIS. These clinics have at a minimum a doctor, a nurse, and a technician to serve a population of between 1,500 and 4,000 people. They were initially established in rural areas, where, historically, citizens had the least access to health care. By 2001, 70 percent of the population had access to this system, and the level of care available for individual communities rose. Decentralization of budgeting and purchasing was encouraged by new kinds of contracts between the hospitals and clinics and the CCSS, and incentives were given for improved performance. Attempts were also made to improve collection of social security contributions,

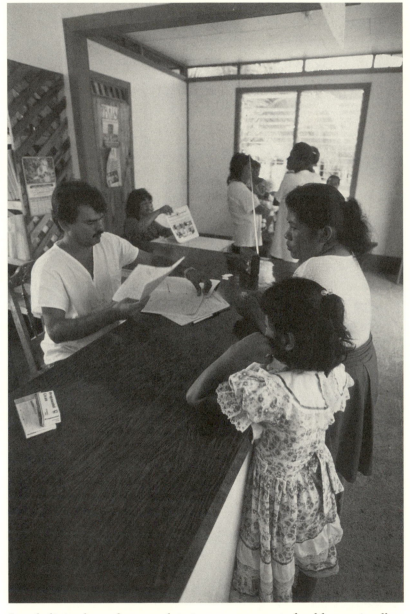

Local clinics have done much to improve access to health care in all parts of Costa Rica, but they require continued investment to meet the needs of a growing population. (Martin Rogers/Corbis)

which, despite all the successes of the Costa Rican system, has always been very low (World Bank 2003, 101, 102; Rosero-Bixby 2004, 1277).

Yet many problems persist. Several recent scandals have diminished the prestige that the Caja always enjoyed, implicating an ex-director and even an ex-president of Costa Rica in corruption (see Rivera and Segnini 2004; Rivera, Feigenblatty, and Segnini 2006). In some ways, Costa Rican health care, ironically, has become a victim of its own success. By gradually improving care and extending coverage, many easily avoidable or treatable illnesses have been eliminated; those that remain require a more sophisticated and more expensive level of care. As the population lives longer, demand for services also increases (Salas and Miranda 1997, 10). Unfortunately, the number of public hospitals has not increased along with the number local clinics. This trend has led to long waiting lists for surgery and appointments with specialists, as well as to the perception of lower quality of care (Rosero-Bixby 2004, 1272). Certain high-tech equipment and certain specialists (particularly anesthesiologists) have been in very short supply, and these shortages have increased wait times for certain necessary procedures (see Avalaos 2005c; Brenes 2006; Avalos 2006c; Stanley 2006a). Shortages of necessary drugs have also occurred in the CCSS pharmacies; hemophiliacs, heart patients, and AIDS patients, among others, have all felt this lack (Avalos 2005a, 2005b, 2006a).

Although Costa Rica still has some of the lowest levels of private health care expenditures in Latin America, a number of new private hospitals opened in the 1990s. For Costa Ricans with the resources to pay for their care and medicines in these facilities, long waiting times or shortages of medicines have not been the problem that they have been in public hospitals. In addition, a marked increase has been seen in "medical tourism"—foreigners (the majority from the United States) who come to Costa Rica to take advantage of good private hospitals that offer services, especially cosmetic surgery, at much lower prices than in developed countries (Arguedas 2006). As was the case with the increase in private education, the growth of private hospitals seems to mark a trend toward segregation of medical services by social class. Another fear is that the opening of the insurance market that could come about as a result of a free trade agreement with the United States would further segregate the system, perhaps allowing wealthy Costa Ricans to opt out of the national system and purchase private medical insurance.

OTHER AUTONOMOUS INSTITUTIONS

The probable approval of the free trade agreement and the resulting open markets seem, to many Costa Ricans, to threaten several other institutions to which they attach great importance. As discussed in the previous chapter, one of the most important of these has historically been the Costa Rican Institute of Electricity (ICE), which has been successful in bringing electric power and telephone service to nearly the entire country; 98.3 percent of homes have electricity (Leitón 2006). This is a particularly impressive achievement considering the difficult geography of much of the country. Unfortunately, many of the hydroelectric plants that provide most of the country's electricity have aging equipment in need of repairs. This problem, combined with lack of rainfall needed to fill the reservoirs that power the plants, necessitated a series of rolling blackouts at the end of the dry season in 2007 (Agüero and Carranza 2007).

Another important institution is the National Insurance Institute (INS). Insurance has been nationalized in Costa Rica since 1924. The INS functions as part of the health care system by providing workers' life insurance and rehabilitation for work-related injuries, but it also provides all car and homeowner's policies. In 1925, the National Insurance Bank (later to become the INS) took responsibility for all the firefighters and firefighting in Costa Rica in an attempt to limit insurance fraud through arson; the INS still provides these services. In recent years, however, the reputation of the INS has suffered. The preferential benefits that its employees receive (in salaries and pensions, among other benefits) have proven a source of resentment (Jaramillo Antillón 1993, 87, 92, 94). Corruption scandals have also implicated a number of high-ranking bureaucrats (Loaiza and Moya 2004; Segnini and Herrera 2006).

The Instituto Costarricense de Acueductos y Alcantarillados (AyA) has contributed greatly to public health by supplying the country with potable water, thus eliminating many water-borne diseases. The AyA was established in 1960, and although it first operated only in urban areas, it now covers the whole country, but not always equally. For instance, although 93.9 percent of San José enjoys clean drinking water, the rate is only 86.5 percent in the province of Guanacaste and 64.2 percent in the province of Alajuela. Recently, however, problems of protection of watersheds, poorly disinfected water tanks, and an aging system of pipes have in many places threatened the clean water supply (Miranda 2006). In some areas, the water supply has been contaminated by the runoff of nitrates and other chemicals from the ever-increasing agricultural production or from gasoline leaks (Avalos 2006b).

The AyA has done less well with its mandate to provide sewage disposal than it has done with providing clean water. Most houses in Costa Rica have septic tanks, a system that works very well when population densities are fairly low. However, as the population in the country has increased and urban areas have expanded, septic systems work less and less well and threaten to contaminate groundwater. Although some cities (such as Limón, on the Caribbean coast) as well as some new condominium developments have their own sewer systems and waste treatment plants, the metropolitan area of the Central Valley as a whole does not (Carvajal 2005).

Only 2.6 percent of the Costa Rican population benefits from a sanitary sewer system and waste treatment plants. Around 97 percent of the sewage produced in Costa Rica flows directly, without any kind of treatment, into the river system. The country has one of the worst systems of sewage treatment in Latin America. Unfortunately, the Rio Virilla (which runs through the Central Valley and drains into the Tarcoles River and ultimately into the Pacific Ocean) has become the recipient of much of this waste and as a result is the most contaminated river in Central America (Agüero R. 2007). Approximately 250,000 cubic meters of waste pours into the Rio Virilla every day. This includes not only sewage but also waste oil, agrochemicals, and industrial and medical wastes. According to the Minister of the Environment, along with Haiti and Nicaragua, Costa Rica shares the dubious distinction of holding first place in Latin America for sewage dumped into its rivers (Loaiza 2006a).

Costa Rica hopes to improve this situation by investing a $127 million loan from the Japanese government in a system of sanitary sewers and treatment plants for the Central Valley. A network of collection pipes and treatment tanks will be constructed beginning in 2007, and by the end of the second stage of the project in 2025, it is hoped that this system will cover 85 percent of the residents of the metropolitan area (ACAN-IFE 2006). This project is to be praised, but considering all the advancements that the country has made in health care and in environmental protection, that something as fundamental as a sewer system for the capital city will not be finished until well into the 21st century is less than laudatory. As with education and health care, it often seems that long-range planning has been lacking, as if the state, despite all the institutional advances made in the 20th century, was somehow caught unaware by population growth and urban development and must now scramble to keep up.

NATIONAL PARKS, PROTECTED AREAS, AND PRIVATE CONSERVATION EFFORTS

Some of these same problems of poor planning and underfinancing have affected another of Costa Rica's most important institutions: the system of national parks and protected areas. As with the systems of education and social security, the system of protected areas—which encompasses not only national parks but also other regions of important natural resources—is an accomplishment of which Costa Ricans are justifiably proud. Around 25 percent of the national territory is under some form of protection. Costa Rica's achievement is particularly impressive considering that as of 1970, it did not even appear on a United Nations' list of countries with established national parks or nature reserves (Evans 1999, 7). In 2006, it possessed 128 protected areas, 32 of which are designated as national parks (Loaiza 2006a).

Although the park system did not take shape until the 1970s, public efforts at conservation had begun earlier. In 1913, the government declared the area around the Poás volcano to be "protected", and in the 1930s, it attempted to establish a system of forest guards. In 1943, biologists successfully lobbied for the legal protection of the land on either side of the newly opened Pan American Highway. Yet all of these well-meaning efforts ultimately failed because of inadequate monitoring and lax enforcement of laws. The law "protecting" the highland oak forests through which the Pan American highway ran was abrogated in the 1970s because "there was nothing left to protect." In the 1950s and 1960s, new laws were passed to preserve forests, soils, and watersheds, but still no consistent national plan was in place for the preservation of natural resources (Evans 1999, 54–56).

It was precisely during those decades when the need for such preservation became urgent. The majority of the deforestation in Costa Rica occurred after 1950. The population of the country tripled between 1950 and 1985, and

An hour from San José, the Poás Volcano National Park is the one most visited by Costa Ricans. The gaseous crater is a source of fascination for tourists, and, from time to time, concern for neighboring farmers. (Photo by Meg Mitchell)

population pressure pushed the agricultural frontier out in all directions from the Central Valley. Before the 1970s and the creation of the national system of protected areas, forestland was generally thought to be valuable only once it had been cleared. As one historian has put it, "Forests were not viewed as resources at all, but as impediments to agricultural expansion; consequently, their destruction was seen not as liquidation of natural capital but as paving the way for development" (Meyers 2001, 4). Government policies reflected this notion: taxes were higher on "unimproved" land, and it was more difficult to prove title to it (Brockett and Gottfried 2002, 16, 14).

With special loans and tax credits, the government encouraged activities that required large tracts of treeless land.

Livestock production destroyed large swaths of dry tropical forest in Guanacaste, and the increase of land under banana cultivation throughout the 20th century led to the clearing of thousands of acres of rain forest in the Atlantic and the Pacific lowlands. In the 1970s and 1980s, Costa Rica annually lost between 2 and 4 percent of its primary forest; this was at the time the highest rate of deforestation in Central America and one of the highest in the world. By 1980, 40 percent of the country was pasture and 20 percent of all land was seriously eroded or degraded. Although the timber industry profited from this deforestation, only an estimated 10 percent of the timber cut was ever used. The rest was left where it fell or was burned (Meyers 2001, 4).

It was in this atmosphere of constant loss of forests and biodiversity, of seemingly irreversible changes to the natural world, that the movement for the creation of a system of national parks developed. In the mid-1960s, Cabo Blanco Nature Reserve and the Santa Rosa National Monument (both on the Pacific side of the country) became the first true protected areas. In 1969, a new forestry law was passed that consolidated these efforts and created a system of national parks meant for research, recreation, environmental education, and tourism (Evans 1999, 72). This system was to provide "the underpinning of Costa Rica's international reputation in conservation" (Allen 2001, 273).

To fulfill these multiple aims, the administration of the national parks and conservation areas has been reorganized several times since the 1970s. These areas were initially placed under the control of the Ministry of Agriculture and Livestock (which is interesting, considering that it was livestock and agriculture that caused many of the problems that necessitated the creation of the parks in the first place). After several reorganizations, the parks are now part of the more recently created Ministry of Environment and Energy (MINAE). They are directly administered by a division of this ministry called the National System of Conservation Areas of Costa Rica

(SINAC), which was created in an attempt to improve administration through decentralization. The national territory is divided by geographical areas into 11 conservation regions. Regional offices coordinate public and private conservation efforts in their areas and attempt to encourage the participation of local citizens in environmental planning and protection in order to better protect and monitor natural resources. Meanwhile, the offices encourage the tourism that will ideally generate revenues for ongoing and future projects (National System of Conservation Areas of Costa Rica 2007).

Although all the protected areas are often referred to generically as "national parks," in fact this is just one designation among several. The category of lands under "strict" protection includes not only national parks but also biological reserves, national monuments, natural reserves, and wildlife refuges (Evans 1999, 8). Not all these designations have the same aims. The national parks are legally established to preserve beautiful areas and important flora and fauna while facilitating public access and environmental education. The principle function of biological reserves is conservation and research. Wildlife refuges focus on the preservation of animal and plant species, especially those in danger of extinction. These are made up of public or private lands, or some combination of the two, and may contain human habitation, although removal of resources from the area is not permitted. National monuments include areas of national historical significance, as well as archeological sites. Another category of protection focuses on what has been called "multiple-use development." These reserves and protected zones aim to protect forested areas and important watersheds, but may also be open to controlled logging and human habitation. Other protected areas have received international designations: the Coco Islands off the Pacific coast have been declared a World Heritage Site by the United Nations, and the Amistad region on the border with Panama is a World Heritage Site and a

Biosphere Reserve. A final type of reserve, obviously meant for people, is the indigenous reserve. Indigenous reserves are meant to preserve "indigenous" ways of life, but as will be discussed in chapter 4, a variety of ways of life can be found in these areas. One feature they have in common is that most of the indigenous residents are very poor (Meza Ocampo 1999, 77; Evans 1999, 9; SINAC 2007)

This system has succeeded in protecting many natural resources important both for their natural beauty and for their scientific value. Some areas are unique in the world. The protected areas of Guanacaste and Santa Rosa on the Pacific coast contain the last important stretches of tropical dry forest on the entire Pacific coast of Latin America. Careful scientific research, a certain amount of political savvy, international contributions, and a commitment to involving, rather than excluding, local people in the process have made this ongoing project of forest restoration a success (see Allen 2001).

Other conservation projects have run up against problems. Management and harvesting plans are required for timber extraction in any protected forest area. These plans, however, have sometimes turned out to be just for show: they are drawn up in order to receive a permit to cut a certain number of trees, but then they are never followed (Brockett and Gottfried 2002, 19). In other cases, although the government has set aside land for new protected areas, it has not always been immediately able to pay the current owners for their property. An estimated 15 percent of national parks and 46 percent of biological reserves are on private lands whose purchase by the government is still pending (Avendaño Flores 2005, 34). In 2006, the government owed $74 million to pay for 800 square kilometers of national parks, biological reserves, and other protected lands. According to a subdirector of the SINAC, Costa Rica would need to spend 3,500 million *colones* a year for 15 years to pay off these debts (Loaiza 2006b).

Financial problems have also prevented hiring the necessary number of park guards to protect land already incorporated into the system. In 2007, no money at all was to be available for more guards or park repairs (such as improved trails, bathrooms, and picnic areas). More guards could go a long way toward ending recurring problems like illegal hunting that, in some areas, threatens to create "empty forest"—land that has forest cover but no wildlife. Because 6 out of every 10 foreign tourists to Costa Rica visit a national park, the maintenance and improvement of park facilities would appear to be a very important task (Loaiza 2006b). The Rainforest Alliance, an organization that has done a great deal of work in Costa Rica and has some of its offices there, has summarized such shortcomings in this way: "Efforts to secure and consolidate Costa Rica's protected areas have been jeopardized by limited human resources, ineffective regulation, neglect of vital ecosystems that lack protected status, insufficient budgets and the failure to effectively engage local stakeholders in conservation stewardship" (Rainforest Alliance 2006).

Other critics have called into question not only certain practices in the establishment and management of public and private lands but the entire geographical structure of the protected areas that has gradually emerged since the 1970s. Although many different areas representing the many ecological niches of Costa Rica have been protected, few spatial connections exist between them. These zones have become "disarticulated islands of preservation" surrounded by unprotected areas, many of which are degraded, eroded, or otherwise adversely affected by environmentally unsound development. This structure may partly have been the result of conflicts inherent in the desire to promote environmental protection while at the same time increasing agricultural production for export. As discussed earlier, many export crops (including products like ornamental plants, pineapples, and bananas) not only require a great deal of land but also rely on the use of large amounts of fertilizers and pesticides that are extremely dangerous to the very plants and animals the national parks system is intended to protect. It was, of course, the production of Costa Rica's original export crop, coffee, that initiated the period of environmental destruction, even as it ensured the country's relative economic prosperity. Tourism—which relies both on Costa Rica's natural beauty and its reputation as a kind of eco-paradise and provides revenue that ought to help to conserve it—places the country in the same paradoxical situation. Tourism brings in money for conservation but could actually harm the environment in the long run by attracting too many visitors and developing too much resort real estate to entertain them (Stonich 1999; see also Vandermeer and Perfecto 2005).

Such problems may at times seem overwhelming, but conservationists in Costa Rica and internationally are constantly looking for solutions. Mario Boza, a scientist who was also one of the original founders of the park system, has asserted that in light of continuing difficulties, "the protected areas system in Costa Rica needs a radical change." Although the establishment of the SINAC was meant to decentralize the system and take regional differences into account, Boza believes that the protected areas would benefit from economic as well as administrative decentralization. Entry fees earned by the parks, instead of going into a general government fund, could go directly toward the maintenance of the parks. Others have suggested that local participation in the conservation areas ought to be increased. This involves improving not only environmental education programs but also the means through which local people could benefit economically from the tourism that parks generate. Both public and private conservation groups have recently been working to find creative ways to sustain and expand the system of protected areas in Costa Rica (Rainforest Alliance 2006).

The white-faced or capuchin monkey is one of the more entertaining of the country's four species of primates. All are endangered due to habitat loss. (Photo by Meg Mitchell)

Costa Rica's Disappearing Monkeys

The National Parks System has managed to protect and preserve a great deal of Costa Rica's beautiful landscape and incredible biodiversity. Yet it alone cannot carry the whole burden of this daunting task. A recent study of the state of the country's monkey population clearly indicates the necessity of the participation of all Costa Ricans, and those who visit Costa Rica, in the work of conservation, both for the sake of the animals and for the continued economic and social development of the country.

There are four species of monkey in Costa Rica: the white faced (or capuchin) monkey, the howler monkey, the spider monkey, and the squirrel monkey. Biologists from the University of Costa Rica and the National University have been studying the monkeys over the last 12 years, and in 2007, they released a new report on their findings. All species of monkeys saw drastic reductions in their numbers over the years of the study, but the spider monkeys suffered the greatest loss. Their population fell about 72 percent—from 26,000 in 1995 to 7,225 in 2007. Over the same period of time, it is estimated that the number of howler monkeys fell from 102,000 to only around 36,000 (a loss of 64 percent). The number of squirrel monkeys fell from 7,300 to 4,200, and the number of white-faced monkeys fell from 95,000 to only 54,000, both representing a decrease of around 43 percent. These are very dire findings: if these same rates of decline continue for 10 more years, Costa Rica may have no monkeys in the wild at all.

Although some species have proven more adaptable than others, all have been severely affected by loss of habitat caused by deforestation for agriculture and development. Many have died, and many others are sick. Scientists have detected a new strain of malaria, never known before to affect Central American monkeys. The animals were also found to suffer from dental problems (which can make eating difficult), cataracts of the eyes, and discoloration of their coats. Some of these problems may be caused, the scientists say, by an excess of solar radiation. Others may be due to the increased use of toxic chemicals on banana, pineapple, and citrus plantations.

Increased deforestation in Costa Rica has forced monkeys into smaller and smaller areas, and this has resulted in increased inbreeding. Less genetic variability means that the animals are less resistant to disease and less able to adapt to new threats to their habitat and sources of food. This is obviously bad news for the monkeys, but it is also bad news for tourism. If tourists cannot come to Costa Rica and see the wildlife and tropical forests that they expect to see, they may simply go somewhere else. As Costa Rican biologist Ronald Sánchez has put it, "We are a country that depends on our natural resources to attract tourism. If we lose that, I don't know what we'll have left."

Source: Sherwood, Dave. 2007. "Monkey Populations Shrinking Fast." *Tico Times,* April 27, 1.

Measures to improve the administration and operation of the protected areas are already underway. The SINAC has tried to improve the management of forest reserves by simplifying the permitting process, improving law enforcement, and increasing efforts at monitoring areas under protection. And although there is still a long way to go, these efforts seem to be paying off. In November 2006, the government announced that illegal logging in Costa Rica had been reduced from 35 percent of all timber harvested in 2004 to only 15 percent in 2006 (Baxter-Neal 2006). Estimates vary on the percentage of land that now has forest cover, but the Food and Agriculture Organization of the United Nations estimates that it is 46.8 percent (FAO 2007). Costa Rica is the only country in Latin America that, despite experiencing a decrease in forest cover during the 1990s, saw an increase from 2000 to 2005. It is not entirely clear if this change is due simply to a reduction in agricultural land or to the use of innovative policies, but in any case, it seems to be a step in the right direction (FAO 2007).

One of the country's most successful initiatives has been the National Forestry Financing Fund. This fund was established in 1996–1997 to encourage small and medium landowners to participate in the recovery of forest cover. It has successfully used loans and tax credits to promote reforestation, sustainable management practices, and new technologies in forestry projects. It also uses money from the Costa Rican government, the World Bank, and other donors to pay private landowners for the environmental services that their forested land provides to the country and, in fact, to the world. These services include the "mitigation of greenhouse gasses; protection of water for urban, rural, or hydroelectric purposes; protection of biodiversity," as well as tourism and scientific research (National Forestry Financing Fund 2007). These and other projects have contributed to Costa Rica's gradual reforestation. From 1990 to 2005, Costa Rica was the only country in Central America—

and one of the few in the world—to experience an increase in its forest cover: in twenty years, it recovered forest areas equivalent to about 10 percent of the national territory (Vargas M. 2007b).

The most recent initiative in this same vein was the announcement in February 2007 of a push by the government to make Costa Rica "carbon neutral." This effort would mean, according to the MINAE, the implementation of a new series of laws, taxes, and budget allocations that could allow the country to compensate for the greenhouse gases and other environmental contaminants that are produced in Costa Rica. The government also says it will commit to promoting the use of cleaner energy sources, like biodiesel, and new technologies, like hybrid cars, that would reduce the overall pollution output. Improvements are promised in the monitoring of air quality, as well as a promise to plant 5.5 million trees. One of the most interesting proposals is a voluntary tax on tourists to compensate for the volume of carbon dioxide produced in bringing them to the country and in their travels while there. This money would then be used to support new programs of environmental conservation and research (Vargas M. 2007a). These new plans are to be applauded, and it is hoped that they indicate a renewed and long-term commitment on the part of the Costa Rican government to extend the country's legacy of environmental concern into the new century.

Costa Rica has a long record of cooperation between public and private, national and international institutions in working toward environmental conservation. For example, various organizations have worked together to connect protected areas into "biological corridors." These connections would ideally prevent the isolation of protected areas in a sea of overdeveloped areas, allowing for freer movement of animals not only in Costa Rica but also throughout Central America. The SINAC, in particular, has worked to create corridors between various national protected areas.

Dairy cattle graze a pasture along the edge of the Monteverde cloud forest. Originally settled by North American Quakers in the 1950s, Monteverde is famous for its cheese and ice cream. (Gary Braasch/Corbis)

Reflecting even grander aspirations, the Mesoamerican Biological Corridor is an ongoing project involving all the countries of Central America, as well as Mexico and Belize, in an attempt to increase cross-border connections linking both public and private lands (National System of Conservation Areas of Costa Rica 2007). While this project has been generally praised for recognizing that it does not make sense for conservation projects to end at political borders, it has also been criticized for its inability to incorporate local projects into higher-level planning and for its slow implementation. Yet despite these problems, the project represents an important opportunity for Central Americans to cooperate in the protection of their distinctive and important natural resources (see Dettman 2006; Youth 2005).

Just as the cooperation across national lines has become more and more important, so has the cooperation within

Costa Rica. Environmental preservation has never been the sole responsibility of state institutions. Since the 1950s and 1960s, when the threat to the region's natural resources was first taken seriously, private conservation efforts have been extremely important. Among the first and the most well known of these efforts was undertaken by a group of Quakers from the United States who immigrated in the 1950s to the cloud forest area of Monteverde in the western highlands. There they established dairy farms as well as private forest reserves that today are some of the most visited in Costa Rica. In 1959, biologist Archie Carr founded the Caribbean Conservation Corporation to protect the sea turtles on the northern Caribbean coast from commercial hunting and egg gathering. Today this area, Tortuguero, has been made a national park. And in the late 1960s, a consortium of U.S. universities established a research station in the Caribbean lowlands. The Organization for Tropical Studies now has three biological stations in different parts of the country and incorporates 52 U.S. and Costa Rican universities (Evans 1999, 25–30).

These are only a few of the better-known private projects in Costa Rica. There are also many private nature reserves, as well as ongoing research and environmental conservation efforts. Public institutions in several cases have worked with private groups, both in funding and research and in the promotion of tourism and environmental education. One of the most well known of these private groups is the National Biodiversity Institute (INBio). This nongovernmental, nonprofit institute was founded in 1989. It was first proposed as a public institution, but when the Costa Rican government was unable to gather the money or the political support to establish it, a group of scientists and conservationists took the project on themselves. It describes itself as a "research and biodiversity management center" that has as its guiding idea that "the best way to conserve biodiversity is to study it, value it, and utilize the opportunities is offers to improve the quality of life of human beings" (National Biodiversity Institute 2007).

Its activities, funded by national and international donors, include the inventory and monitoring of biodiversity in Costa Rica; it has an extensive collection and catalogue that has been compiled into a database available to the public on the INBio Web site. It has also worked with SINAC in conservation projects around the country. One of its most important goals is to "create awareness of the value of biodiversity" through environmental education. More controversial has been its involvement in bio-prospecting: the search to find and study chemical substances or genes in forest areas that might be useful to the pharmaceutical, biotechnology, or other industries. Useful and marketable findings, in this way of thinking, would provide another reason to protect natural areas from deforestation and development (INBio 2007). It is only such willingness to try out new ideas, along with a commitment to cooperation between public and private, national and international institutions, and donors, that may eventually lead to solving the thorny problem of how best to conserve and protect natural resources.

POLITICAL INSTITUTIONS

The reason that institutions that oversee aspects of society like education, health care, and the environment have succeeded to the extent that they have in Costa Rica is that political institutions functioned so well over the last 50 years of the 20th century. Yet the relationship between social and political institutions is not a strictly one-way relationship. To use a biological metaphor to describe a country so rich in biodiversity, it is a symbiotic relationship. While stable democratic politics created the necessary environment for strong institutional development, strong institutions (including the so-called autonomous institutions in which

Costa Ricans have come to have so much faith), have also played an important political role. This relationship faces many challenges at the beginning of the 21st century, but it is to be hoped that the strengths that each element brings to Costa Rican society will allow the country to continue to peacefully confront and solve new problems.

The roots of this relationship are found in the 1948 Civil War. A constituent assembly elected to write a new constitution in 1948–1949 rejected the draft document proposed by the Founding Junta of the Second Republic and decided instead that its point of departure would be the constitution that had governed the country since 1871 (Wilson 1998, 45). However, as discussed in chapter 1, the 1871 Constitution permitted too much power to accumulate in the hands of the Costa Rican president. Presidential abuse of power, particularly in election years, and resistance to those abuses made the political system unstable. The 1948 Civil War was only the last in a series of conflicts provoked by the malfunctioning of the political machinery inherited from the 19th century. Perhaps the greatest achievement of the assembly that drafted the new constitution is that no such conflict has occurred since.

Indeed, since that time Costa Rica and Mexico are the only two Latin American countries not to experience a military coup. And of those two countries, only Costa Rica's political transitions have been completely democratic. How was this stability achieved? Principally by setting up a system of checks and balances that governed the sharing of power among legitimate players in domestic politics, and by neutralizing two actors that caused a considerable amount of political instability in the rest of Latin America in the second half of the 20th century—the military and the U.S. government.

The Supreme Electoral Tribunal (TSE), established in the 1949 Constitution and officially designated as a fourth branch of government in 1975, is the key institution guaranteeing the legitimacy of the rest of the political system. The TSE is responsible for maintaining the civil registry and issuing the *cédulas,* or identification cards, which Costa Ricans proudly carry and which serve, among other functions, to give them access to the ballot box. Additionally, the TSE convokes elections, organizes polling places, trains poll workers, and resolves disputes over electoral matters. It has intervened in the workings of the political parties to enforce laws that demand that the parties function more democratically and that they ensure the required minimum participation by women (40 percent). It has removed popularly elected municipal officials when they have been found to be derelict in their duties. The Tribunal's rulings cannot be appealed (Programa Estado de la Nación 2005b, 236–239).

The TSE enjoys much more popular support and respect than electoral tribunals in other Latin American countries (Programa Estado de la Nación 2005b, 236). It was edifying to witness the equanimity of Costa Ricans in February 2006 as the TSE patiently supervised a hand recount of the votes and resolutely resisted projections and speculations until the process was concluded and the winner of the presidential race (Óscar Arias Sánchez, by roughly 18,000 votes) officially declared. Perhaps this respect is due to the fact that the members of the TSE are selected in an entirely nonpartisan procedure. Each member of the Tribunal, which consists of three magistrates and six substitutes, is chosen by a two-thirds vote of the Supreme Court and given an initial term of six years (Wilson 1998, 45). One new or returning magistrate is elected every two years along with two substitutes, thus further guaranteeing the continuity and impartiality of the Tribunal (Salazar and Salazar 1992, 85).

The TSE took elections entirely out of the hands of the Costa Rican president. The 1949 Constitution restricted the power of the president in other ways as well, making him "probably the weakest executive in Latin America," unable to "(1) veto the national budget as determined by the legislature; (2) use a pocket or line-item veto; (3) assume emergency powers without a supporting vote by a two-thirds majority of the legislature; (4) legislate by decree" (Clark 2001, 23). To be elected president, a candidate must win at least 40 percent of the votes. If no candidate wins 40 percent, the election moves into a second round between the two candidates with the most votes. Until the 2002 election, there had never been need for a second round. And until a 2004 decision by the Supreme Court in favor of Óscar Arias, it was impossible for an individual to stand for election to the presidency more than once. With the new decision, Costa Rica reverts to the state of affairs before 1969 when only immediate reelection to the presidency was prohibited.

The 57 members of the Legislative Assembly, who are elected every four years at the same time as the president, gained the powers lost by the president. The Legislative Assembly is empowered, along with the president, to propose new laws. The assembly controls its own agenda during its two mandatory annual sessions; however, the president can, and often does, call an extraordinary session for which he establishes the agenda. And yet *diputados,* as the legislators are known, are also subject to severe limits on individual power. They depend for their nomination on the political parties, which put forward a list of candidates to voters; voters vote for the list rather than for individual candidates. When the votes are counted, parties are assigned seats based on the proportion of total votes won. Diputados are prohibited from seeking immediate reelection, and very few seek reelection even after sitting out the mandatory four years (Wilson 1998, 51, 52).

Like other legislatures throughout the world, much of the work of the Legislative Assembly is done in committees, the chairpersons of which are selected by the leaders of the majority party. However in Costa Rica, one never encounters the powerful committee members and legislative leaders that one finds, for example, in the U.S. House of Representatives. The Legislative Assembly elects a new assembly president every year, who in turn tends to rotate diputados to new committees every year. As a result, the individual power of the diputados (along with, perhaps, expertise in particular fields of legislation) is further diminished (Wilson 1998, 53).

The Legislative Assembly, therefore, is strong relative to the president, while individual legislators are fairly weak. Indeed, Costa Rica's government would appear to function according to rules that make the president and each legislator a "lame duck" from the day he (or increasingly she) is elected. Thus, legislators have little interest in, and gain little leverage from, forming coalitions that last much beyond the first few years following an election. Yet the country managed to pursue a unique, fairly coherent, and successful path of economic and social development for more than 30 years (1948–1982). This curious situation has led analysts to probe deeper to determine where and how policy is really made in Costa Rica.

Recalling the autonomous institutions discussed at some length in this and the previous chapter can dispel much of the confusion. Seemingly every aspect of Costa Rican community life, from infrastructure to health care to women's rights, falls within the purview of an autonomous institution. At the peak of the development of the "tropical welfare state," 200 of these bodies were in place (Wilson 1998, 54). It is important to remember that the whole point of their "autonomy" was to remove them from the direct influence of politicians; this objective was largely achieved. Boards of directors appointed to terms that span more than one presidential administration govern the autonomous institutions. Directors cannot be removed from their posts for political reasons; this rule insulates them from the normal swings of electoral politics. Civil service regulations insulate the middle and lower ranks of the autonomous institutions, as well as the executive branch bureaucracy, from political manipulation. Therefore, one could argue that a good deal of the potential weakness associated with the lame-duck status of elected officials is compensated for by the relative permanence of the bureaucracy that made many of the important decisions determining Costa Rica's path of development.

Seen from this perspective, an important part of the task of Costa Rican presidents and legislatures, particularly prior to the era of neoliberal reforms, was to create, staff, and fund autonomous institutions to address the problems of modernization and development that surfaced during their term in office. If the institutions could not be politically manipulated, their creation could still be used as a kind of safety valve for social pressures. Indeed, these institutions are seen by some as convenient tools for politicians who are perhaps more interested in opening channels of communication with unhappy political constituencies than in actually solving their problems (Wilson 1998, 56; Palma 1989, 134). This preferred approach to the problems of development—creating a space in a growing bureaucracy to institutionalize, discuss, and even sometimes ameliorate them—depended heavily, however, on favorable economic conditions. These conditions ended abruptly with the debt crisis of the 1980s.

In the 1990s, however, several new institutions were created. One that has turned out to be particularly influential is the Constitutional Court, known as the Sala IV because it is actually the newest of four subdivisions of the country's Supreme Court. Prior to the creation of this court in 1989, Costa Rica's Supreme Court had been a very passive institution. To a great extent, this is because Costa Rica follows a civil law tradition (as is the case in nearly all of Latin America) that does not give judges much latitude for the sort of judicial review exercised, for example, by the U.S. Supreme Court. Until 1989, the Supreme Court in Costa Rica operated on the presumption that laws passed by the Legislative Assembly were constitutional and consequently accepted very few constitutional cases. The Sala IV, however, was empowered to decide the constitutionality of government laws and administrative actions by a simple majority vote. Costa Ricans, with or without the aid of a lawyer, suddenly could bring before the court claims for protection from the violation of the rights guaranteed to them in the 1949 Constitution or in international treaties ratified by Costa Rica (Wilson 1998, 58).

The court's caseload has grown astronomically. In the first year of its existence, 2,000 cases were brought before the Sala IV, and in its first three years, it declared 974 government acts unconstitutional. Between 2001 and 2004, the number of new cases stabilized at around 13,000 a year (Poder Judicial 2004;Wilson 1998, 58). The majority of these cases involve the right to *amparo*—individual protection from arbitrary treatment by public institutions in violation of one's rights. These petitions can stem from something as small as denial of a permit affecting one individual's ability to earn a living, or as large as stopping a government-approved tuna farming project in Costa Rica's Golfo Dulce that the plaintiffs argued (successfully) would constitute a serious threat to the ecosystem in general, and to sea turtles in particular (PRETOMA 2006). Costa Ricans also have often turned to the Sala IV for resolutions of disputes that are strictly local in nature.

In the second half of the 20th century, local government in Costa Rica was a very passive element in the country's political system. Costa Rica is formally divided into provinces, cantons, and districts. No provincial government exists, although the provinces do function as electoral districts for the Legislative Assembly and are granted diputados based strictly on population. This formula results in a pronounced dominance of the Legislative Assembly by representatives of the provinces of the Central Valley. The central government and the autonomous institutions, which provide most important services in Costa Rica (education, electricity, roads, water, etc.), also collect the vast majority of tax dollars and service fees. Perhaps the most important responsibility of local government is garbage collection, but frequently a garbage crisis breaks out in municipalities unable to pay for the upkeep of the trucks because they are unable to efficiently collect the already low local property taxes and service and license fees (Rojas 2006). No clear solutions are on the horizon, and Costa Ricans, habituated to looking to the central government and national institutions, are not prepared to invest a lot of confidence or tax dollars in *la muni,* as they refer to local government (Wilson 1998, 54).

POLITICAL PARTIES

Along with the growing body of autonomous institutions, the National Liberation Party (PLN) is the other dominant and, until now, permanent presence in Costa Rican politics. The PLN, founded in 1951, traces its political and intellectual roots to the Center for the Study of National Problems that was active before the 1948 Civil War. Its original program was steeped in the belief that impersonal, technical government and permanent, ideological political parties were indispensable to progress in Costa Rica. Ironically, the party owed much of its allure to its personalistic identification with the victors of the 1948 Civil War and particularly to the national hero, José "Don Pepe" Figueres. Figueres himself was known to speak out strongly against personalistic politics and even favored, at one time, a weaker presidency than the one created in the 1949 Constitution (Ameringer 1978, 100). However, the PLN was in many ways a vehicle for his election to the presidency in 1953; he was nominated for the post without any internal party vote. He was elected president a second time in 1970, and his son, José Figueres Olsen, was elected to the office in 1994. Don Pepe remained president of the PLN until his death in 1990 (Salazar and Salazar 1992, 95).

The Figueres name and personality were powerful forces in Costa Rican politics in the second half of the 20th century, and the PLN was the only modern political party in the country until the founding of the Social Christian Unity Party (PUSC) in 1983. In the 14 national elections since 1951, the PLN has won the presidency eight times, an absolute majority in the Legislative Assembly on six occasions, and has been the largest individual party in the assembly on all but five occasions (Clark 2001, 25–26). The PLN worked successfully to establish a presence throughout the country and to build strong relationships with the urban and rural middle classes, as well as with leaders in important economic sectors like cattle, sugar, and industry. Yet one of its earliest and strongest pillars of support was the workers who filled the rapidly growing government bureaucracy. Between 1950 and 1958 the percentage of the economically active population employed in government grew from 6 to 10 percent, and many of those workers had the PLN to thank both for their jobs and for the civil service legislation passed in 1953 that made those jobs stable (Wilson 1998, 96). They could also thank the PLN, and Don Pepe in particular, for the dramatic expansion to all government workers of a benefit known as the *aguinaldo*—a 13th month's salary paid before the Christmas holidays in December. Because the most active unions in Costa Rica have been state worker unions, the influence of the PLN spread beyond individual voters to potentially important pressure groups (Salazar and Salazar 1992, 94; Winson 1989, 71–72). During the 1960s and 1970s, the Costa Rican bureaucracy continued to grow, and the PLN continued to control the presidency and/or the legislature. Thus, the party could function, at least in part, as a political machine that provided jobs and other benefits for its supporters.

In spite of the PLN's political dominance, the opposition to the party of Figueres was constant. Mostly this opposition came from forces still known to this day as Calderonistas or anti-Liberacionistas. These included sectors nursing resentments from the conflicts of the 1940s and sectors tied to interests in finance, commerce, and coffee that were ideologically opposed to the nationalized banking system and the new role of the state in the "mixed economy" built by the PLN. The opposition had much more success winning the presidency than it did in wrenching control of the Legislative Assembly from the PLN, which controlled the legislature from 1953 to 1974 (Wilson 1998, 93).

Until the founding of the PUSC in 1983, opposition forces formed temporary coalitions around a popular presidential candidate rather than a permanent party infrastructure. Through the efforts of these coalitions, the PLN has only been able to succeed itself in the presidency on two occasions (1970–1978 and 1982–1990). And while most opposition politicians talked a good deal about slowing down the growth of government and reigning in spending, for the most part they failed to stop the momentum of the "managerial" and ultimately the "entrepreneurial" state. They rarely controlled the Legislative Assembly, where the national budget was decided and where the laws to reduce the size of the state would need to be passed. This failure was also due, no doubt, to the popularity of the welfare state and the difficulty in taking away benefits once they have been granted (Wilson 1998, 97). In the end it was the financial collapse of the 1980s, rather than opposition arguments against a bloated government bureaucracy, that ended the growth of the welfare state.

One other important element contributed to the political stability achieved by Costa Rica during the Cold War years. With the start of the Cold War in 1947, reformist governments throughout the developing world, and particularly in Latin America, had to proceed with extreme caution. Several historical experiences suggested that the combination of a professional army and an unfriendly relationship with the United States caused by perceived or real communist

After his 1948 victory, José Figueres formed the "Founding Junta of the Second Republic." Political divisions rooted in the civil war persisted, but "Don Pepe" was a hero to most Costa Ricans. (Bettmann/Corbis)

sympathies could lead to a military coup and the end of reform. Perhaps the case most relevant to Costa Rica was the Guatemalan coup of 1954. There, the Guatemalan army and a band of exiles funded and directed by the U.S. Central Intelligence Agency brought down a reformist government (one that had lent crucial support to Figueres in the 1948 Civil War). Prior to the coup in Guatemala, but no doubt responding to the same historical conditions, Figueres and the Founding Junta took steps that would insulate the Second Republic from its potential enemies. Immediately following the signing of the Pact of the Mexican Embassy, Figueres and the Junta proceeded to violate the guarantees given to the communists and other members of the Calderonista coalition. In July 1948 the Junta issued decree #105, which, without mentioning it by name, effectively prohibited the

Communist Party by prohibiting all political parties that "oppose the regime of democratic representative government of the Republic; or who threaten national sovereignty." Although this decree was subsequently included as Article 98 of the 1949 Constitution, it was annulled in the 1970s (Salazar and Salazar 1992, 109).

Costa Rican communists were persecuted both in the Popular Vanguard Party (into which they had been united since the 1940s) and in associated labor unions; the Junta dissolved 51 unions by 1949. Possession or circulation of the party newspaper, *Trabajo*, was punishable by 10 years in prison, and the hitherto respected founder of Costa Rica's communist movement, Manuel Mora, was unable to express his opinions in print or on the radio until 1958. Some 7,000 people, both Calderonistas and communists, emigrated to Mexico, Nicaragua, and Panama following the 1948 decree, and 3,000 people were imprisoned in Costa Rica (Salazar and Salazar 1992, 110–111). While all evidence indicates that anticommunism had been integral to the ideology of Figueres and the members of the Junta even before the civil war, the prohibition and persecution of communists during the Cold War era certainly helped Costa Rica avoid any potential misunderstanding with the United States about the character of the fairly radical reforms (particularly bank nationalization) that the Junta was to carry out.

THE ABOLITION OF THE ARMY AND COSTA RICAN FOREIGN POLICY

Another source of potential opposition was removed—and Costa Rica gained instant and lasting fame—when the Junta abolished the armed forces on December 1, 1948. The powerful symbolism of the decision was given concrete expression when Figueres himself helped take a sledgehammer to part of the Bellavista barracks and later turned this still imposing building into the National Museum. Yet it is important to remember that military tradition and military budgets had almost always been meager in Costa Rica. Figueres's guerrillas had defeated the army with ease, and it really had no popular support to continue in existence. The Junta's decree abolishing the army was incorporated without debate into the 1949 Constitution. This fact suggests that most Costa Ricans, and not just Figueres, were ready to be done with it and to "reasonably assume, as they had since the 1920s, that they could go on looking to the United States for unilateral protection against Panama or Nicaragua" (Holden 2004, 217–218).

Curiously, the formal abolition of the army did not eliminate Costa Rica's interest in military aid from the United States. Ongoing conflict with Figueres's arch enemy Anastasio Somoza in Nicaragua and the fear of Calderonista subversion from across the northern border led to repeated requests for U.S. military assistance. In 1953, President Figueres proposed to spend nearly a half-million dollars on rifles, mortars, machine guns, rocket launchers, and hand grenades purchased from the United States. The United States sold him the weapons after he agreed to abandon his support of the embattled Guatemalan government. In 1955, the United States sold Costa Rica four fighter planes in response to an attempted rebel invasion from Nicaragua. The United States renewed its military mission to the "republic without an army" from 1950 to 1966, yet repeatedly resisted Costa Rican pressures for a further "military collaboration agreement that would have made it one of the strongest military powers in the isthmus" (Holden 2004, 221, 224).

Clearly, the Costa Ricans of the generation who very pragmatically abolished the armed forces as an institution were not pacifists. They did, however, eliminate an institution that in the rest of Latin America served as a constant threat to civilian reformist governments like the one that would be built in Costa Rica after 1949. Some observers

This building in San José was a barracks until Costa Ricans abolished their armed forces in 1948 and converted it for use as the National Museum. (Photo by Meg Mitchell)

in the 1950s believed that this regime would have been vulnerable to a coup by Figueres's enemies had an army existed (Bowman 2004, 175–182). The abolition of the army was possible because of the Costa Ricans' expectation that the United States would protect them. The ban on communist political and union activity guaranteed continued friendly relations with the United States during the tense decades of the Cold War.

This close relationship with the United States did not, however, prevent Costa Rica from criticizing its powerful ally. Pepe Figueres was famous for his willingness to expose the hypocrisy of the United States' support for Latin America's dictators. In 1958 he asked the members of a committee of the U.S. House of Representatives, who called him to testify about violent protests that had greeted Vice President

Richard Nixon on a visit to Venezuela, "If you talk human dignity to Russia, why do you hesitate so much to talk human dignity to the Dominican Republic?" (quoted in Ameringer 1978, 146). The Dominican Republic was ruled by the dictator Rafael Leonides Trujillo, an ally of the United States in the Cold War and, according to Figueres (and many others), a brutal, corrupt, but reliable protector of U.S. business interests in that country. Figueres argued that democracy and development were the best weapons against the threat of communism, and his was an influential voice in the discussions that led up to inauguration of the Alliance for Progress in 1961 by President John F. Kennedy (Ameringer 1978, 174–178).

In a similar show of independence, Óscar Arias devoted much of his first presidency to putting together a peace plan to end the civil wars that were devastating Central America in the 1980s. In the case of the war between Nicaragua's elected Sandinista government and the U.S.-backed rebels known as *contras,* the conflict threatened to draw Costa Rica into the regional conflict. The United States not only provided material support to the contras but it was also deeply committed to military support of the government of El Salvador in its war with the leftist Farabundo Martí National Liberation Front. The Reagan administration viewed the conflicts in Central America as part of its larger Cold War struggle, and it was not interested in Arias's proposal that Central America's problems be solved through internal dialogue and democratic elections and without outside military interference. Despite U.S. opposition, and despite Costa Rica's absolute dependence on U.S. economic assistance to weather the debt crisis, Arias persisted. In August 1987, all five elected Central American presidents signed the peace plan. For his patience in working out the plan, and no doubt for his courage in defying the United States, Óscar Arias was awarded the Nobel Peace Prize in 1987 (see Edelman and Kenen 1989, 362).

INSTITUTIONAL CHANGE IN THE NEOLIBERAL ERA

Some suggest that the price of Costa Rica's defiance of U.S. foreign policies in the 1980s was its acquiescence to the aggressive neoliberal reforms pushed by the United States Agency for International Development discussed in chapter 2. There is no doubt that those reforms changed the dynamics of the country's domestic politics. As the PLN's state-led development model lost momentum, traditional anti-Liberacionista forces were coalesced into an effective opposition party, the PUSC. Rafael Ángel Calderón Fournier, the son of the controversial leader of the 1940s, founded the PUSC in 1983. Under Calderón Fournier's leadership, the PUSC established itself nationwide and elected him to the presidency in 1990.

Until the 2006 elections, when the party was nearly eliminated from the political scene as a result of corruption scandals and widespread dissatisfaction with political parties, the PUSC shared power with the PLN in what many analysts thought to be a stable two-party system. Together, these two parties carried out a gradual process of neoliberal reforms that many think will be brought to their logical conclusion with ratification of the Dominican Republic–Central America Free Trade Agreement with the United States (DR-CAFTA). While the PUSC was generally understood to represent a more enthusiastic attitude toward neoliberal reform, leaders of both parties understood that promising to cut back on benefits and to privatize valued autonomous institutions like the ICE and the INS was certain to bring electoral defeat. Thus, a pattern has taken shape whereby neoliberal reform is criticized or its necessity minimized in election campaigns, and then inexorably pushed forward to the extent possible by the winning party. The constitutional prohibition against reelection to the presidency or the legislature made this tactic feasible: no individual president or diputado would have to answer to the electorate for his or her failure to follow through on campaign promises. Furthermore, a law prohibiting elected officials from simultaneously serving in official party posts means that the political parties can, and do, assume a critical posture toward elected officials of their own party, especially during election campaigns. Thus, for example, PLN party leaders and candidates can "maintain their commitment to social democratic programs even as the party in government is abandoning those programs" (Wilson 1998, 141).

On the other hand, these same prohibitions make it difficult for any victorious presidential candidate to actually implement neoliberal reforms once in government, as diputados have no incentive to fall in line behind a lame-duck president. Indeed, at some point in the political cycle, diputados are more interested in determining who might be their party's next candidate for the presidency and, therefore, the person most able to help an unemployed diputado continue his or her political career in the bureaucracy. As candidates are loathe to support cutbacks in government services, diputados testing the political winds can become very uncooperative when it comes to supporting initiatives—even by a president of their own party—that involve unpopular reforms (Wilson 1998, 132).

This set of obstacles to rapid reform and Costa Ricans' own deep attachment to the public institutions created during the era of PLN dominance meant that neoliberal reform could only progress slowly. Yet the ideological tenor of the times and the pressure of international and domestic creditors have pushed Costa Rica down the path toward a smaller state and a restructured, often reduced, network of social benefits for its citizens. Some of those citizens, habituated to hearing one thing during election years and experiencing another when a new government comes to power, have found other ways to resist reforms. Infrequently, Costa Ricans take to the streets, as they did in March 2000 to protest what was known as the Combo ICE, a package passed by the Legislative Assembly that would have opened the telephone and electricity monopoly to 49 percent participation by private investors (*La Nación* 2000). The protests became ugly by Costa Rican standards and led to the abandonment of the new law. In August 2004, truckers blocked strategic sections of Costa Rica's already strained highway system to protest a vehicle inspection monopoly administered by a Spanish company. In the fall of 2006, several days of peaceful street protests took place against the signing of the free trade agreement with the United States, and more protests were predicted both before and after the expected passage of the treaty.

CORRUPTION AND THE 2006 ELECTIONS

Costa Ricans' frustration with neoliberal reform, worry over the future, and disgust with political corruption at the highest levels could be seen in the 2006 election results. Thirty-five percent of eligible voters did not go to the polls; abstention was even higher (45 percent) in the poorer peripheral provinces of Limón and Puntarenas. In a country where Election Day is a national fiesta and where the vote is considered sacred, this record level of abstention is troubling. Nonetheless, one's attention quickly shifts to the results, which were also dramatic. The PUSC, which had shared the political spotlight with the PLN since 1990, almost disappeared. In 2002, the PUSC had won the presidency for the second consecutive time and elected 19 of its diputados to the Legislative Assembly. In 2006, its presidential candidate won only 3.5 percent of the vote, and only five of its diputados were elected to the Legislative Assembly (Alfaro Redondo 2006, 128, 126).

The PUSC's demise had everything to do with allegations of corruption. In 2004, both the party's founder, Rafael Ángel Calderón Guardia, and the country's most recent PUSC president, Miguel Ángel Rodríguez (1998–2002), were detained on charges of accepting payments in exchange for using their influence to benefit government contractors. Ironically, Calderón was accused of benefiting from a complicated scheme involving the public health care system founded by his father in the 1940s. Rodríguez, who had recently been inaugurated as secretary general of the Organization of American States, resigned his post in October 2004 and flew home to face corruption charges. The pictures of his arrest as he stepped down from the plane further damaged the image of a party whose founder was already being held by authorities.

The self-destruction of the PUSC left the field to the PLN and two new parties to its left and right on the political spectrum. The PLN, however, did not escape the wave of corruption stories unleashed in the press in 2004. Another son of a leading politician, ex-president José María Figueres Olsen, was accused (and later exonerated) of receiving payments in exchange for lobbying the ICE—the signature institution founded by *his* father, Don Pepe Figueres. Unlike ex-President Rodríguez, Figueres Olsen at first refused to return from Switzerland, where he was serving as head of the World Economic Forum, to face charges in Costa Rica. Fortunately for the PLN, the Liberacionistas were able to nominate an untarnished, if not much loved, Óscar Arias for the presidency. A decision of the constitutional court lifted the ban on reelection, permitting the Nobel Prize winner to stand again for election.

To the right of the PLN a small but significant Libertarian movement was visible in the 2006 election. Its candidate, Otto Guevara, was well financed and a very familiar face in the campaign. However, his support for the free trade agreement and opposition to corruption and taxes did not resonate with voters. He received only 8.5 percent of the votes, and his party merely held onto the same five seats it won in the previous legislature. The Libertarian movement, however, has shown itself to be adept at using those seats to exercise a disproportionate influence in the Legislative Assembly. Through appeals to the constitutional court and parliamentary maneuvering, they have proven to be very skillful in blocking reforms—particularly tax increases—that they oppose.

Many expected Arias to win the election easily; however, the Partido Acción Ciudadana (PAC) and its candidate, Ottón Solís, were only 18,000 votes short of defeating him. The PAC first became prominent in the 2002 election when it won enough votes to deprive the PUSC and PLN candidates of the 40 percent minimum majority required to avoid a second round in the presidential election. The PAC is considered to be slightly to the left of the PLN; its founder, Solís, was a planning minister in Arias's first term as president and resigned his post to protest neoliberal reforms.

In the 2006 campaign, Solís resolutely refused to offer voters the sorts of promises (a new bridge here, a new school there) that are commonly made in Costa Rican campaigns. Solís's opinion was that these sorts of promises were a product of the corrupt political culture represented by the two dominant parties. In addition to this austere image, Solís also attracted voters opposed to the ratification of DR-CAFTA as it is currently drafted. Arias is in favor of ratifying the agreement and addressing its possibly damaging effects through a "complementary agenda" of tax and other reforms to be passed by the Legislative Assembly.

FROM GRIDLOCK TO REFERENDUM IN 2007

The PAC's astounding success (17 seats in the Legislative Assembly and 39.8 percent of the presidential votes) was seen as a referendum on the trade agreement and made its passage more complicated for Arias (Alfaro Redondo 2006, 126). Indeed, as the new Legislative Assembly struggled through its first year of debates over the treaty, it became far from certain whether it could be passed before the March 2008 deadline for entrance into the new trading block. The Legislative Assembly is notoriously slow under the best of circumstances, and with a determined opposition coalition skilled in the use of parliamentary procedures, a train wreck of sorts appeared imminent. Either the treaty would be passed over the objections of the PAC and its coalition partners, or the opposition would succeed in using delaying tactics to "run out the clock" on the treaty and its implementing legislation. According to one political commentator, Costa Ricans were running the risk that whichever side won, the political environment might be so poisoned that lawmakers would be unable to work together on the country's long list of problems (Vargas Cullel 2007).

And then, surprisingly, in April 2007 the Supreme Electoral Tribunal ruled in favor of a group of citizens requesting a referendum to decide the fate of the treaty. The citizens' group wanted to convene the referendum by gathering signatures, but President Arias acted decisively. Taking advantage of a constitutional provision permitting a referendum to be called by an executive decree that is subsequently approved by the legislature, he immediately proposed the referendum himself, claiming it was time for Costa Ricans to settle the question, "in the way most in keeping with our idiosyncrasy: voting in peace and tranquility; not in the streets but at the ballot box." (Arias Sánchez 2007). The Legislative Assembly overwhelmingly approved the decree, despite considerable mistrust of President Arias's motives (and perhaps resentment of his political acumen) by some opponents of the treaty. In October 2007, Costa Rican voters will determine whether to join the free trade agreement. It will be the first referendum in Costa Rican history, and the first time in Latin America that a free trade agreement with the United States will be decided by a popular vote.

The 2006 elections and the 2007 referendum, then, open up uncharted territory in Costa Rican politics. The old Calderonista-Liberacionista divide, institutionalized in the 1980s and 1990s as the PLN-PUSC two-party system, appears to be gone. The new PAC-PLN contest pits the center (PLN) against the center-left (PAC), and the key issue dividing them presently is the free trade agreement. Notably, support for the PAC and the PLN is a rural/urban phenomenon. Roughly speaking, the PAC does very well in the metropolitan region of the Central Valley, where human development indicators are higher. The PLN was able to win the election of a president and 25 diputados because of its disproportionate success in the peripheral provinces of Guanacaste, Limón, and Puntarenas (Alfaro Redondo 2006, 131, 134). It is interesting to speculate that the PLN's success in Costa Rica's poorer periphery has to do with the loyalty its past and future promises of useful infrastructure projects have inspired. The PLN's future may depend on its ability to deliver these goods in a free trade environment, and to convince more skeptical metropolitan voters that the free trade agreement will bring jobs to the urban industrial economy. For the PAC, the challenge is twofold. It must rally its forces again to attempt to defeat the trade agreement in the September 2007 referendum. If the treaty is defeated, the PAC will be expected to articulate a new development agenda for Costa Rica that can work without a special trading relationship with the United States. If the treaty is ratified by the voters, the PAC will need to move beyond its opposition to the free trade agreement and work to build support for its brand of politics in peripheral regions oscillating between political apathy and acute need for basic public services.

References

ACAN-IFE. 2006. "Japón ofrece 127.2 millones de dólares para proyecto sanitario." *La Nación,* March 9, sec. "Centroamérica Hoy."

Agüero R., Mercedes. 2007. "97% de las aguas negras van a los ríos sin ningún tratamiento." *La Nación,* March 5, sec. "Nacionales."

Agüero R., Mercedes, and Juan Pablo Carranza. 2007. "ICE ordena racionar electricidad en todo el país." *La Nación*, April 26, sec. "Nacionales."

Alfaro Redondo, Ronald. 2006. "Elecciones nacionales 2006 en Costa Rica y la recomposición del sistema de partidos políticos." *Revista Chilena de Política* 26:1.

Allen, William. 2001. *Green Phoenix: Restoring the Tropical Forests of Guanacaste Costa Rica.* Oxford: Oxford University Press.

Ameringer, Charles D. 1978. *Don Pepe: A Political Biography of José Figueres of Costa Rica.* Albuquerque, NM: University of New Mexico Press.

Arguedas, Carmen. 2006. "Turismo médico creció un 15% en Costa Rica el año pasado." *La Nación*, July 15, sec. "Nacionales."

Arias Sánchez, Óscar. 2007. "Respeto y emoción." *La Nación*, April 16, sec. "Opinión."

Avalos R., Ángela. 2005a. "Hemofílicos sin medicina coagulante." *La Nación*, January 12, sec. "Nacionales."

Avalos R., Ángela. 2005b. "CCSS esta sin medicina para pacientes cardiacos." *La Nación*, August 6, sec. "Nacionales."

Avalos R., Ángela. 2005c. "Médicos admiten colapso en hospital San Juan de Dios." *La Nación*, September 20, sec. "Nacionales."

Avalos R., Ángela. 2006a. "Enfermos de SIDA reclaman medicina." *La Nación*, March 3, sec. "Nacionales."

Avalos R., Ángela. 2006b. "Material fecal, nitratos y gasolina amenazan 4,000 fuentes de agua." *La Nación*, May 22, sec. "Nacionales."

Avalos R., Ángela. 2006c. "Enfermos de cáncer esperan más de 3 meses por examen." *La Nación*, May 28, sec. "Nacionales."

Avendaño Flores, Isabel. 2005. *La relación ambiente sociedad en Costa Rica: Entre gritos y silencio, entre amores y odios.* Serie Cuadernos de Historia de las Instituciones de Costa Rica, no. 15. San José: Universidad de Costa Rica.

Baxter-Neal, Leland. 2006. "Illegal Logging Greatly Reduced." *Tico Times*, November 10, 1.

Biesanz, Mavis, Richard Biesanz, and Karen Zubris Biesanz. 1999. *The Ticos: Culture and Social Change in Costa Rica.* Boulder, CO: Lynne Rienner.

Bowman, Kirk. 2004. "Democracy on the Brink: The First Figueres Presidency." In Steven Palmer and Iván Molina, eds., *The Costa Rica Reader: History, Culture, Politics.* Durham, NC: Duke University Press, 175–182.

Brenes Z. Harold. 2006. "Falta de especialistas y equipos retrasa atención en radiología." *La Nación*, February 12, sec. "Nacionales."

Brockett, Charles D., and Robert R. Gottfried. 2002. "State Policies and the Preservation of Forest Cover: Lessons from Contrasting Public-Policy Regimes in Costa Rica." *Latin American Research Review* 37 (1): 7–40.

Carvajal, Marvin. 2005. "Sistema de aguas negras de Limón opera al 100%." *La Nación,* November 26, sec. "Nacionales."

Chavarría Navas, Soledad, et al. 1998. *La política educativa: hacía el siglo XXI: propuestas y realizaciones.* San José: Ministerio de Educación Pública.

Clark, Mary A. 2001. *Gradual Economic Reform in Latin America: The Costa Rican Experience.* Albany, NY: State University of New York Press.

Cordero, José Abdulio. 1985. "Análisis histórico de la situación educativa." In *El modelo educativo costarricense.* San José: Asociación Nacional de Fomento Económico.

de Bertodano, Isabel. 2003. "The Costa Rican Health System: Low Cost, High Value." *Bulletin of the World Health Organization* 81 (8): 626.

Dengo, María Eugenia. 1995. *Educación costarricense.* San José: Editorial Universidad Estatal a Distancia.

Dettman, Stephen. 2006. "The Mesoamerican Biological Corridor in Panama and Costa Rica: Integrating Bioregional Planning and Local Initiatives." *Journal of Sustainable Forestry* 22 (1): 15–34.

Edelman, Mark, and Joanne Kenen, eds. 1989. *The Costa Rican Reader.* New York: Grove Weindenfeld.

Evans, Sterling. 1999. *The Green Republic: A Conservation History of Costa Rica.* Austin, TX: University of Texas Press.

Feigenblatt, Hazel. 2005 "Padres gastaron millones para enviar hijos a clases." *La Nacion,* February 7, sec. "Nacionales."

Food and Agriculture Organization of the United Nations. 2007. "State of the World's Forests." www.fao.org/forestry/sitc/sofo/cn/.

Holden, Robert H. 2004. *Armies without Nations: Public Violence and State Formation in Central American, 1821–1960.* Oxford: Oxford University Press.

Jaramillo Antillón, Juan. 1993. *Salud y seguro social.* San José: Universidad de Costa Rica.

Leitón, Patricia. 2006. "Hogares mejores equipados." *La Nación,* April 23, sec. "Nacionales."

Loaiza, Vanessa. 2006a. "250,000 metros cúbicos diarios de desechos ahogan al Virilla." *La Nación,* April 27, sec. "Nacionales."

Loaiza, Vanessa. 2006b. "Parques nacionales sin dinero para arreglos ni mantenimiento." *La Nación,* October 23, sec. "Nacionales."

Loaiza, Vanessa, and Ronald Moya. 2004. "Dictan impedimentos de salida a jerarcas del INS." *La Nación,* October 20, sec. "Nacionales."

Meyers, Mark C. 2001. "Economic Development Policy and the Protected Areas System in Costa Rica: A Historical Review and Prospects for the Future." *Vida Silvestre Neotropical* 10 (1–2): 3–18.

Meza Ocampo, Tobías A. 1999. *Costa Rica: naturaleza y sociedad.* Cartago, Costa Rica: InstitutoTecnológico de Costa Rica.

Miranda, Yendry. 2006. "Casi un 40% de gente sin agua potable en Alajuela." *La Nación,* June 7, sec. "Nacionales."

Molina Jiménez, Iván. 2003. *Identidad nacional y cambio cultural en Costa Rica durante la segunda mitad del siglo XX.* Serie Cuadernos de Historia de las Instituciones de Costa Rica, no. 11. San José: Editorial Universidad de Costa Rica.

La Nación. 2000. "Guía sobre el 'Combo ICE'." *La Nación,* March 23, sec. "Nacionales."

La Nación. 2005. "Hoy, hace 65 años nació la UCR." *La Nación,* August 26, sec. "Aldea Global."

National Biodiversity Institute (INBio). 2007. "What Is INBio?" www.inbio.ac.cr/.

National Forestry Financing Fund (FONAFIFO). 2007. Home page. www.fonafifo.com/english.html/.

National System of Conservation Areas of Costa Rica (SINAC). 2007. "Información General." sinaccr.net/informacion.php/.

Palma, Diego. 1989. "The State and Social Co-optation in Costa Rica." In Marc Edelman and Joanne Kenen, *The Costa Rica Reader.* New York: Grove Weidenfeld, 132–136.

Poder Judicial. "Sala Constitucional." www.poder-judicial.go.cr/salaconstitucional/.

Programa Estado de la Nación. 2005a. *Estado de la educación 1.* San José: Programa Estado de la Nación.

Programa Estado de la Nación. 2005b. *Estado de la Nación en Desarrollo Humano Sostenible: Un análisis amplio y objetivo sobre la Costa Rica que tenemos y a partir de los indicadores más actuales (2004).* 2005. San José: Programa Estado de la Nación.

Programa Restauración de Tortugas Marinas (PRETOMA). 2006. "Sala IV acoge recurso de amparo contra granjas atuneras." www.tortugamarina.org/content/view/183/1/lang,es/.

Quesada, Juan Rafael. 2003. *Estado y educación en Costa Rica: Del agotamiento del liberalismo al inicio del estado interventor: 1914–1949.* San José: Universidad de Costa Rica.

Rainforest Alliance. 2006. "Massive Effort Underway in Costa Rica to Save a Leading Source of Income: The Country's Famed National Park System." *Eco-Exchange Bulletin,* July. www.rainforest-alliance.org/neotropics/eco-exchange/2006/july_06_02.html/.

Rivera, Ernesto, and Giannina Segnini. 2004. "Presidente de la CCSS alquila casa de gerente de Fischel." *La Nación,* April 21, sec. "Nacionales."

Rivera, Ernesto, Hazel Feigenblatt, and Giannina Segnini. 2006. "Fiscalía indaga hoy a siete imputados en caso Caja-Fischel." *La Nación,* June 21, sec. "Nacionales."

Rojas, José Enrique. 2006. "CNE declara emergencia por problemas con basura en Tibás." *La Nación,* May 18, sec. "Nacionales."

Rosenberg, Mark B. 1981. "Social Reform in Costa Rica: Social Security and the Presidency of Rafael Ángel Calderón." *Hispanic American Historical Review* 61 (2): 278–296.

Rosero-Bixby, Luís. 2004. "Spatial Access to Health Care in Costa Rica and its Equity: A GIS-Based Study." *Social Science and Medicine* 58: 1271–1284.

Salas, Álvaro, and Guido Miranda. 1997. "Costa Rica Reforms 'Model' Health Care System." *World Health* 150 (5): 10.

Salazar Mora, Orlando, and Jorge Mario Salazar Mora. 1992. *Los partidos políticos en Costa Rica.* San José: Editorial Universidad Estatal a Distancia.

Segnini, Giannina, and Mauricio Herrera. 2006. "Funcionarios del INS ocultaron sobreprecios en póliza del ICE." *La Nación,* May 17, sec. "Nacionales."

Stanley, Katherine. 2006a. "Arias: Those Children Must Not Pardon Us." *Tico Times,* July 7, 1.

Stanley, Katherine. 2006b. "Country Grapples with Education Spending." *Tico Times,* July 14, 1.

Stocker, Karen. 2005. *"I Won't Stay Indian, I'll Keep Studying": Race, Place, and Discrimination in a Costa Rican High School.* Boulder: University Press of Colorado.

Stonich, Susan. 1999. "Review of *The Green Republic: A Conservation History of Costa Rica* by Sterling Evans." *Journal of Political Ecology: Case Studies in History and Society.* jpe.library. arizona.edu/volume_6/stonichonevansvol6.htm/.

United Nations Children's Fund (UNICEF). 2004. "Background." www .unicef.org/infobycountry/costarica.html.

Vandermeer, John, and Ivette Perfecto. 2005. *Breakfast of Biodiversity: The Political Ecology of Rain Forest Destruction.* 2nd ed. Oakland, CA: Food First Books.

Vargas Cullel, Jorge. 2007. "Enfoque." *La Nación,* April 12, sec. "Opinión."

Vargas M., Alejandra. 2006. "País estrena Parque Nacional los Quetzales." *La Nación,* April 26, sec. "Aldea Global."

Vargas M., Alejandra. 2007a. "País quiere ser primera nación con balance neutro de carbono." *La Nación,* February 21, sec. "Aldea Global."

Vargas M., Alejandra. 2007b. "Costa Rica es ejemplo mundial en reforestación." *La Nación,* March 14, sec. "Aldea Global."

Villasuso, Juan Manuel. 2005. "Interrogantes sobre la educación costarricense." In Marcos Arroyo F. and Juan Manuel Villasuso, eds., *Dimensiones de la educación en Costa Rica.* San José: CEDAL, 15–26.

Villegas S., Jairo. 2006. "Bachilleres relegados a puestos con bajo salario." *La Nación,* August 25, sec. "Nacionales."

Villegas S., Jairo. 2006. "UCR procura ser protagonista." *La Nación,* June 6, sec. "Nacionales."

Wilson, Bruce M. 1998. *Costa Rica: Politics, Economics, and Democracy.* Boulder, CO: Lynne Rienner.

Winson, Anthony. 1989. *Coffee and Democracy in Modern Costa Rica.* Toronto: Between the Lines.

World Bank. 2003. "Social Spending and the Poor in Costa Rica." www.worldbank.org/.

World Health Organization (WHO). 2004. "The World Health Report: Costa Rica." www.who.int/whr/2004/annex/country/cri/en/.

Youth, Howard. 2005. "Chain of Dreams: The Mesoamerican Biological Corridor." *Zoogoer* (September/October). nationalzoo.si.edu/Publications/.

CHAPTER FOUR
Society and Culture

A successful society is created by balancing the competing tensions that exist within it: the forces that pull it apart, and the forces that draw it together. In this balance, a defining element is the image that a society creates of itself—how it describes itself to itself, and how it presents itself to the rest of the world. As discussed in chapter 3, since 1948 this image has become intricately linked in Costa Rica with the success or failure of the country's most important democratic and social institutions. Yet this is only one of the most recent manifestations of an image whose outlines were first drawn by national leaders in the 19th century. This image has changed over time, but its basic elements remain the same. Costa Rica generally thinks of itself as an inherently democratic, peaceful, and ethnically homogeneous society. A Costa Rican historian has characterized this image as "agricultural, egalitarian, peaceful and white, but located in the wrong place (that is to say, not in the heart of Europe or at least near Chile, Argentina, or Uruguay, but rather next to 'volcanic' [*plutónica*] Nicaragua)." This is, then, an image of Costa Rica as *exceptional,* not at all like its Central American neighbors. Catholicism is another part of the picture; it is still the official state religion, although the practice of other religions is allowed, and even flourishes. A final element is the generalized belief in Costa Rica as a middle-class society. All of these factors create an image that is not only widespread (both within and outside the country) but also a "cultural construction that resists disappearing despite decisive changes experienced by Costa Rican society since 1950" (Molina Jiménez 2003, 2).

Nineteenth-century national leaders intent on forging a national identity, as well as numerous historians since then, found the origins of this image in the colonial period. This was an era, it has been asserted, in which the isolation and poverty and the tradition of small landowning in the Central Valley led to a kind of natural "rural democracy" and a distinctive national psychology inclined toward compromise rather than conflict (Sandoval-García 2004, 64–65). The other important element is that the population is considered to be of generally European heritage. This idea also had its roots in the 19th century when, because the various regions of the country remained so isolated from one another, the national leaders in the capital city were able to define the characteristics of the population of the Central Valley as the "national" characteristics. This characterization meant that by the late 1800s, "most Costa Ricans saw themselves as a racially pure society who were the direct descendants of poor 'white' Spanish immigrants" (Harpelle 2000, 29). As a Costa Rican commentator has pointed out, despite the fact that this image of Costa Rica as a "white" society is not entirely accurate, "the construction of an imagined homogeneous society seems to be a fundamental element of the country's *ethos*" (Monestel 2005, 16).

Costa Ricans are very conscious of their image and of what they like to call their "idiosyncrasies"—the traits they believe make them special. These idiosyncrasies may include everything from the use of many diminutive suffixes in their speech ("*-illo*" or "*-ico,*" from which they get their nickname, the *ticos*) to an obsession with their national breakfast food, *gallo pinto* (beans and rice), to a distaste for militarism and a commitment to peaceful resolution of conflicts. For many, the more serious of these traits explain why in the second half of the 20th century, in contrast to many Latin American nations, Costa Rica experienced neither civil wars nor dictatorial interludes, accomplishments of which it has every right to be proud. But there is a problem with the explanatory power of such "self-centered" identities. As a Costa Rican social scientist has described it, they tend to "impose political controls limiting dissent and, in turn, represent certain 'others' as a threat to a timeless and 'unique' democracy" (Sandoval-García 2004, 72). In order to understand these images of Costa Rican society and to see the impact they have had on the country's ability to adapt its democratic traditions to changing circumstances and to integrate new groups into society, it is first necessary to look at the social changes that since 1950 have affected all members of society.

URBANIZATION, POPULATION GROWTH, AND THE ROLE OF WOMEN

Besides improvements in transportation and communication, one of the most obvious changes in the second half of the 20th century was from a predominantly rural to an urban society. In 1950, 63 percent of the population was employed in agriculture; in 2002, this number was only 16 percent. From 1973 to 2000, the percentage of urban residents increased from 43 percent to 59 percent; over this same period, the population density increased from 36.6 people per square kilometer to 74.6 (Programa Estado de la Nación 2006, 63). As urbanization increased, the rate of poverty decreased. In 1960, one-half of the population lived in poverty; by 1980, only one-quarter did (Vargas Cullel, et al 2005, 3, 6). Over the last 50 years of the 20th century, the government bureaucracy grew enormously, as did the size of the middle class. The most "tico" character could no longer be said to be the poor farmer with a machete and a canvas hat, but rather the urban office worker with a briefcase and, increasingly, a car (Cuevas Molina 2003, 23).

In this way, Costa Rica achieved peacefully what its Central American neighbors have been unable to accomplish even through revolution: raising large numbers of people to the middle class. In Nicaragua, for instance, per capita income in 2005 was only $950 a year. In comparison, in Costa Rica in the same year, per capita income was $4,700 (World Bank 2005). The poverty rate in Costa Rica as calculated by the country's National Institute of Statistics and Census decreased from 21.2 percent in 2005 to 20.2 percent in 2006 (Leitón 2006b). It varies a great deal, however, depending on the region of the country. While in the central region it was only 16.2 percent, in the Brunca region (in the far south) it was 32.8 percent and in the Chorotega region (in the northwest) it was 34.4 percent (Leitón 2006c).

In 2006, Costa Rica fell in the United Nations Index of Human Development for the fifth straight year. In 2001, it was ranked number 41 among 177 nations in human development; in 2006, it was number 48. This index analyses three variables: life expectancy at birth, education (measuring enrollment rates), and the economy (evaluating economic growth and annual income). Although both the poverty rate and the rate of unemployment decreased in 2006, 7.5 percent of the population still lives on $2 a day or less (Rojas and Lara 2006a). Distribution of income has also worsened; the richest 20 percent of the population has an income 10 times that of the poorest 20 percent (Leitón 2006d). Thus, although Costa Rica has been economically "exceptional" in many ways, not everyone can be considered middle class or even on the way to being so. It could be said, then, that in comparison with its Central American neighbors, Costa Rica is exceptional only in degree, not in kind.

As in many Latin American countries in the 20th century, the population has increased exponentially. In 1950 the total population was 877,000; by 2006, it was nearly 4.5 million. The "millionth child" remembered fondly by so many Costa Ricans was not born until 1956. Population growth combined with increased urban employment accelerated the expansion of San José and the surrounding towns

Plans for revitalizing San José and improving its public spaces include building many more pedestrian boulevards like this one near the National Museum. (Photo by Meg Mitchell)

of the Central Valley. The metropolitan area received many migrants from rural areas along with immigrants from other Central American countries. In 1880, San José had only 13,000 inhabitants, and by 1950, barely 100,000 (Hall and Pérez 2003, 250). By 2000, the population of the city was 1,345,750 (and that of the entire metropolitan area was even larger) (INEC 2000). A general lack of planning during this growth process led to overcrowding, pollution, lack of public green space, and a general sense of disorder in the capital city. Most old buildings in the center of San José were destroyed in order to construct unattractive multistory modern buildings (Hall and Pérez 2003, 251). As San José grew, small towns and municipalities lost their traditional functions as the organizing frameworks of civic life; citizens came more and more to live a commuter's existence and to rely upon and identify with the central government (Molina Jiménez 2003, 5).

Another striking change has been in the structure of the family and the role of women. The average family in 1960, accustomed to farm life, had seven children—thus the population boom. Yet by 2004, the average number of children per family had fallen to only two (Programa Estado de la Nación 2005, 388). Women have more opportunity to play different roles in the family and in the wider society. But other changes have occurred as well. The divorce rate increased between 1976 and 2000 from 9.1 percent to 39.8 percent. And by 2000, 52.7 percent of all births took place out of wedlock (Molina Jiménez 2003, 25). A very large number of births occur to women age 15 to 19 years old—more than 30 times the worldwide average (Programa Estado de la Nación 2005, 68). Therefore, not only did women enter the workforce in ever-greater numbers, but they did so in many cases as the sole support for their families. In 2006, women were the heads of household in 26 percent of all families in Costa Rica. Fifty-nine percent of these women only finished primary school or never attended school at all, meaning that these households are most likely poor (Leitón 2006a).

The *Estado de la Nación,* a yearly survey of social, political, and economic conditions in Costa Rica, has noted that, "Historically, in patriarchal societies like that of Costa Rica, men have been responsible for public life and decision-making, just as women have been in charge of reproduction, education, the care of the family, and thus confined almost exclusively to private life" (Programa Estado de la Nación 2000, 258). This framework is changing, but the transition has not been easy. In national surveys in 1995 and 1997, 73 percent of those interviewed said that the man ought to be the principle provider for the family; 75.5 percent believed that the woman ought to dedicate herself to her home and her family. Despite this vision of rather sharply divided family roles, 58.4 percent thought that the control of the household should be shared between husband and wife (Rodríguez Saénz 2003, 35).

The legal and political position of women in society changed greatly during the 20th century. After many years of effort, women were finally granted the right to vote with the 1949 Constitution. It was only beginning in the late 1980s and early 1990s, however, that further modification of the law accorded women greater protection and support. In 1990, the Law for the Promotion of Social Equality for Women initiated a period of change and gave impulse to the growth of many women's organizations that succeeded in focusing more attention on women's issues (see Leitinger 1997). Importantly, this law affected the electoral code that, in 1996, required political parties to nominate women for at least 40 percent of the posts that they compete for. In 2006, 22 women, 38.6 percent, were elected to the 57-seat national legislature (Global Database of Quotas for Women 2006). In 1998, a new autonomous institution, the National Institute for Women was formed to coordinate policies and programs in favor of women (INAMU 2007). This effort may have signified a new level of commitment on the part of the central government to support women's rights, but since 2003, administrative and budgetary conflicts within this new institution have gravely limited its abilities to support new initiatives (Programa Estado de la Nación 2006, 120).

New legislative initiatives have addressed problems like domestic violence and sexual harassment in the workplace, and at the beginning of the 21st century much greater awareness of these problems exists. Yet many protections for women are still lacking, and certain social and economic forces disproportionately affect women (Programa Estado de la Nación 2005, 69). The rate of domestic violence against women in 2005 reached its highest rate since 1996 (Programa Estado de la Nación 2006, 119). Although women now make up 40 percent of the workforce in Costa Rica, unemployment still tends to affect women more than men. In 2005, 9.6 percent of women were unemployed, while the rate for men was only 5 percent (Cantero 2006). Women who are employed also tend to earn less money than men with the same level of education. For every dollar that a man earns, a woman earns only 46 cents. Of 160 countries ranked by the United Nations in terms of male/female earning power, Costa Rica ranked 111 (Rojas and Lara 2006b). One factor that gives hope for improvement, though, is that in terms of education, things are looking up for women. Women now have a higher average level of education than men—8.4 years as opposed to 8.3. Women also have a higher rate of enrollment in universities. In 2004, almost 60 percent of the graduates from Costa Rican universities were women (Programa Estado de la Nación 2005, 67).

SOCIAL COHESION AND POLITICAL PARTICIPATION

A 2004 study of public opinion determined that "in Costa Rica, there exists almost unanimous pride in being Costa Rican" (Vargas-Cullel, et al 2005, 26). This finding mirrors almost exactly the results of a survey of 100 years before. In 1904, the city of San José performed a census in which many respondents, when asked their nationality, responded, "*Costarricense, por dicha*"—Costa Rican, thank goodness (Molina Jiménez 2003, 134). Even despite economic growing pains and corruption scandals, to judge from the more than enthusiastic support for the national soccer team during the 2006 World Cup soccer tournament and Costa Ricans' love of talking about their idiosyncrasies, the pride in simply *being from* Costa Rica continues unabated. As pointed out in chapter 3, a good measure of this pride comes from Costa Ricans' perceptions of their democratic institutions.

This same survey of political attitudes found that in 2004, Costa Ricans expressed the highest level of popular support

Masked dancers are a festive complement to the typical costumes and schoolchildren marching in formation that dominate the independence day celebrations. (Photo by Meg Mitchell)

in all of Central America for their political institutions (Vargas-Cullel, et al 2005, xv). The survey pointed out, however, several trends that seem to be contradictory in a society that has for so long considered itself a democracy. For example, the authors assert that although theirs is the "oldest and most stable democracy in Latin America," Costa Rican citizens demonstrate levels of "intolerance" similar to those in Mexico and other Central American nations—countries that have not enjoyed long periods of democratic development. "Tolerance" was defined as the belief that even those who hold different opinions ought to have the same rights; almost half of the Costa Rican population had "predominantly intolerant attitudes" (Vargas-Cullel, et al 2005, xvi). Only a little more than 60 percent approved of the notion that people who are critical of the government should have the right to vote; just 50 percent agreed that those critical of the government ought to be able to give public appearances, appear on television, or hold public office. More than 60 percent opposed the right of homosexuals (long the most disparaged group in Costa Rican society) to hold public positions. The analysis of the results of this study determined that these were the same levels of intolerance that existed in 1994. That is to say, 10 more years of democracy in Costa Rica had not resulted in a more tolerant population (Vargas-Cullel, et al 2005, 36, 37).

Political scientists generally suppose that a broad tolerance for different points of view is one of the bases of a stable democracy, yet this does not seem to have been the case in Costa Rica. The authors of this study hypothesize that this anomaly could be due to the fact that the Costa Rican political development took place among a population that perceived itself to be very homogeneous and therefore did not need to test the limits of its tolerance. For much of the 20th century, groups such as Afro-Caribbeans and indigenous peoples were excluded from meaningful political participation. The Constitution of 1949 forbade the participation of certain political parties (i.e., the Communist Party) until the 1970s, institutionalizing the idea that some political positions were simply not to be considered (Vargas-Cullel, et al 2005, 37–38).

Another element that seems to be in conflict with Costa Rica's self-image as a thoroughly democratic society is that it has a rather low level of citizen participation in public life. Despite its democratic ideals, Costa Rica does not record any higher community participation than other Latin American countries (including its neighbors in Central America), and it has some of the lowest rates of citizen participation in political parties. "Electoral participation in Costa Rica basically consists of voting" (Vargas-Cullel, et al 2005, xviii). And as discussed in chapter 3, abstentionism is increasing. In the national elections of 2006, abstentionism rose to

35 percent from 30 percent in 2002 (Programa Estado de la Nación 2006, 65). In a 2006 survey about voting participation in an upcoming municipal election, 44 percent said they planned not to vote. In 2002, only 33 percent said the same thing. Sixty-one percent of those interviewed said they were "indifferent" or "uninterested" in this election (Villalobos 2006). Mayors have been popularly elected only since 2002, and municipalities have been notorious for their financial and structural problems. It might be supposed that citizens would be interested in addressing these at the ballot box, yet this does not seem to be the case. The results of another recent survey suggest that though support for institutions is still strong, it has in some cases changed greatly over the last 20 years. When asked in 1988 if they could trust the systems of justice in Costa Rica, 43.4 percent of respondents answered yes. When asked the same question in 2006, only 22.9 answered in the affirmative. Of those interviewed, 53.1 percent believed that the Supreme Electoral Tribunal handled the last elections badly, and 70.8 percent think that services in hospitals have deteriorated (Poltronieri 2006, 19, 36, 48). These results, although not analyzed in the same depth as those in the 2004 survey, do point to the fact that Costa Ricans, even if they still have relatively high levels of social trust and faith in their institutions, have over the last few years come to have certain doubts about the functioning of their society.

After Chile, Costa Rica has in the past had the fewest problems with corruption of all countries in Latin America. Despite this fact, a very broad *perception* of corruption was held, even before the scandals of 2004. This level of perception is very similar to that found in Guatemala or Nicaragua, where *actual* public corruption is much greater (Vargas-Cullel, et al 2005, 66, 67). This dissonance seems to indicate that since Costa Ricans have historically had a greater faith in their public institutions, they also hold these institutions to a higher standard. Thus, any amount of corruption is more destructive to the sense of Costa Rican identity that is so tightly bound up with these institutions. The general faith in public institutions (which, interestingly, does not extend to political parties) still seems to be a force for cohesion in society, even if levels of support for specific institutions have declined over the last 10 to 15 years.

Thus, although Costa Ricans still feel a great deal of pride in their democracy and the peaceful functioning of their government, levels of actual participation (beyond voting) are not very high. Levels of tolerance and cooperation in society also are not as high as might be imagined. These factors have almost certainly been affected in some way by the economic and social changes the country has experienced as it is integrated more completely into the global economy. Rapid and unplanned urbanization and loss of a sense of community are testing Costa Rica's ability to adapt their beliefs to their reality. Yet it is to be hoped that even if the Costa Rican image of democracy has not fully encompassed these new realities, the tradition of democratic governance will be flexible and strong enough to carry the country peacefully into the next century.

RELIGION

An element that has traditionally drawn Costa Rican society together is Catholicism and its most important festivity of the year, the pilgrimage to the Basilica of the Virgen del los Ángeles in Cartago. The feast day of *La Negrita,* as the image is known, is August 2 and is a national holiday. In many Latin American countries, apparitions of a dark-skinned Virgin Mary during the colonial period served to symbolically tie the Catholicism of the conquerors to the religion of the conquered indigenous people and to ameliorate ethnic tensions. Mexico's Virgin of Guadalupe is perhaps the most dramatic example of this phenomenon. It is interesting that in Costa Rica, where secular traditions minimize the country's

The striking basilica in Cartago welcomes more than a million pilgrims every August during Costa Rica's most popular religious festival, which honors the Virgin of the Angels. (Photo by Meg Mitchell)

ethnic diversity, the single most important religious tradition bears witness to the need to unite diverse people through a common devotion.

Every year at the beginning of August, more than one million people walk to Cartago from all over Costa Rica, usually in gratitude for a miracle or with a particular intention in mind (a cure, a job, a winning season). When they arrive at the basilica the pilgrims fall on their knees and inch forward to the altar toward the small stone image that is clothed in a tiny gown chosen from hundreds sent in each year by seamstresses among the faithful. Afterward, the pilgrims line up to partake of the holy water that bubbles up from the spot where they believe the Virgin appeared to a young Indian woman in 1635 (Villegas 2006). At the large public mass, the president of the republic and other important political figures listen patiently (perhaps even attentively) as the presiding bishop gives a homily that will be reproduced in the nightly news and the next day's newspaper.

The pilgrimage can be a dangerous event. Every year deaths and injuries occur as an old tradition shares space on Costa Rica's crowded roads with the nation's newer infatuation with the automobile. The persistence of the pilgrims despite these perils highlights the importance of religious tradition in Costa Rican society, even as the world around it changes rapidly. The pilgrimage itself has changed since the 1970s. Before that, pilgrims might dress in Indian costumes as a way to remember the festival's colonial origins. There were also more and livelier public celebrations including popular music, dancing, and food. Now the festivities are more strictly religious, and the pilgrimage is a more personal or family event consisting mainly of the long walk.

Devotion to a *mestizo* apparition of Mary is one of the few typically Latin American characteristics of modern Costa Rican Catholicism. In particular, the Costa Rican church, with a very few important exceptions, has not played a significant role in the nation's political life since the pact with President Calderón Guardia and the Communist Party in the 1940s. Perhaps that pact—which restored to the Catholic Church many of the privileges it had lost in the late 19th century—gave the Catholic bishops everything they really wanted from the government. The 1949 Constitution made Catholicism the state religion but did not prohibit the practice of other faiths. Yet this status gave important privileges to the church, such as the right to teach religion in the public schools; the right to receive government funding for charitable, educational, and religious projects; and exemption from all taxes (Sawchuk 2004, 13; Picado 1989, 75).

These benefits, together with the generally progressive policies of the National Liberation Party (PLN), permitted the church to avoid the conflicts over poverty and human rights that emerged in almost every other Latin American country after World War II. Indeed, some refer to the period stretching from the death of Archbishop Sanabria in 1952 until the elevation of Monseñor Roman Arrieta Villalobos to Archbishop of San José in 1979 as the "long period of silence" of the Costa Rican church. Other than some acerbic warnings about the threat of communism, the bishops rarely spoke critically of social or economic developments in this period, despite the dramatic changes that were affecting the rural and, increasingly, urban lives of Costa Ricans (Sawchuk 2004, 4).

The silence was also curious given the changes that swept through the Catholic Church beginning with the Second Vatican Council (1962–1965). Vatican II encouraged regional bishops' conferences to take the lead in articulating the church's teachings in local contexts, and the Conference of Latin American Bishops (CELAM) was perhaps the most vocal of these new collegial bodies in the world. At various meetings, CELAM issued statements condemning the "structural sin" of the region's poverty and calling on Catholics to make a "preferential option for the poor" in lives committed to building social justice. To bring the church closer to the poor, and particularly to migrants living in precarious settlements on the margins of Latin America's mushrooming cities, CELAM promoted the formation of ecclesial base communities (CEBs), where people could come together to read the scriptures and to pray, often without the presence of a priest.

The Costa Rican bishops did not embrace these changes in Latin American Catholicism. The Costa Rican delegate to an important CELAM meeting in Medellín, Colombia, even refused to sign the final documents issued by his brother bishops (Sawchuk 2004, 81). According to one writer, when faced with the phenomena of urbanization and modernization, the Costa Rican church chose a "preferential option for the middle class" (Meléndez 2003). This option implied a close and submissive relationship with the PLN as it sought to build a middle-class society. It also implied a different way of meeting the pastoral challenges of a middle-class flock. While CEBs grew elsewhere in the region, Costa Rica's bishops favored charismatic movements and other efforts aimed at personal, as opposed to social, renewal (Picado 1989, 49, 90).

Some observers have also seen these sorts of movements as the Costa Rican church's response to the threat of rapid Pentecostal and Evangelical church growth during this same period (Picado 1989, 99). The number of Protestants (including mainline denominations) grew by 313 percent between 1956 and 1974, mostly due to the growth of Pentecostal and Evangelical congregations (Steigenga 2001, 111). This growth was and is very much in line with developments in the rest of Central America and Latin America as a whole. While some very important institutions are tied to mainline Protestant denominations in Costa Rica (like the excellent Clínica Bíblica hospital, the Colegio Metodista school, and the Universidad Bíblica Latinamericana), the most notable growth is in the Evangelical and Pentecostal churches that spring up in working-class and marginal neighborhoods, often in very humble houses decorated with holiday lights, cut paper banners, and other simple adornments.

While reliable numbers are hard to come by, a survey conducted in 1997 estimated that nearly 18 percent of Costa Ricans are members of non-Catholic churches (Holland 2002). It is possible to attribute this success to the sense of community that such churches create for people living in difficult circumstances. Although these churches are not notably politicized, they do seem to open spaces for active participation in community life that are not easy to find elsewhere. One survey of this topic found that only 34 percent of Catholics attended weekly religious services, while nearly 60 percent of mainline Protestants and 54 percent of Pentecostal church members did so. Perhaps due to

Some Protestant churches in Costa Rica represent traditional denominations, but many, like the "World of Faith" pictured here, do not and may be found in working-class neighborhoods mixed in among commercial establishments. (Photo by Meg Mitchell)

this more intense connection with their religious community, Protestants were much more likely to do volunteer work for their church (Steigenga 2001, 172, 114).

Another indication of the loss of influence of the Catholic Church is the rapid rise in civil marriage. In 1980, out of every 100 marriages in Costa Rica, 77 were performed by a Catholic priest and 23 were civil marriages. By 2006, this trend had been reversed: 76 of every 100 were civil marriages and 24 were Catholic. Of the 18,182 civil matrimonies of 2006, perhaps 10 percent were performed by a Protestant pastor, according to representatives of Protestant churches; even adding these to the 5,698 Catholic marriages performed, civil weddings still far outnumber religious services. These changes not only indicate the secularization of

Costa Rican society but they also reflect the fact that the divorce rate has so greatly increased over this same period of time. Since the Catholic Church does not recognize divorce, if someone originally married in the Catholic Church has divorced and wants to remarry, he or she must opt for a civil marriage the second time around (Rojas 2007).The Costa Rican Catholic Church might be losing ground to its competitors in religious intensity and church membership, and it may not have opted for the more typical paths of political influence pursued by the church elsewhere in the region. However, since the onset of Costa Rica's economic crisis in the 1980s, it has shown signs of taking a more active role in the workplace. It has done so, however, in two diametrically opposed directions. In the Diocese of Limón, where poverty and labor unrest have been much more widespread, the local church began in the late 1980s to embrace the preferential option for the poor, to promote CEBs, and to side openly with workers against the transnational fruit companies that operate in the region. In 1989, to the shock and dismay of business interests, and to the discomfort of many of his colleagues in the Costa Rican Bishops Conference, the bishop of Limón released a pastoral letter criticizing the "uncontrolled expansion of the banana industry" in his diocese, and the human and environmental costs such expansion brought (Sawchuk 2004, 169).

On the other end of the political spectrum, a church-sponsored institution known as the Pope John XXIII Social School (named for the pope who called the Second Vatican Council), has interpreted Catholic social teaching in a much more conservative way. The school, which has been heavily financed by the fruit companies and other business interests since its founding in 1971, has been one of the most important agents promoting the concept of "solidarism" among Costa Rican workers. Solidarism is a movement directly opposed to union organization, collective bargaining, and strikes. Supporters of solidarism argue that workers' problems can best be solved, and the common good best served, through cooperation with management. Workers who join solidarist associations give up the right to collective bargaining and strikes in exchange for electing representatives to a joint worker/management committee at the company that employs them. This committee manages a savings fund to which both workers and management contribute 5 percent of their monthly salary. The fund is used to provide benefits like supplementary health care, support for housing and education, recreational opportunities, and perhaps a subsidized store or cafeteria. The 1949 Constitution guarantees Costa Rican workers the right to organize unions and to strike under certain circumstances. In fact, however, striking legally is very difficult to do. Between 1969 and 1996, for example, the government declared all but three attempted strikes illegal for various reasons (Sawchuk 2004, 35, 37). Despite these obstacles, union activity in Costa Rica continued, particularly in the banana-growing regions where strikes occurred into the 1980s. The Pope John XXIII Social School, however, has proven particularly adept in working with business executives and with the banana companies to promote the *solidarista* alternative. The school opened offices to promote associations throughout the banana zones, and a worker education center in the San José suburb of Tres Ríos to train movement leaders. Since the beginning of the school's promotion work in 1971, solidarista associations have grown 60 times over, and between 4,000 and 5,000 workers can pass through the center in Tres Rios in a given year (Sawchuk 2004, 143–144).

While the Catholic Church in Costa Rica no longer dominates religious and cultural life the way it once did, it still is the primary focus of attention of people looking for a religious perspective on public affairs. The church's history and its organization, which permits easy identification of its leaders, certainly account for some of this continuing influence.

Even if Catholic parishes are not always the most fervent in their religious practices, nor as full as some Pentecostal churches on a given Sunday, the country's Catholic hierarchy is frequently consulted as to its positions on public affairs. Whether it is in the annual pilgrimage to Cartago or in the papal audience sought by President Óscar Arias to suggest that Costa Rica's bishops should throw their support behind the ratification of the free trade agreement with the United States (which they have not), Costa Ricans still look to Catholic practices and Catholic leadership to hold their society together.

ETHNIC MINORITIES AND THE COSTA RICAN SELF-IMAGE

If Costa Rica is not religiously homogeneous, neither is it ethnically homogeneous—despite its long-standing self-image as the "whitest" country in Central America. Besides a European (mainly Spanish) heritage, Costa Rican society also owes a debt to its indigenous, Afro-Caribbean, and Chinese inhabitants for their contributions. In the 2000 census, about 6 percent of the population was self-described as a member of one of these three groups. The remaining 94 percent was neither described as "white" nor as "mestizo" (either of which designations might have been expected) but rather as "other." Although, for better or worse, we usually think of minority rather than majority groups as "other," this usage was justified as appropriate by the government agency in charge of the census because "the rest of the population does not seem to clearly ascribe to itself a definite ethnicity." Perhaps this could be because the last time that the Costa Rican government tried to determine the ethnicity of its population was in the census of 1950. But 50 years later, both governmental and nongovernmental agencies were vocal in their opinion that it was necessary to make even small ethnic groups visible through the census so that their socioeco-

While the United Fruit Company no longer dominates the Atlantic region (as it did when this photo was taken in 1910), bananas are still a very important and sometimes controversial export. (Library of Congress)

nomic and demographic situations within the country could be properly understood (Solano Salazar 2003, 17–18).

That certain ethnic groups could remain invisible for so long was due in part to the difficult geography of the country. Because the various regions remained isolated from one another even up into the 20th century, it was easy for the national leaders in the capital city to define the characteristics of the relatively homogeneous population of the Central Valley as the "national" characteristics. As late as the 1970s, one Spanish commentator living in Costa Rica observed that "in his daily life, the Costa Rican [i.e., someone living in the Central Valley] does not even acknowledge the existence of" port cities like Limón (on the Atlantic coast) or Quepos or Golfito (on the Pacific coast) (Láscaris 1992, 48). Thus, "others" were those not only perceived to have a different ethnicity but also those who simply lived outside the Central Valley. Such characterizations became much more difficult to sustain as improvements in transportation and communication tied the country more closely together, and migrants from the Central Valley moved to other parts of the country looking for land or work. It is interesting to point out as well that a good portion of the Chinese, indigenous, and black Costa Ricans have always lived outside the Central Valley.

In 1862, the Costa Rican government passed a law forbidding all non-European immigration to the country (Harpelle 1993, 104). That such a law was created indicates that fear already existed that "different" types of people might dilute Costa Rica's "European" blood. That the law could never be strictly enforced indicates that the need for labor was bound to override certain prejudices. Chinese workers and black workers (mostly from Jamaica, but also from other areas of the Caribbean) were contracted to build the railroad from San José to the Atlantic coast; because of the discriminatory law, they had not been the first choice of the Costa Rican government to fill their labor needs. The first railroad workers contracted were Italians and prison laborers from the United States. But when the Italians went on strike to protest the conditions of their labor contract and all the prisoners died, there seemed to be no choice except to ignore the law that barred non-Europeans and hire Chinese and black West Indians to finish the job (Harpelle 1993, 104). Both groups still maintain a presence in Costa Rica in the 21st century. In the 2000 census, 7,873 people self-identified Chinese and 72,784 people identified themselves as black or Afro-Caribbean (INEC 2000).

Both black and Chinese workers arrived as contract labor, but also independently, that is, without a specific contract. Chinese working on the railroad mostly arrived on the Atlantic coast, but others arrived on the Pacific coast. They were hoping to get all the way to California to participate in the legendary Gold Rush, but, for one reason or another, they found their trip cut short in Costa Rica. Most Chinese immigrants since then have been Cantonese, but in the last decades of the 20th century, a number of immigrants have alse come from Taiwan. Many men came alone to work and married Costa Rican women. Chinese families who have lived many generations in the country may have lost or changed their Chinese surnames at some time and now have many of the same last names as their Hispanic neighbors. As a Chinese Costa Rican professor of history has put it, "The majority of the descendents of the first Chinese immigrants no longer speak Cantonese nor its dialects; they are Catholic and feel themselves to be Costa Rican. Nevertheless, the feeling of belonging to a different ethnic minority still persists." The towns with the largest Chinese populations, like Limón, Puntarenas, Nicoya, and San José, have Chinese associations. One of the most well-known public figures in the country is the Chinese Costa Rican scientist Dr. Franklin Chang Díaz, who was the first Latin American to become an astronaut and fly on U.S. National Aeronautics and Space Administration missions (Chen Apuy 1992). Franklin Chang returned to Costa Rica in 2006 with great fanfare to open a plasma rocket lab in Guanacaste, and he is frequently lauded in the national media for his contributions to Costa Rica's science and economy (ACAN EFE 2006).

The black community has also made important contributions to Costa Rican society, but for both cultural and geographical reasons, for many years it remained isolated from the rest of the country. Although the railroad was finished in 1890, other work in Limón Province continued to attract Jamaican laborers: as the railroad had opened up new land, banana cultivation and export became one of Costa Rica's most important economic activities. This trade came to be controlled by the United Fruit Company (UFCo), which found it convenient to continue to employ English-speaking

West Indians in its operations. Between 1900 and 1913, 20,000 Jamaicans migrated to Costa Rica. Work on the banana plantations was exhausting but paid relatively high wages. The Jamaican immigrants hoped to earn enough to return home and buy their own land, or to set up as independent farmers in Costa Rica. Many achieved this goal, often growing bananas on their own land as subcontractors for UFCo (Chomsky 1996, 35, 43).

Until the 1920s, an Afro-Caribbean culture flourished in Limón Province without much interference from highland Costa Rica. There were three reasons for this. The first was that UFCo exercised almost complete control (economic and otherwise) over the Caribbean province. It paid workers' salaries and bought the produce of independent growers, but it also controlled what the Caribbean residents could buy by importing goods and selling them to the workers in exchange for the money they had just earned working for the company. UFCo paid no taxes to the Costa Rican government for what it imported and sold the goods to the workers at inflated prices (Chomsky 1996, 56).

The second reason for the relative isolation of the Caribbean community was geographical: even with the railroad, it was not very easy to get to the coast from the Central Valley. Finally, the Jamaican workers had brought with them a distinct Afro-Caribbean culture—a different language and a different religion, as well as a taste for their own food and their own pastimes. In coastal settlements, they established their own English-language schools and Protestant churches. Until World War II, when it became impossible to import the necessary equipment, cricket was the most popular sport. After the middle of the century, baseball and soccer became popular (Palmer 2005, 83, 187). From Jamaica (as well as other islands), people brought their own customs, folklore, popular medicine, and popular music. The province of Limón developed its own style of calypso music that reflected influences from mento music from Jamaica, calypso from Trinidad, and *son* from Cuba. Costa Rican calypso has remained alive into the 21st century by also being able to incorporate new influences like reggae and salsa (Monestel 2005, 22).

Community organizations in Limón were strong throughout the first half of the 20th century. One of the most important was the Universal Negro Improvement Association (UNIA), founded by Marcus Garvey in Jamaica in 1919. Garvey had worked for UFCo in Costa Rica and returned there in 1921 to bring UNIA's program of education and promotion of black culture to the residents of Limón and the smaller communities south down the coast. Garvey also brought to Costa Rica a ship of his Black Star Line to promote a plan to carry blacks from around the Americas back to Africa. This venture ultimately failed. When Garvey ran into legal problems in the United States in the 1930s, UNIA also began to fall into decline, but both were long remembered by the residents of the Caribbean coast (Palmer 2005, 171–176).

In the 1920s, the relatively high wages and year-round work on banana plantations (as opposed to seasonal work on highland coffee plantations) began to attract Hispanic workers to the coast. They resented the preferential treatment they felt the English-speaking West Indians received from the fruit company. The United Fruit Company, however, was concerned about the West Indians only so long as it served its interests. In the late 1930s, after labor unrest (in which black workers for the most part were not involved) and the increase of disease in the banana crops, UFCo moved its operations to the Pacific coast. It negotiated contracts with the Costa Rican government, exchanging Atlantic for Pacific lands and agreeing not to employ "colored" labor in its new operations. Restricting Afro-Caribbean workers to Limón assuaged fears among certain Costa Rican elites that, as one well-known scientist put it in 1939, "OUR BLOOD IS BLACKENING" (quoted in Palmer and Molina 2004, 244; emphasis in original). If little out-and-out race conflict has

Costa Rica's Caribbean Culture

Beginning in the first few years of the 20th century, the Caribbean coast of Costa Rica was colonized by Jamaicans, Panamanians, Nicaraguans, and Colombians, among others. Many came to work on the railroad, others came to grow bananas for the United Fruit Company, and some were independent farmers. In Paula Palmer's fascinating oral history of the coast, *"What Happen,"* men and women described what life was like in the Talamanca region of the coast from the early years of the 20th century through the 1970s—when improved transportation and communication, as well as the advent of the tourist industry, began to more fully integrate the Caribbean with the rest of Costa Rica.

One of her sources, Mr. Augustus Mason, who was born in Jamaica but came to the town of Old Harbour (now called Puerto Viejo de Talamanca) as a boy in 1910, had a lot to say about the old ways of doing things. Immigrants had to be self-sufficient in many ways, and life was not always easy. As Mr. Mason said in the distinctive English idiom of the coast, "The Jamaicans was the hardest working people that you could ever come across. They live from nothing but they make something. And they start to go inside the land and plant their own provisions and cocoa, and they build their own boats that run with sail. They build those out of any kind of wood and use calico cloth for sail."

Especially in the early years of settlement, farmers planted a variety of crops to sell in the city of Limón. Besides bananas, these crops included coconut, pineapple, yuca (cassava), melon, cocoa, cabbage, tomato, and okra. Transportation was mostly by sea and was very unreliable, but that was the only way to get crops to market. Yet much of what farmers grew was for their own consumption. Mr. Mason claimed that "We never left for hungry. We make sugar from sugar cane and give everybody a portion who didn't have cane. We was living very easy that way. Rice and beans we don't have to buy because we cultivate that. We cut the wild palm [*palmito*] in the bush and use it for vegetable as cabbage, turnip, or anything." Mr. Mason also remembered that the sugar cane could be used to make home-brewed liquor for parties, the biggest of which were at Christmas and Easter.

The residents of coastal Limón were also self-sufficient in entertainment. Mr. Mason described how they could make various instruments: "To make the drum they get the bark log, the down-tree, *balsa* the Spanish call it . . . And they will get the wild bamboo in the bush to make a flute with different holes. We call it fife . . . And that was the way we make our bands down here and we dance and enjoy ourselves." Over the years, the musical traditions that the immigrants brought from places like Jamaica, Trinidad, and Cuba merged to create a unique form of Costa Rican calypso music that is still performed, but with more modern instruments, especially the guitar.

As roads were built and telephones lines were strung, a national park was opened in the town of Cahuita, and tourists began to arrive, things along the coast began to change. Some of the old-time residents saw great opportunities in these changes for themselves and their children; others became nostalgic for the past and worried that unique aspects of the Caribbean culture would be lost as the region modernized. But Mr. Augustus Mason, who had always adapted to the changes that came along during the seventy years he lived along the coast, was optimistic about the future. "Well, you can see and you can hear," he said. "There is a great future in Old Harbour. Plenty of things will happen. I can't tell you, but there is a lot of improvement coming in the future."

Source: Paula Palmer. 2005 [1979]. *"What Happen": A Folk History of Costa Rica's Talamanca Coast.* Miami: Zona Tropical, 46–49, 274.

arisen in Costa Rica, this pernicious sort of racism has, unfortunately, occasionally come to the surface.

In the 1930s, the government also tightened immigration and naturalization rules for West Indians and put more pressure on black residents of Costa Rica to register with the government, even though it was no easier than before to become a legal resident. Descendents of West Indian immigrants born in Costa Rica were not automatically citizens but had to apply for citizenship. In this same decade, police in Limón began enforcing the segregation of public spaces like beaches and movie theaters for the first time. And in 1942, the government passed a law that prohibited the immigration of "the black race, Chinese, Arabs, Turks, Syrians, Armenians, Gypsies, Coolies, etc." This law technically remained in force until 1960, although it was not enforced. In this atmosphere, in the 1930s and 1940s, many blacks left Costa Rica, particularly to find work in Panama. Others tried to accommodate themselves to the new laws, but naturalization remained a difficult process (Harpelle 1993, 109, 115–118).

The situation of the black population definitively changed with the Civil War of 1948 and the subsequent presidency of José Figueres. As one of Costa Rica's most important Afro-Caribbean writers has described it, "José Figueres arrived in Limón and visited the villages speaking English, kissing black children, dancing with black women. Never before had a president of Costa Rica done such a thing. The blacks for the first time felt part of the country" (quoted in Chomsky 1996, 257). And, in fact, after 1950, the Afro-Caribbeans finally began to be incorporated into Costa Rica, increasingly becoming citizens and gaining the right to vote. The government set up new schools—but these were Spanish-language, not English-language schools. The Ministry of Public Health built new clinics and began a campaign to eradicate malaria. The Ministry of Public Works began to improve roads and build roads where none had existed before. A national park was established on land in the town of Cahuita (Palmer 2005, 255–256).

All of these changes brought certain benefits, but they also exacted certain costs from the Afro-Caribbean communities. To continue their education, children had to be proficient in Spanish, and if they were, they might be more likely to leave their communities to look for opportunities elsewhere in the country. Roads finally connected the

Caribbean coast to the rest of the country; gone were the long trips involving rail, bus, and boat travel to get to the southernmost point of the Atlantic coast. These same roads brought tourists and investors who would ultimately change the Caribbean coast entirely; in the end, it may have been tourism that finally integrated this region into modern Costa Rica. But the modern world was bound to mean change, and loss, for the Afro-Caribbean cultures that had existed in semi-isolation for so long. In some cases, the loss can be marked concretely in land lost to foreign investors or to the national park. In others, perhaps, it is less tangible, like the loss of language or weakening of community ties.

Since the 1980s, thanks to more study of this facet of Costa Rican history, "the question of ethnicity now has a place on the political agenda." Writers whose work reflects their Afro-Caribbean roots, such as Quince Duncan and Eulalia Bernard, have won a place in the Costa Rican literary canon. But most Afro-Caribbeans still live in Limón Province, one of the country's poorest. Black Costa Ricans have become more prominent as television announcers and sports figures, but, at least according to one Costa Rican academic, the stereotype of "white" Costa Rica is still apparent in advertising and "in the admissions systems of public universities (on whose campuses students, professors, and administrators of Afro-Caribbean origin are an exception to the rule)" (Molina Jiménez 2003, 20–22)

Some of these same kinds of prejudices have also affected indigenous Costa Ricans. Black Costa Ricans did not become citizens until 1949. Indigenous peoples were not full citizens until 1991, when they were finally recognized as Costa Ricans by right of birth and received the identity cards (*cédulas*) that allowed them to vote and take advantage of state services (Programa Estado de la Nación 2006, 254). That indigenous people have been generally excluded and their presence even denied is due, in part, to the fact that unlike in some Latin American countries, an attempt has never been made to incorporate indigenous heritage into the national image. Costa Rican leaders and intellectuals of the late 19th and early 20th centuries preferred to find the origin of Costa Rican culture in things and peoples purely European (Sandoval-García 2004, 66, 84). Even at the beginning of the 21st century, stereotypical images of smiling native people greeting friendly Spanish friars with gifts of gold could be found decorating school bulletin boards on Columbus Day. A change in the law is not always enough to change attitudes.

Although a few towns in the Central Valley still have strongly indigenous populations (like Quitirrisí near San José) almost all Indian groups live outside the center of the country. In the colonial period, many indigenous people fled from the Central Valley and from coastal areas to the remote north to hide in the heavily forested Guatuso plains below Lake Nicaragua; others fled to the far south to live in the inaccessible Talamanca Mountains. Indigenous populations all over the region decreased rapidly after the arrival of the Spanish. When Europeans arrived, estimates indicate that 400,000 Indians lived in the region. Because of overwork, war, disease, and flight, by 1611, only about 10,000 remained (Palmer and Molina 2006, 19). Fewer indigenous people live in Costa Rica today than in most other Latin American countries, but that fact does not seem to justify ignoring the existence of the approximately 65,000 that do live in Costa Rica (Marín 2006).

The Costa Rican government first tried to address the question of where indigenous Costa Ricans fit into the larger society in 1973 with the creation of the National Commission for Indian Affairs (CONAI). In 1977, provisions were made in the national constitution to create Indian reserves encompassing areas where native people continued to live and large populations were known to exist before the conquest. Eight ethnic groups were recognized—Chorotega, Bribri, Cabécar, Huetar, Guaymi/Nobegue, Maleku/Guatuso,

The indigenous groups of Costa Rica have been left out of the country's development and must struggle (often in peaceful marches like this one) for recognition of their rights to land and other resources.
(AFP Photo/Teresita Chavarría)

Térraba, and Brunca (sometime called Boruca)—and 23 reserves have since been established around the country (Stocker 2005, 40). Perhaps because these reserves were established at such a late date, different indigenous groups have had very different reactions to them. The various groups had different characteristics and needs (for instance, only four out of the eight still spoke indigenous languages) that a single law could not take into account.

In the northwestern part of the country, for instance, land was given to people of Chorotega descent. However, by the time the town of Nambue received reservation status, its residents no longer spoke a Chorotega (Mangue) language or had a distinctive structure of land tenure or local leadership. Only about half of the residents of the reservation chose to identify themselves as indigenous, and many resented that they had no rights to sell their portion of the land. Some believed that the existence of the reservations only increased discrimination against them as "Indian," more because they came from a certain town than that they looked or lived differently from others in nearby areas (Stocker 2005, 43–50). Other groups, particularly those living further from urban areas and still maintaining traditional customs and languages, found the reservations to be of great benefit. The Bribri and Cabécar people who live on the KéköLdi reserve in Talamanca have said, "The Reserve makes us feel that we are valued equally with all other people. With the Reserve, we are more united as a people, more identified as a people. We can work together to strengthen our traditions and our language. We feel more protected and at ease" (Palmer, et al 1991, 68).

What almost all indigenous groups have in common is that they are among the poorest in the country. Seventy percent of indigenous homes have no electricity; 90 percent of indigenous people take their drinking water from contaminated sources, and 30 percent are illiterate. A Costa Rican commentator has pointed out that "in the middle of our everyday reality of 'civilization,' the indigenous are an invisible people, another Costa Rica." (Mayorga 2006). Indigenous people often lack access to the health care services that most other Costa Ricans enjoy. A recent UNICEF report noted that children and adolescents, in particular, have suffered from this lack, and almost half (47.6 percent) of the indigenous population is under 17 years of age. Infant mortality rates in indigenous communities have not improved along with those of the rest of the country: at the beginning of the 21st century they are equivalent to what they were in the rest of the country in 1980 (Cantero 2007).

Groups living in relatively more accessible areas have tried to improve themselves economically by taking advantage of the increase of tourism in Costa Rica. The Chorotega are known for making beautiful ceramics that

These masks were made in Escazu, a suburb of San José, by artisans interested in preserving Costa Rican crafts. When inspired by a cimarron, a traditional brass band, dancers bring them to life. (Photo by Meg Mitchell)

they sell to visitors and in San José. The residents of the KéköLdi reservation opened their land to eco-tourists interested in their way of life and their environmental projects, like the raising of green iguanas. The Brunca, also in the south, eagerly market textiles and masks in the style of the ones used in their annual Fiesta de los Diablitos. In Quitirrisí, just 45 minutes from San José, visitors can discuss various aspects of indigenous spirituality and contemporary life while learning about artisanal and medical uses of native plants. Other groups, however, particularly in the far south, remain very isolated from any of the benefits of modern civilization—roads, schools, clinics. Their communities may be several hours' walk away from the nearest highway. The residents find it harder and harder to exist in their traditional ways as the animals and plants they have always depended on become scarcer, but they have not become integrated into the modern life of the rest of the country, either.

Unfortunately, the CONAI often has provided more problems than solutions for the indigenous communities it was supposedly created to serve. It has been accused of seriously mismanaging Indian affairs and particularly of failing to protect indigenous land from the encroachment of nonindigenous settlers (Vargas Rojas 2006). In the last months of 2006, indigenous groups and the national legislature debated a plan to dissolve the CONAI and replace it with another sort of indigenous council that would allow the reservation areas direct representation and more control over local affairs (Murillo M. 2006). Such reorganization has proven difficult because of divisions within the indigenous community itself and because still, in the broader society, as one member of a national indigenous group has put it, the native population in Costa Rica suffers from "intolerance, lack of respect, and the intransigence of political leaders and of society itself" (Swaby 2003, 11).

If black and indigenous Costa Ricans still occupy an ambiguous position within Costa Rican society, if they need to be included economically and politically, but desire at the same time to be able to maintain aspects of their traditional cultures, there is still hope that this may be accomplished. One Costa Rican musician and historian has put it this way: "The incorporation of calypso and other manifestations of Afro-Caribbean culture into the process of the construction of the Costa Rican identity is part of a cultural debate. In this debate is expressed the necessity to create a national consciousness of the participation of the Afro-Costa Rican, the indigenous, the Chinese and other ethnic and cultural groups that have been part of Costa Rican social life for many years" (Monestel 2005, 17).

NICARAGUAN IMMIGRANTS

The most recent group to feel the impact of "intransigence" is Nicaraguan immigrants to Costa Rica. The relationship between Costa Rica and Nicaragua has always been somewhat difficult. In 1824, almost immediately after independence was declared, Costa Rica annexed the northwestern area of Guanacaste, which during the colonial period had been administratively under the control of Nicaragua. In the Central Valley, a certain prejudice still exists against Costa Ricans from Guanacaste. It is sometimes said that they are *"Nicas regaladas"*—Nicaraguans given to Costa Rica by the annexation. That is, more like Nicaraguans than "real" Costa Ricans. This notion is ironic, because if those in the Central Valley have not always been personally accepting of the residents of the northern Pacific coast, they have gladly adopted many of their folkloric traditions, music, and dance. It has been said that "an idealized image of [Guanacaste's] cultural tradition is plundered freely by state intellectuals and the tourist ministry in order to fill with dances, dress, and marimba music what would otherwise be a rather empty basket of national folklore" (Palmer and Molina 2004, 249).

An 1858 treaty gave Nicaragua control over the San Juan River, which separates the two countries, but also gave Costa Rica the right of free transit. Nicaragua has several times raised the ire of Costa Rica through actions that seemed to limit this freedom. In 1876, Nicaragua signed a treaty with France to cut Costa Rica out of the deal regarding any future canal that passed along the river (Edelman 1998, 356). Of course, the interoceanic canal was eventually built not in Nicaragua but in Panama, yet disputes over the San Juan still continue. In 2005, Costa Rica brought complaints in the International Court of Justice at The Hague against Nicaragua over a fee that country charged to anyone who entered by crossing the river and over whether or not

Costa Rican border guards patrolling the river had a right to be armed (Villalobos 2005).

Despite these conflicts, Nicaraguan immigrants to Costa Rica were not always unwelcome. They have, in fact, been arriving in Costa Rica off and on since Nicaragua was occupied by the United States from 1927 to 1932. Many were welcomed later in the century as they fled the decades-long dictatorship of the Somozas in Nicaragua, others as they fled the Sandinista government and the civil wars that followed the fall of the dictatorship in 1979. In the aftermath of the destruction caused by Hurricane Mitch in 1999, another wave of immigrants arrived. But the combination of the removal of the socialist Sandinistas from power in 1990 and the decline in investment in Costa Rican public services beginning in the 1980s made Nicaraguan immigration seem less appealing than before (Sandoval-García 2004, 137).

Because of natural disasters and political uncertainty in Nicaragua, economic conditions have remained very bad there. It is the second poorest country in the Western Hemisphere, after Haiti, and suffers from very high un- and underemployment rates (U.S. Department of State 2007). Jobs in Costa Rica are relatively more plentiful and better paid. Most of the Nicaraguan immigrants to Costa Rica at the beginning of the 21st century are economic migrants instead of political refugees, as they were during the civil wars of the 1980s. They take many of the low-paying jobs that Costa Ricans no longer want to do—harvesting coffee, for example, or working in construction or domestic service.

Yet to Costa Ricans, Nicaraguans often seem to be competing for the same jobs, pushing down wages, pushing up crime. They have been accused of putting pressure on the educational and health systems. Nicaragua's tumultuous history has contributed to a popular perception that individual Nicaraguans are more prone to violence, and the generally darker tone of their skin has led them to be stereotyped as

Nicaraguan immigrants line up on August 20, 2001, in front of an immigration office in San José to ask for permission to work or live in Costa Rica. (AFP Photo/Teresita Chavarría)

more "Indian." Costa Ricans call the immigrants "*nicas,*" which is also something Nicaraguans call themselves. Yet in this situation, it has taken on a pejorative meaning and generally signifies to Costa Ricans not *all* people from Nicaragua, but only poor immigrants who came to Costa Rica looking for work (Sandoval-García 2004, 143). A 2005 poll found that 8 out of every 10 of Costa Ricans believe that immigrants take work that ought to go to ticos, and 6 out 10 think that the country would be better off without so many immigrants. Women tend to be the most hostile toward immigration and to believe that immigrants are responsible for most of the crime in Costa Rica. On a more positive note, though, 55 percent of Costa Ricans surveyed said that immigrants do help to enrich the country's cultural diversity (*La Nación* 2005).

These perceptions seem to have their basis in fear, rather than in fact. In the 2000 census, Nicaraguans made up only

6 percent of the residents of the country. (This figure may rise by 2 percent during harvest times.) Only 3 percent of the total school population is made up of Nicaraguan children. Although Nicaraguans are often blamed for the increase in crime in Costa Rica, in 1998 they were only 5 percent of the prison population. Interestingly, xenophobic sentiments seem not to have extended to Europeans or North Americans in Costa Rica; they are not seen so much as "foreigners" as "tourists" (Sandoval-García 2004, 145, 147, 155, 163).

Discrimination against Nicaraguans has taken many forms, including "workplace exploitation, aggressively stereotypical images, rejection in everyday life, the obscuring of their cultural and social contributions, and the creation of jokes that hide violence and hostility under a humorous façade." Jokes have been a particularly insidious form of discrimination because they are so common and because "they create an anonymous (or impersonal) space that permits laughter and complicity, where images are constructed out of fear, hatred, and rejection of the 'other'" (Masís 2006). Many Costa Ricans, however, have recognized that in their society a pernicious undercurrent of xenophobia exists, and they have strongly supported efforts to overcome these misunderstandings and prejudices.

Such prejudices have occasionally resulted in violence. Toward the end of 2005, two Nicaraguan nationals were killed in violent incidents in and around the capital city. After these incidents, a general outcry arose against xenophobia and racism; but a surge in anti-Nicaraguan jokes was also seen. The rector of the University of Costa Rica, Yamileth González, was prompted to write in an editorial in *La Nación* that "Costa Ricans have become xenophobic, intolerant, discriminatory, and this is a grave problem." She pointed out that the government agency, the Defensoría de los Habitantes, had asserted its obligation to defend the rights of *all* inhabitants of the country, not just those who were citizens. She insisted that the university must not remain on the sidelines of these debates, but should "lift up its voice to turn back this process and find a path where solidarity exists" (González 2005).

Because of these incidents, in 2006, the Nicaraguan government brought a complaint against the Costa Rican government to the Interamerican Commission on Human Rights accusing it of "deep-rooted xenophobia" and of lack of action in the cases of the Nicaraguans killed. The Costa Rican government countered that the Nicaraguan government had not gone through the proper channels to make its complaint and, in any case, the Nicaraguans should be more concerned with why so many people have to immigrate to Costa Rica from Nicaragua in the first place (Associated Press 2006; EFE 2006). Yet in November 2006, the Costa Rican authorities formally indicted two police officers involved in one of the incidents for having taken no action to save the life of the Nicaraguan in question (Argüedas and Gutiérrez 2006).

One Costa Rican historian has indicated a parallel in the treatment that the Nicaraguans have received and the experiences of previous "others" in Costa Rican society. "The coming to the country of Afro-Caribbeans, Chinese, Jews, and of the Nicaraguans," he wrote, "brought into being distinct discriminatory measures and a public discourse centered on the defense of the racial purity of Costa Rica." Yet unlike some of the other groups who remained geographically as well as culturally separate, the Nicaraguans have come to live and work mostly in and around the capital city. And this happened at a time when Costa Ricans tended to feel that their social security and educational institutions are in a period of crisis. Perhaps this is why the new immigrants seem so particularly threatening (Molina Jiménez 2003, 106). Nicaraguans and other groups perceived to be different have suffered "various forms of exclusion and racialization" perhaps because they have threatened the "emphasis on the country's uniqueness"—in particular, the long-standing image of Costa Rica as a homogeneous society (Sandoval-García 2004, 62).

INSECURITY AND CRIME

At the beginning of the 21st century, many Costa Ricans feel threatened not only by foreign immigration but also by crime. This feeling of insecurity is much greater in San José than in rural areas, but more than half the country's population now lives in the metropolitan area of the Central Valley. The number of crimes committed in Costa Rica has increased since the late 1980s. In 1986, 20 percent of all homes reported that some member of the family had been the victim of a crime. In 2004, 38.7 percent reported this occurrence. Most are crimes against property. To put these numbers in perspective, however, it is necessary to point out that although crime rates are higher than they once were, they are still relatively low in comparison with the rest of Latin America. The rate of individual victimization in metropolitan San José is less than one-third of what it is in other Latin American cities like Bahia, Brazil; San Salvador, El Salvador; or Caracas, Venezuela. Homicide rates in Costa Rica were 3.9 per 100,000 people in 1970 and 6.6 per 100,000 in 2004. Homicide rates for Latin America in general in 2004 were 28.4 per 100,000. And at 6.6 per 100,000, mortality rates in Costa Rica are still much lower for homicide than for traffic accidents (14.8) or suicide (7.6) (PNUD 2006, 8–9).

Despite these statistics, surveys over the last 20 years have shown that Costa Ricans still feel that security is one of the biggest problems facing their country. Most fear aggression from strangers in public places, but for women at least, domestic violence is still a much greater threat. And, over the entire population, it seems that the perception of crime is much greater than the probability of crime. The

Bars, and very often razor wire, are the norm in most urban neighborhoods. Many ticos believe that crime and insecurity are some of the most pressing problems the country now faces. (Photo by Meg Mitchell)

perception of risk—that is to say, how likely that someone *thinks* he or she will be a victim—is 1 in 2 for crimes against property, 1 in 3 for physical aggression, and 1 in 5 for sexual aggression. The *actual* probabilities that one will be a victim of crime are 1 in 4 (property), 1 in 31 (physical), and 1 in 89 (sexual). The most fearful groups are those that feel they have the most to lose: the middle and upper classes. Of these groups, those who feel the most threatened are people under age 25 living in urban areas and women (PNUD 2006, 15, 16).

As discussed earlier, many tend to blame foreigners (especially Nicaraguans and Colombians) for the increase in crime. Yet most crimes are committed by Costa Ricans (PNUD 2006 11). Citizens generally seem to feel that the institutions of public safety do not protect them: 86.9 percent say that the police should share some of the blame for rising crime rates. Yet, unlike in some other Latin American countries, a very low number of inhabitants feel actively threatened by the police. Costa Rican police do not have the dreadful reputation for human rights abuses that many of their counterparts in other countries have. The system of public security is highly segmented, with various government ministries controlling their own specialized police forces, and a general lack of coordination, sharing of intelligence, and standardized training is seen. Financing for training and equipment has not been a priority, and thus the ability to successfully investigate crimes and prosecute criminals has been seriously impaired (PNUD 2006, 17–19).

As people have lost faith in the police and the justice systems, they have more frequently turned to private security firms. In Costa Rica about the same number or slightly more private guards than police officers are actively engaged in security. In addition to the heavily armed guards in front of every bank and in the parking lots of most shopping centers, large numbers of (usually unarmed) watchmen guard the gated entrances and the streets of middle- and upper-class neighborhoods. (Ironically, considering their generally low status in public opinion, many of these low-paid guards are Nicaraguans.) Two-thirds of all Costa Ricans have taken some kind of security measures in their homes: 39.2 percent have guard dogs, 64.2 percent have bars on their windows and doors, 59.9 percent say that they never leave their house empty for fear of robbery, and 6.2 percent have bought firearms (PNUD 2006, 20).

Iron bars, razor wire, and snarling dogs have made most neighborhoods in the capital city aesthetically unappealing. As an article in *La Nación* put it in 2005, it looks like ticos of all social and economic classes have traded their *casas* (houses) for *cárceles* (jails). "*Casa por cárcel*" is the phrase commonly used to describe "house arrest": out of fear, honest citizens seem to put *themselves* in jail (Salguero 2005). Fear has also changed the social lives of Costa Ricans. If people are afraid to leave their houses, their social and community lives will by necessity be impaired to some extent. Public urban spaces have generally been abandoned by the middle and upper classes, and this trend makes such spaces seem even more empty and dangerous than they might actually be. All of these factors contribute to a sense of "social deterioration." As a 2005 United Nations report concluded, "[the population] has stopped considering that a different way of life is possible . . . In other words, the fear is winning out" (PNUD 2006, 2, 21).

The factors that contribute to this phenomenon are complex. They involve not only the rising crime statistics but also a "complex interaction of variables that are the product of economic crisis, social polarization, corruption, institutional crisis, [and] violence, among other things" (Quesada 2006). One very important factor may be the role of the media. Most Costa Ricans get their news from television; only 3.4 percent do not watch news on any TV channel. Costa Ricans watch an average of 6.3 hours of TV programming a day from Monday to Friday, and 95 percent of all adults watch television between 6:00 and 11:00 p.m. (Fonseca and Sandoval 2006, 10, 22). Young people spend more hours in front of the television than they do in school and with their parents (Cuevas 2003, 33). Costa Rica is probably not very different from most developed or developing countries in this way, but what do these statistics have to do with crime?

A 2004 study found that in the most viewed news media—Telenoticias (channel 7) and *Diario Extra* (a tabloid newspaper)—the two most frequently represented categories of news were homicides and traffic accidents. The majority of the population that watches this news is thus much more likely to perceive that society is very dangerous. According to one study, "the feeling of insecurity is not only a consequence of the increase in criminal acts, but also of the increase in what is presented by the media in terms of crime news [*sucesos*]." Television media's presentation of crime news could go a long way toward explaining why 62 percent of those surveyed considered that their own neighborhood was safe, while only 33.6 percent believed that the country as a whole was safe or very safe: their experience every day where they live may not be very frightening, but the exaggerated presentation of crime news in the media gives people the impression that the rest of the country is increasingly dangerous (Fonseca and Sandoval 2006, 16, 23, 33).

Costa Ricans have recognized these problems, and many people have committed themselves to improving the situation. But such an undertaking implies not only physical transformation of the city but also a transformation in thinking. Costa Ricans must agree that at some point, more and more razor wire does more harm than good. Better options would, in the words of a commentator in *La Nación,* "allow us to break down physical and mental barriers in order to have space for a society and a city that is more stable and more open, while recuperating public spaces in danger of extinction and creating a more democratic urban area" (Quesada 2006).

One of the most interesting and visible projects working toward this end has been *San José Posible.* Realizing that fear of crime is exacerbated by the abandonment of the urban center and the physical deterioration of public spaces and services, this project emphasizes the revitalization of downtown San José and the creation of a new urban environment. San José Posible is sponsored by the Institute of Tropical Architecture (a nonprofit organization supported by some of the country's most renowned architects) and strongly encouraged by the mayor and municipal government of San José. In 2006 and 2007, the project had already begun to make improvements downtown like the creation of pedestrian malls, the renovation of sidewalks and drainage, and the relocation of bus stops. To improve the area visually, electric and phone lines were being placed underground (Instituto de Arquitectura Tropical). Several areas of downtown have also been decorated with public murals. And another project recently begun by the Institute of Tropical Architecture and the municipal government of San José, Urban Flowering, ambitiously hopes to revive San José's parks and pedestrian areas by planting many species of tropical trees and plants (Díaz 2007a). Successful urban reclamation projects in other Latin American cities like Curitiba in Brazil and Mexico City provide hope that San José might become again an attractive and livable urban area.

SOCCER

It is impossible to end a discussion of Costa Rican society without addressing one of the strongest forces that draws Costa Ricans together: their love of soccer. (Of course, when a national championship is on the line, you might also say it draws them apart, depending on the professional team to which they owe their loyalties.) At the end of the 19th century, young men of the upper classes who had completed their studies in Europe brought soccer to Costa Rica, and enthusiasm has apparently never waned since. By 1912, a full-fledged national league was in place with five teams in the first division and three in the second. By 1921, the first division had 7 teams, and the second division had 10 (Fumero Vargas 2005, 12). In 2006, six leagues were active, including first division teams (12), second division teams (22), many third division teams, as well as an amateur league, an indoor league, a beach soccer league, and a women's league (Fedefutbol).

When the national team qualified to compete in the 2006 World Cup soccer tournament in Germany and, even better, to play in the opening match against the host team, the entire country went almost mad with joy. In their enthusiastic support of the national team, nearly every other issue was forgotten. As a sports commentator put it in *La Nación,* "when the national team [the *sele,* or national 'selection'] plays, above all in the World Cup, the country is paralyzed and the high price of gasoline, the rise in inflation, the street protests against the free trade agreement, and the new tax package announced by the government, are all of very little importance" (Marín M. 2006). Most government employees and schoolchildren were given the morning off to watch the game against Germany.

When the sele lost every single one of its World Cup games in 2006, the entire country entered a period of depression. The only good thing about being knocked out in the first round, according to one commentator, was that at least then "the fans could watch the rest of the tournament without the fear of a new national humiliation" (Jiménez 2006). These losses were widely felt to reflect not only Costa Rica's shortcomings in soccer but also its many shortcomings in other areas. One editorial writer opined that Costa Rica could not get ahead in soccer, just as it could not get ahead in politics because there was no "plan of attack." Such a plan meant "taking positions, defining boundaries, setting goals, advancing by confronting problems and these are not exactly attributes of our soccer, nor of our politics, nor of our idiosyncrasies" (Carvajal 2006).

Thus, in Costa Rica, *fútbol* has become more than merely a sport or a pastime; it has become tied up with the country's self-image and self-definition. It is a phenomenon studied not only by sports writers but also by social scientists. One Costa Rican academic has written that perhaps apart from soccer, no other activity "offers the possibility of constructing a sense of nationhood among people of diverse social backgrounds who, except for soccer, have little common ground in their everyday lives. In fact, the national team is known as *el equipo de todos* [everybody's team]." As politics has come to be seen as a realm where only elites participate

Soccer is more of a passion than a pastime in Costa Rica. Even the smallest towns, like Tortuguero pictured here, have well-tended soccer fields. (Martin Rogers/Corbis)

and "traditional foods, oral stories, founding fathers" and other symbols have become less important, it may be that soccer has become the essential marker of Costa Rican-ness (Sandoval-García 2005, 213–215).

But another important marker must be, perhaps inevitably for a country that has been so long preoccupied with its image, that Costa Ricans are intensely aware of their social, economic, and political problems. They do not always agree on the solutions, but they do seem to tacitly agree that to know is better than not to know. Every year, *El Estado de la Nación* publishes a meticulously researched project discussing the most pressing problems and detailing possible solutions (or at least perspectives) from the country's most notable experts. Its very aim is spelled out on its cover: "To know the Costa Rica that we have and to think about the Costa Rica that we want." Whenever there is a new United Nations or World Bank study involving Costa

Rica, its results are widely published and its ramifications are widely discussed on the editorial pages and radio discussion shows. As occurred in the 1940s with the *Centro de Estudios de los Problemas Nacionales,* again in Costa Rica an important segment of the population is not content simply to contemplate the country's supposed "exceptionalism" in Central America, nor to allow its problems to be hidden in order to attract tourists. In this matter, they exemplify one of the country's principle cultural strengths—a knack for coming up with solutions to its problems at critical moments. It is to be hoped that despite the many obstacles modern life (and timeless human folly) have placed between the Costa Rica that is and the country most Costa Ricans would like to have, the nation is again poised to renew the traditions and institutions of which it is justifiably proud.

ARTS AND LITERATURE

One commentator on the visual arts and literature in Costa Rica has pointed out that the country's "unique history of development results in large part from isolation. While this situation favored the development of a substantial middle class and a stable democracy, Costa Rica suffered, and continues to suffer to some degree, from intellectual isolation" (Paul-Ureña 2001, 475). This isolation has not meant that the country failed to produce a number of talented writers, musicians, and artists, of whose work it is possible here only to provide the briefest outline. Costa Ricans have creatively reflected on many aspects of life and society. Yet isolation has meant that their work has not, for the most part, been widely known outside of their country, or at least outside of Central America. It has also meant that, at times, artists and writers have been of two minds about intellectual and creative influences coming from outside of Costa Rica. "During the epoch of the construction of the national identity," two Costa Rican historians of literature have asserted, "Costa

Rica manifested ambivalent positions toward foreign influences: on the one hand, they were perceived as an attractive model, but on the other hand, they were regarded fearfully as an undesirable intrusion into the national 'family'" (Rojas and Ovares 1995, 42).

Any history of art in Costa Rica must certainly begin in the pre-Hispanic period. Costa Rica did not have as many indigenous people as other areas of Latin America, but as mentioned earlier, they produced an astounding range of beautiful objects in ceramic, stone, gold, and jade, many examples of which are now preserved in museums in San José. A few indigenous musical instruments from the pre-Columbian era have also survived. These include the *quijonge* (a single-stringed instrument), the *juque* (a percussion instrument made from a gourd), and the *ocarina* (a kind of flute or whistle made out of clay or wood). Yet indigenous musical traditions have had very little influence on later developments in Costa Rican music (Griffin 1988, 438). The same thing might be said for the development of the plastic arts.

Soon after the arrival of the Spaniards, the majority of the indigenous population died from disease or violence or fled to isolated regions in the north and the south. There was in Costa Rica a sharp break between indigenous and European artistic traditions. In Mexico, Guatemala, and Peru during the colonial period, indigenous artists mastered European styles of (usually religious) painting, sculpture, and architecture but added their own characteristics to produce a distinct mestizo tradition. Such a tradition never developed in Costa Rica where religious art in colonial times was almost all imported from somewhere else in the Spanish empire. Because Costa Rica was always very poor, this imported art did not amount to very much. For the same reasons, there was never much colonial architecture to speak of, and what existed often was destroyed in later periods by earthquakes. Some of the only surviving

churches from the colonial era are found in the towns of
Orosi and Cot in the Central Valley and in Nicoya on the
Pacific coast.

Perhaps because of the lack of the development of a dynamic mestizo culture in colonial Costa Rica, or because until the 20th century the population of the country was so
small and dispersed, there was never much folk culture in
Costa Rica. Almost all the typical dances, music, and costumes that visitors might see today came not from the Central Valley but from the province of Guanacaste, and some
of these cultural productions had their origins only in the
19th century. Perhaps for lack of any other, the rest of the
country has adopted Guanacastecan folk culture as its own.
The "national" dance is the "Punto Guanacasteco," which is
usually accompanied by the marimba and often interrupted
by *bombas*. These humorous exchanges between the dancing partners have the form of rhyming couplets, and usually
refer to love, courtship, or the battle between the sexes.
Costa Ricans still take great enjoyment in bombas, and
many people have a whole repertoire they can recite at a
moment's notice.

But if Costa Rica historically had relatively little folk culture, what of "high" culture? If there was little in the way of
visual arts or music or literature that emerged from the colonial era, this was true for the period just after independence
from Spain as well. Costa Rica had no printing press until
1830. It was only in the middle of the 19th century, when
the coffee boom finally brought some measure of prosperity
to the country, that art and literature began to flourish to
any extent. The coffee elite now had money to obtain from
Europe art and household objects in the latest fashions. The
Costa Rican government also had money to invest in public
monuments and commissioned European artists to design
and construct public buildings and monuments. The most
important and beautiful of these was the National Theater,
which was inaugurated in 1897. A debate was waged at that

Oxcarts were an important part of Costa Rica's transport system well into the 20th century. However, now they are most likely to be seen as here, in a parade at a small-town festival. (Photo by Meg Mitchell)

The Costa Rican Oxcart

The brightly painted wooden oxcart is one of Costa Rica's most visible folkloric symbols. Miniature oxcarts are popular souvenirs, available in almost any tourist store. But, interestingly, the cart *(la carreta)* with its enormous oxen *(los bueyes)* and their driver *(el boyero)* with the long pointed stick he uses to keep the animals in line can occasionally still be seen at work in some parts of the country. They are much more likely to be seen, though, in parades on festive days in the capital city and in small towns.

These two-wheeled carts were first used in the 19th century to carry coffee from the Central Valley to the Pacific port of Puntarenas, but were also adapted for use carrying rice or

(continues)

sugarcane in other parts of the country. Their heavy wooden construction and solid wheels made the carts the perfect vehicle for Costa Rica's difficult, often roadless, terrain. In the second half of the 19th century, farmers and artisans began to decorate the solid wheels and wooden sides of the carts with bright colors and elaborate geometric and floral designs, and this tradition has been maintained since. In 2005, the United Nations Educational, Scientific and Cultural Organization proclaimed oxcarts and the tradition of oxcart herding as one of the Masterpieces of the Oral and Intangible History of Humanity (www.unesco.org).

An interesting history of the oxcart by Láscaris and Malavassi (1985) first published in the late 1970s shows how the bright colors of the oxcarts and the hard work of the drivers represented even then for Costa Ricans something that ought to be preserved, but that was being lost in the modern world. The authors pointed out that "the pressures of technology and media are standardizing" the ways of life of people around the world (including, of course, in Costa Rica). Thus, "the particular ways of life developed in periods of isolation are slowly relegated to the level of 'folklore' . . . [and] the attempt to maintain a living folklore begins to change it into mere spectacle." That is to say, the skills that people developed in the past, the ways they entertained themselves, the clothes they wore, begin to seem like nothing more than props for a show put on for tourists. In the modern world these kinds of artifacts and practices lose their inherent meaning as they lose their useful function.

The authors believed that the turning point in this process for the oxcart in Costa Rica was the decade of the 1960s, in which agricultural production was mechanized. They pointed out that "the function that the oxcart had for a century is now filled by pickup trucks, tractors, large trucks, and four-wheel-drive vehicles." But the most interesting element of their argument is not technical or economic, but rather cultural. They noted that at the same time that the oxcart was disappearing from the countryside and ceasing to do useful work, it was undergoing a "spectacular folklorization." By this they meant that the oxcart was becoming a symbol, coming to represent "all that is truly 'Costa Rican'"; yet it had very little meaning itself once it was taken out of its historical context. Visitors to Costa Rica can easily buy a brightly painted toy oxcart, but they are very lucky if they really get to see one at work.

The authors may not have been able in the 1970s to predict the coming wave of tourism that would change their country so completely, but they could, perhaps, see that the decline in the usefulness of the oxcart foreshadowed future economic and social changes. "The useful life of the oxcart in Costa Rica" was effectively over. "With it was born our means of transport," they wrote, "with its substitution the isolation of Costa Rica is ending. Not even the trains to Limón and Puntarenas or the highways managed to make the oxcart obsolete. It has been the jeep, that strange vehicle that looks like a car but needs no asphalt under its wheels, and the airplane, which needs no harbors along the coast, that have finally brought about the change."

Source: Láscaris, Constantino, and Guillermo Malavassi. 1985. *La carreta costarricense.* San José: Editorial Costa Rica.

time over whether the inaugural performance should be of a foreign work (to showcase the fine modern tastes of the elite) or of a work by a Costa Rican (to illustrate the country's own achievements). The advocates of foreign style won out, and a French company performed the opera *Faust* (Rojas and Ovares 1995, 33).

In the same year that the theater opened, the first National School of Fine Arts was opened in San José (Fumero Vargas 2005, 34). At this time, the most important artists were formed in the German or Italian "academic" traditions, the style preferred by the Europeanized coffee elites (Sullivan 1996, 70). This style is evident in the paintings that adorn the inside of the National Theater, yet these works also contain an interesting local element. Corpulent, half-naked

The National Theater inspires more pride in Costa Ricans than any other building. Built in the heyday of coffee, the theater is still a busy place that welcomes both local and international performers. (Photo by Meg Mitchell)

angels and muses fly across the ceilings playing musical instruments and proudly displaying the plans for the very theater in which they themselves are painted. In the main stairway, this same style is used to represent a more authentically Costa Rican scene: beautiful farm girls pick coffee while burly workmen pack up boxes of the beans to be taken to Europe by waiting ships. This is an interesting (and idealized) reference to the labor that earned the money that allowed the coffee elites to build the theater and enjoy its modern entertainments.

At the turn of the 20th century and in its first decades, these entertainments often featured music. The Costa Rican state became interested in supporting local bands, military bands, and music schools, believing that "through music, they could spread a way a life, of values, and of entertainment that was *civilized*"—that is to say, European. Concerts were frequently held in the parks of San José and in the provincial towns where bands played an assortment of music: fox trots, tangos, and other popular styles, as well as arrangements of classical music. In 1928, the first symphony orchestra was organized (Fumero Vargas 2005, 23–24). Contemporary composers in Costa Rica today, much as they were in earlier periods, have continued to be influenced by European and U.S. musical trends, are often educated abroad, and have not been much influenced by their country's folk music (Sider 1984, 264).

By the end of the first decades of the 20th century, however, nationalist themes had become very important in the work of a new generation of painters. Although stylistically they have clear European roots, these "depictions, even idealizations, of the tranquility of rural life [were used] as symbols of Costa Rica's national identity" (Sullivan 1996, 70). One of the most common themes of these paintings was the traditional adobe house set in a beautiful Costa Rican landscape. The colors of the national flag (white adobe, red tile roof, blue sky) were prominent, and the almost complete absence of human figures is notable. The paintings in this style done in the 1920s, 1930s, and 1940s, however, depict dwellings that had not been widely used since the colonial period. In search of a national style, these painters beautified a rural lifestyle that was in reality much dirtier and more difficult and that, in many places, was being replaced by a more conflictive, urban way of life. As one Costa Rican historian has put it, "The distant blue of the landscape and the adobe house in the countryside allowed the painters to escape an urban universe that they found unpleasant, especially with the increasingly visible poverty aggravated by the crisis of 1930" (Molina Jiménez 2002, 53).

Some of the artists who are now considered the most important of their era had broader interests and themes.

Francisco Zúñiga (1912–1998) is best known for his drawings and sculptures of indigenous women. He felt underappreciated in his native country and in 1936 left Costa Rica for Mexico, where his work became very well known (Sullivan 1996, 70). Francisco Amighetti (1907–1998) was the most important graphic artist of his generation. He was self-taught, but influenced by German expressionism, Mexican art, and Japanese printmaking. His prints and murals, inspired by his interest in social issues and scenes of everyday life, are still greatly esteemed in Costa Rica where, in 2007, the centenary of his birth was celebrated with great fanfare (Díaz 2007b).

In the literature of the first decades of the 20th century can be seen the same attempt to create a national identity and to answer the question of what it meant to be a Costa Rican. These issues had begun to be addressed in the middle of the 19th century by a growing number of journalists who found employment at daily newspapers. They soon began to publish not only essays but also stories, fables, chronicles, and novels. In 1890 and 1891, the first anthology of Costa Rican poetry was published, and in 1900 the first novel (*El Moto,* by Joaquín García Monge) appeared (Rojas and Ovares 1995, 15–16, 35). Books and magazines from Europe, the United States, and other Latin American countries were available in Costa Rica, but most writers of this period seemed most interested not in integrating themselves into more cosmopolitan currents but in defining themselves and describing Costa Rican "types." The best known example of this was *Concherías,* published by Aquileo Echeverría in 1905. The *concho* was a particular rural type with his own vocabulary and his own way of life. City folks might think him a rube, but he had his own wily intelligence. By defining and describing the concho, Echeverría was also pointing clearly to the existence of another type of Costa Rican: the more educated, urban Costa Rican who might buy the book and who would need the glossary the author provided at the back to understand some of the expressions used by his fellow countrymen. The national identity, though still in the process of being defined, was already divided by geography, economic status, and manner of speech, and, just as was the case in the visual arts, a nostalgia was already emerging for an "authentic" rural way of life that was being gradually lost (Rojas and Ovares 1995, 38–39).

By the 1920s and 1930s, reactions were arising against such nostalgia. Many writers were less interested in idealized types and more interested in the emerging social dynamic of the 20th century. One of the most important manifestations of this trend was the journal *Repertorio Americano* (American Repertory) published by Joaquín García Monge in San José from 1919 to 1958. It published essays, criticism, and poetry and showed a particular interest in education and Hispanic identity. It became an important point of contact and exchange between Costa Ricans and contributors from other Latin American countries and from Spain. Some of its most important contributors included Rubén Darío (Nicaragua), Pablo Neruda (Chile), and Miguel Ángel Asturias (Guatemala) (Rojas and Ovares 1995, 61–62). The generations of Costa Rican writers influenced by *Repertorio* turned their attention away from nostalgia for a lost past and toward the changes taking place within modern society. Educator, folklorist, social critic, and political activist Carmen Lyra published novels in the 1920s and 1930s that addressed the problems she saw in the Costa Rican society of her day (see Paul-Ureña 2001). Carlos Luís Fallas, a labor organizer and novelist, published *Mamita Yunai* in 1941, addressing the problems of the Caribbean banana workers and their exploitation by the United Fruit Company (Rojas and Ovares 1995, 177, 187, 232).

Changing themes in literary expression could be seen into the second half of the 20th century when writers like Carmen Naranjo took as representative of Costa Rican life "not the *concho* . . . but the office worker, the middle class, the city-dweller" (Cuevas Molina 2003, 23). Writers like Quince Duncan, who addressed the theme of the marginalization of Afro–Costa Ricans, began to incorporate the experiences of other groups of Costa Ricans who did not necessarily live in the Central Valley. Costa Rica never again became as integrated into a pan–Latin American literary scene as it had been during the heyday of the *Repertorio*. If it has produced no writers of the status of Gabriel García Márquez of Colombia or Mario Vargas Llosa of Peru, Costa Rica has many active writers who, leaving behind idealized depictions of their society, have examined many important themes. Issues such as the role of women in society have been addressed by writers like poet and dramatist Ana Istarú. Novelist Anacristina Rossi has tackled the ever-present issue of the importance of environmental protection in Costa Rica. Some writers have explicitly focused on "identity, national or continental. In many cases, this preoccupation has formed itself around the critical re-examination of historical eras or events that have determined the traits that define the country or the region." Other writers have examined broader themes and problems affecting modern society in every country: isolation, lack of communication, and violence (Rojas and Ovares 1995, 231, 242–243). And thus we see again the dynamic that pulls at the same time toward the particular and the universal.

In the visual arts over the course of the 20th century, an evolution away from idealized depictions of Costa Rican life and toward a greater influence of foreign ideas and trends is evident. Abstract painting did not really become influential in Costa Rican art until the end of the 1950s, when artists who had studied abroad began to show their work in San José. A number of them joined together to form the Grupo Ocho (the Group of Eight), whose subsequent work left behind the adobe houses and the bucolic landscapes, "break[ing] the entrenched regionalist tradition by introducing the formal languages of post-war contemporary art."

Another important group of artists, the Bocaracá group, organized themselves in 1987 to exhibit together and have shown an interest in a variety of styles, from figurative to abstract, from realistic to symbolic (Sullivan 1996, 73). Yet, it must be said that at art fairs and the stands of street vendors, paintings of the adobe house in the lovely countryside still have a great deal of popular appeal.

Beginning in the 1970s, the government became more involved in the promotion of culture in all of Costa Rica. The Ministry of Culture, Youth, and Sports was established, as was the National Theater Company; the National Symphony Orchestra and the National Museum of Art were reorganized. Programs were organized to bring "culture" to all classes of society and all regions of the country. Costa Rican theater became an especially vital and popular form of expression (Cuevas Molina 2003, 28). With the economic crises of the 1980s, this level of support was not consistently maintained, but by the 1990s, both government and corporate sponsorship of the arts was again increasing. In 1992, the first International Arts Festival was organized in San José and has since begun to alternate its venues between the capital city and the provincial capitals around the country, inviting both national and international performers in dance, theater, and music, as well as visual artists. An annual chamber music festival and a yearly season of the National Symphony Orchestra are also held. Both the National University and the University of Costa Rica have very active modern dance companies. Thus, many cultural offerings are available, at least in the capital city, but most reflect foreign influences more than any characteristic that could really be called uniquely Costa Rican. And all must compete today to one degree or another with the true "popular" culture of the modern world—television and movies, the great majority of whose content is imported. Despite this situation, it must be said that pride in past achievements and ongoing efforts in the fields of the arts is an element that draws together segments of Costa Rican society.

It is worth mentioning, however, one more interesting cultural expression that, even if it represents folk or popular culture more than it does high culture, has achieved a kind of integration of the foreign and the native in Costa Rica. This is the calypso music of the Caribbean province of Limón. This music is a unique combination of calypso music (from Trinidad), mento (from Jamaica), and son (from Cuba). By the 1980s, it also incorporated elements of reggae and salsa music. The "calypsonians," as the men who write and play this music call themselves, have usually come from the lower socioeconomic strata, not from the elite. Through their songs, they have told stories of the history of Limón and of everyday life there. Since the 1980s, the music had become more widely known in the Central Valley and has had an influence on other kinds of Costa Rican popular music. And, in part, it is also preserved by continuing interest in it by foreign tourists. The true achievement of Limón calypso is not only that it is very entertaining but that it also preserves a whole genre of music that reflects "situations, historical events, characters, customs, anecdotes, and the lived experiences of the Afro–Costa Rican community. In this way, what came to Costa Rica years ago as a form of song from the Antilles, was with time transformed into a musical form with traits unique to Costa Rica" (Monestel Ramírez 2005, 27, 28, 124). And is this not the end toward which all artistic endeavors are ultimately striving?

References
Agencia Centroamericana de Noticias (ACAN EFE) San José. 2006. "Franklin Chang abrirá laboratorio para motor de plasma." *La Nación,* January 27, sec. "Sala de Redacción."
Argüedas C., Carlos, and Fernando Gutiérrez. 2006. "Dos policías acusados por muerte de Canda." *La Nación,* 11 November, sec. "Sucesos."
Associated Press (Managua). "CIDH dirimirá caso de xenofobia en Costa Rica." 2006. *La Nación,* November 3, sec. "Sala de Redacción."
Cantero, Marcela. 2006. "Desempleo golpea más a mujeres." *La Nación,* March 9, sec. "Aldea Global."

Cantero, Marcela. 2007. "Salud de niños indígenas ticos tiene 25 años de rezago." *La Nación,* March 15, sec. "Aldea Global."

Carvajal B., Franklin. 2006. "El fútbol nos retrata." *La Nación,* June 22, sec. "Opinión."

Chen Apuy, Hilda. 1992. "La minoría china en Costa Rica." www.reflexi ones.fcs.ac.cr/documentos/5/la_minoria.pdf/.

Chomsky, Aviva. 1996. *West Indian Workers and the United Fruit Company in Costa Rica: 1870–1940.* Baton Rouge: Louisiana State University Press.

Cuevas Molina, Rafael. 2003. *Tendencias de la dinámica cultural en Costa Rica en el siglo XX.* Serie Cuadernos de Historia de Las Instituciones de Costa Rica, no. 10. San José: Editorial de la Universidad de Costa Rica.

Díaz, Doriam. 2007a. "San José impulsa proyecto para convertirse en bosque urbano." *La Nación,* January 21, sec. "Aldea Global."

Díaz, Doriam. 2007b. "Con 4 exposiciones celebran del centenario de 'Paco' Amighetti." *La Nación,* May 31, sec. "Aldea Global."

Edelman, Marc. 1998. "A Central American Genocide: Rubber, Slavery, Nationalism, and the Destruction of the Guatuso-Malekus." *Comparative Studies in History and Society* 40 (2): 356–390.

EFE. 2006. "Nicaragua y Costa Rica enfrentados por acusaciones de xenofobia." *La Nación,* October 18, sec. "Centroamérica hoy."

FEDEFUTBOL (Federación Costarricense de Fútbol) www.fedefutbol.com/.

Fonseca Vindas, Karina, and Carlos Sandoval García. 2006. *Medios de comunicación e (in)seguridad en Costa Rica.* San José: Programa de las Naciones Unidas para el Desarrollo.

Fumero Vargas, Patricia. 2005. *Cultura y sociedad en Costa Rica, 1914–1950.* Serie Cuadernos de Historia de las Instituciones de Costa Rica, no. 16. San José: Editorial de la Universidad de Costa Rica.

Global Database of Quotas for Women. 2006. "Country Overview." www .quotaproject.org/country.cfm/.

González, Yamileth. 2005. "Xenofobia, responsabilidad ¿de quién?" *La Nación,* December 21, sec. "Opinión."

Griffin, Robert J. 1988. "The Folk Music of Costa Rica: A Teaching Perspective." *Hispania* 71 (May): 438–441.

Hall, Carolyn, and Héctor Pérez Brignoli. 2003. *Historical Atlas of Central America.* Norman: University of Oklahoma Press.

Harpelle, Ronald N. 1993. "The Social and Political Integration of the West Indians in Costa Rica: 1930–50." *Journal of Latin American Studies* 25: 103–120.

Harpelle, Ronald N. 2000. "Racism and Nationalism in the Creation of Costa Rica's Pacific Coast Banana Enclave." *The Americas* 56 (3): 29–51.

Holland, Clifton. 2002. "Table of Statistics on Religious Affiliation in the Americas." www.prolades.com/prolades1/documents/latamtbl00 .htm/.

Instituto Nacional de Estadística y Censos (INEC). 2000. Home page. www.inec.go.cr/.

Instituto Nacional de Mujeres (INAMU). 2007. Home page. www.inamu .go.cr/.

Instituto de Arquitectura Tropical, "San José Posible." www.arquitectur atropical.org/sjposible/INDEX.htm.

Jiménez M., Gustavo. 2006. "Mundial: La sele termina hoy paseo por Alemania." *La Nación,* June 20, sec. "Deportes."

Láscaris, Constantino. 1992. *El costarricense.* San José: Editorial Universitaria Centroamericana-EDUCA.

Leitinger, Ilsa, ed. and trans. 1997. *The Costa Rican Women's Movement: A Reader.* Pittsburgh, PA: University of Pittsburgh Press.

Leitón, Patricia. 2006a. "Mujeres dirigen 300,000 hogares." *La Nación,* April 8, sec. "Economía."

Leitón, Patricia. 2006b. "Bajan pobreza y desempleo." *La Nación,* November 1, sec. "Economía."

Leitón, Patricia. 2006c. "Crecen hogares pobres en Guanacaste." *La Nación,* November 1, sec. "Economía."

Leitón, Patricia. 2006d. "Empeora distribución del ingreso." *La Nación,* November 1, sec. "Economía"

Marín M., Douglas. 2006. "Costa Rica olvida sus problemas cotidianos ante el Mundial." *La Nación,* June 7, sec. "Centroamérica Hoy."

Masís, Karina, and Laura Paniagua. 2006. "Chistes de nicas: 'humor' y xenofobia." *La Nación,* April 30, sec. "Áncora."

Mayorga, Armando. 2006. "Ticos en el olvido." *La Nación,* June 8, sec. "Opinión."

Meléndez, Guillermo. 2003. "Especial: Iglesia de la Liberación en Costa Rica: Iglesia Católica Costarricense se renueva." *ADITAL: Noticias de América Latina y el Caribe.* www.adital.com/br/site/noticia.asp ?lang=ES&cod=9508/.

Molina Jiménez, Iván. 2002. *Costarricense por dicha: Identidad nacional y cambio cultural en Costa Rica durante los siglos XIX y XX.* San José: Editorial de la Universidad de Costa Rica.

Molina Jiménez, Iván. 2003. *Identidad nacional y cambio cultural en Costa Rica durante la segunda mitad del siglo XX.* Serie Cuadernos de Historia de las Instituciones de Costa Rica, no. 11. San José: Editorial de la Universidad de Costa Rica.

Monestel Ramírez, Manuel. 2005. *Ritmo, Canción, e Identidad: una historia sociocultural del calipso limonense.* San José: Editorial Universidad Estatal a Distancia.

Murillo M., Álvaro. 2006. "Impulso a nueva ley indígena reactiva lucha entre dirigentes." *La Nación,* October 30, sec. "Nacionales."

La Nación. 2005. "Idiosincrática: Ticos al borde de xenofobia." *La Nación,* June 22, sec. "Nacionales."

Palmer, Paula. 2005 [1979]. *"What Happen": A Folk History of Costa Rica's Talamanca Coast.* Miami: Zona Tropical.

Palmer, Paula, Juanita Sánchez, and Gloria Mayorga. 1991. *Taking Care of Sibo's Gifts: An Environomental Treatise from Costa Rica's KéköLdi Indigenous Reserve.* San José: EDITORAMA.

Palmer, Steven, and Iván Molina, eds. 2004. *The Costa Rica Reader: History, Culture, Politics.* Durham, NC: Duke University Press.

Palmer, Steven, and Iván Molina, eds. 2006. *The History of Costa Rica: Brief, Up-to-Date, and Illustrated.* San José: Editorial de la Universidad de Costa Rica.

Paul-Ureña, Jeana. 2001. "Review of *The Subversive Voice of Carmen Lyra* by Elizabeth Rosa Horan." *Hispania* 84 (3): 475–476.

Picado, Miguel. 1989. *La iglesia costarricense entre el pueblo y el estado (de 1949 a nuestros días).* San José: Editorial Lascasiana-Ediciones Guayacan.

Poltronieri, Jorge. 2006. "Proyecto de Investigación Estructuras de la Opinión Pública Comunicado de Prensa—encuesta 2006: Panorama General." San José: University of Costa Rica. www.ucr.ac.cr/documentos/Encuesta_opinion_2006.pdf/

Programa de Naciones Unidas para el Desarrollo (PNUD). 2006. *Venciendo el temor: (In)seguridad ciudadano y desarrollo humano en Costa Rica: Informe Nacional de Desarrollo Humano 2005. Resumen.* San José: PNUD.

Programa Estado de la Nación. 2000. *Estado de la Nación en Desarrollo Humano Sostenible: Un análisis amplio y objetivo sobre la Costa Rica que tenemos, a partir de los indicadores más actuales.* San José: Programa Estado de la Nación. www.estadonacion.or.cr/.

Programa Estado de la Nación. 2005. *Estado de la Nación en Desarrollo Humano Sostenible: Un análisis amplio y objetivo sobre la Costa Rica que tenemos, a partir de los indicadores más actuales.* San José: Programa Estado de la Nación. www.estadonacion .or.cr/.

Programa Estado de la Nación. 2006. *Estado de la Nación en Desarrollo Humano Sostenible: Un análisis amplio y objetivo sobre la Costa Rica que tenemos, a partir de los indicadores más actuales.* San José: Programa Estado de la Nación. www.estadonacion.or.cr/.

Quesada, Florencia. 2006. "La ciudad-cárcel." *La Nación,* May 14, sec. "Áncora."

Rodríguez Sáenz, Eugenia. 2003. *Las familias costarricenses durante los siglos XVIII, XIX, y XX.* Serie Cuadernos de Historia de las Instituciones de Costa Rica, no. 4. San José: Editorial de la Universidad de Costa Rica.

Rojas, José Enrique. 2007. "Matrimonio civil se impone sobre el religioso." *La Nación,* February 18, sec. "Nacionales."

Rojas, José Enrique, and Juan Fernando Lara. 2006a. "País cae por quinto año en índice de desarrollo humano." *La Nación,* November 9, sec. "Economía."

Rojas, José Enrique, and Juan Fernando Lara. 2006b. "Mujeres ocupan 26% de puestos gerenciales." *La Nación,* November 9, sec. "Economía."

Rojas, Margarita, and Flora Ovares. 1995. *100 años de literatura costarricense.* San José: Ediciones Farben.

Salguero M., Karina. 2005. "El encierro es la norma." *La Nación,* May 8, sec. "Proa."

Sandoval-García, Carlos. 2004. *Threatening Others: Nicaraguans and the Formation of National Identities in Costa Rica.* Athens, OH: Ohio University Press.

Sandoval-García, Carlos. 2005. "Football: Forging Nationhood and Masculinities in Costa Rica." *International Journal of the History of Sport* 22 (2): 212–230.

Sawchuk, Dana. 2004. *The Costa Rican Catholic Church, Social Justice, and the Rights of Workers, 1979–1996.* Waterloo, ON, Canada: Wilfred Laurier University Press.

Sider, Ronald R. 1984. "Contemporary Composers in Costa Rica." *Latin American Music Review/Revista de Música Latinamericana* 5 (2): 263–276.

Solano Salazar, Elizabeth. 2003. "El estudio de los grupos étnicos a través del IX Censo Nacional de Población y Vivienda." In *II Congreso sobre pueblos indígenas: del conocimiento ancestral a conocimiento actual: visión de lo indígena en el umbral del siglo XXI.* San José: Universidad de Costa Rica, 15–23.

Steigenga, Timothy J. 2001. *The Politics of the Spirit: The Political Implications of Pentecostal Religion in Costa Rica and Guatemala.* Lanham, MD: Lexington Books.

Stocker, Karen. 2005. *'I Won't Stay Indian, I'll Keeping Studying': Race, Place, and Discrimination in a Costa Rican High School.* Boulder, CO: University Press of Colorado.

Sullivan, Edward J. 1996. *Latin American Art in the Twentieth Century.* London: Phaidon Press.

Swaby, Alejandro. 2003. "Perspectivas, retos, y desafíos de los pueblos indígenas en el nuevo milenio." In *II Congreso sobre pueblos indígenas del conocimiento ancestral al conocimiento actual: visión de lo indígena en el umbral del siglo XXI.* San José: Universidad de Costa Rica, 11–14.

U.S. Department of State. 2007. "Background Note: Nicaragua." www.state.gov/r/pa/ei/bgn/1850.htm/.

Vargas-Cullel, Jorge, Luis Rosero-Bixby, and Mitchell Seligson. 2005. *La Cultura política de la democracia en Costa Rica, 2004:*

Un estudio del Proyecto de Opinión Pública en América Latina (OPAL). San José: Centro Centroamericano de Población.

Vargas Rojas, Gerardo. 2006. "Realidad de territorios indígenas." *La Nación,* February 17, sec. "Opinión."

Villalobos, Carlos A. 2005. "Costa Rica demandará a Nicaragua ante La Haya." *La Nación,* September 29, sec. "Nacionales."

Villalobos, Carlos A. 2006. "Solo el 30% está decidido a votar en elecciones de alcaldes." *La Nación,* September 27, sec. "Nacionales."

Villegas, Jairo. 2006. "Miles visitan 'La Negrita' llenos de fe y devoción." *La Nación,* August 1, sec. "Nacionales."

World Bank. 2005. "Country Statistics." www.worldbank.org/.

PART TWO
REFERENCE SECTION

Key Events in Costa Rican History

3 million years ago	The land bridge between North and South America closes, separating the Atlantic Ocean from the Pacific Ocean and creating what is now Panama and Costa Rica.
30,000–12,000 B.C.	Hunter-gatherer peoples cross the Bering Strait and begin to move south. There is still much debate over exactly when and how this happened. The date seems to get pushed further and further back, and some scientists now suggest that people may have moved south by sea, staying close to the coast, as well as overland.
12,000–8,000 B.C.	Earliest human settlements are established in the region that would become Costa Rica.
4,000–1,000 B.C.	Settled village groups in Costa Rica begin to practice agriculture.
Around A.D. 1,000	The high point of the culture centered at Guayabo in northeastern Costa Rica.
1502	Columbus lands on the Caribbean coast on his fourth voyage to the New World.
1523	The Spanish establish their first permanent settlement in the Pacific region at Villa Brusellas.
1564	The city of Cartago is founded for the first time.

1574	Cartago is founded again, this time on its present site.
1635	According to tradition, the Virgin of Los Angeles appears to Juana Pereira near Cartago.
1709	Pablo Presbere leads an Indian uprising in Talamanca against the evangelizing efforts of the Spanish. The revolt is suppressed and Presbere is executed in Cartago the following year.
1736	The city of San José is founded.
1821	Mexico and Central America declare their independence from Spain. Costa Rica finds out about it a month later when the mail arrives from Guatemala.
1823	The Battle of Ochomogo is fought between residents of Cartago, who wish to remain allied to Mexico's empire, and residents of San José, who want to separate from Mexico. Those from San José emerge victorious, and that city will be made the new capital. But by the time the battle is decided, the Mexican empire had dissolved. Costa Rica will become a part of the new Central American Federation.
1824	Slavery is abolished in Costa Rica.
1825	The residents of the northwest region of Guanacaste vote to separate from Nicaragua and annex themselves to Costa Rica.
1830	The first printing press arrives in Costa Rica. This very machine can

	still be seen in the National Museum in San José.
1835	The War of the League, another brief war between the cities of the Central Valley, is won by San José, which further consolidates its position as the most important city.
1838	Costa Rica withdraws from the rapidly failing Central American Federation.
1840s	The coffee boom begins and unites Costa Ricans in growing and processing the "golden bean."
1842	General Francisco Morazán invades Costa Rica and tries to bring it back into the Federation; he fails and is shot in San José.
1843	Costa Rica's first university, the University of Santo Tomás, is established.
1848	The Republic of Costa Rica is proclaimed.
1856–1857	Costa Rica participates in the National Campaign, fighting along with other Central American countries to defeat William Walker, the North American adventurer who took advantage of civil conflict in Nicaragua to intervene, name himself president, and pursue his dream of creating a slave state to be annexed someday to the United States. In the aftermath of the war, Costa Rica suffers a terrible cholera epidemic.
1870	Following more than a decade of political instability, General Tomás Guardia establishes a military dictatorship that lasts until his death in 1882. Paradoxically, the

Guardia dictatorship succeeded in reinforcing the rule of law in Costa Rica (a new constitution was adopted in 1870), ending the role of the military in Costa Rican politics, and establishing the basic institutions of 19th-century liberal society.

1871   The construction of the railroad to the Atlantic begins under a contract with British investors. They do not finish the project, and an American, Minor Keith, gets the concession.

1881   Banana exports to New York begin.

1882   The death penalty is abolished.

1885   In an effort to mobilize Costa Ricans against a perceived threat from Guatemala, the name of Juan Santamaría, a humble, and up to that point unknown, soldier from the campaign against William Walker, is put forward as a model of heroism and patriotism. Within 10 years, Santamaría and the struggle of 1857 become central to Costa Rican national identity.

1888   The University of Santo Tomás is closed.

1890   The railroad to the Atlantic coast is finished.

1897   The beautiful National Theater is inaugurated in downtown San José. The railroad to the Pacific is begun, but will not be finished for another 10 years.

1899   Minor Keith establishes the United Fruit Company.

1903	Costa Rica gains a new southern neighbor with the independence of Panama from Colombia.
1910	A massive earthquake nearly destroys the city of Cartago.
1917–1919	The dictatorship of Federico Tinoco does not prove to be very long lasting; he is overthrown and flees the country.
1924	The Reformist Party is established under the leadership of former priest Jorge Volio. Although his party is short lived, Volio is recognized as an important figure in Costa Rica's path to social and political reform in the 20th century.
1931	The Communist Party is established under the leadership of Manuel Mora. Costa Rica's "creole communism" never challenged the country's democratic political institutions, but was instrumental in pushing from below for the rights of workers.
1934	Costa Rica's biggest labor strike to date is called by the banana workers in Limón and led by communist organizers against the United Fruit Company.
1937	Construction begins on the stretch of the Interamerican Highway that runs through Costa Rica.
1941	The University of Costa Rica is founded; Carlos Luís Fallas "Calufa" publishes *Mamita Yunai*, a novel exposing the harsh working conditions and corruption characterizing the Atlantic coast banana

zone dominated by the United Fruit Company.

1943   President Calderón Guardia establishes the Caja Costarricense de Seguro Social to administer a national medical and pension system.

1948   José "Pepe" Figueres overthrows the elected government in a five-week civil war; Figueres abolishes the armed forces and nationalizes the banks.

1949   A new constitution establishes the Second Republic and gives women and black Costa Ricans the right to vote.

1951   Figueres founds a new political party, the Partido de Liberación Nacional (the Party of National Liberation, or PLN).

1960   The Central American Common Market, a regional trade agreement, is established; television comes to Costa Rica.

1971   The National Parks System is created.

1973   A second public university, the National University (UNA) is established in Heredia.

1979   The Sandinistas come to power in Nicaragua, overthrowing Costa Rica's long-time enemy, dictator Anastasio Somoza. Costa Rica's relationship with Somoza's socialist successors and their U.S.-backed opponents will not always prove easy. These ongoing conflicts increase Nicaraguan immigration to Costa Rica.

1981	Costa Rica is the first Latin American country to default on its foreign debt obligations. This initiates a decade of economic crisis and economic restructuring.
1982	The Caribbean Basin Initiative, a trade agreement with the United States, is passed.
1987	Costa Rican President Óscar Arias wins the Nobel Peace Prize for his negotiation of a peace plan for Central America.
1990s	The boom in tourism begins to reconfigure the economy; by 1993, it is the leading earner of foreign exchange.
1990	The national soccer team wins two matches to advance to the second round of the World Cup championships in Italy, but is ultimately eliminated.
1995	President José María Figueres signs a pact with ex-president and opposition leader Rafael Ángel Calderón to accelerate neoliberal reforms and privatize state-owned entities.
2000	Large street protests are held against the planned privatization of the Costa Rican Electrical Institute (ICE), and the plan is dropped.
2004	Corruption scandals implicate three ex-presidents: Rafael Ángel Calderón Guardia, Miguel Ángel Rodríguez, and José María Figueres Olson. Calderón and Rodríguez return to Costa Rica to face charges and are arrested. As of mid 2007, Figueres has refused to return and remains in Europe.

2006   The national soccer team earns a spot at the
                World Cup championships in Germany but
                fails to win any matches. Óscar Arias is
                elected president for a second time after the
                constitution is modified to allow him to run
                again, but he is closely challenged by the
                candidate of the Partido Acción Ciudadana
                (PAC), Ottón Solís, in San José. Street
                protests are held against the probable
                approval of the free trade agreement
                with the United States, the Dominican
                Republic–Central America Free Trade
                Agreement (DR-CAFTA).

2007   The Supreme Electoral Tribunal approves
                Costa Rica's first-ever referendum to
                determine the fate of DR-CAFTA. If events
                play out as anticipated, Costa Rica will be
                the only country in Latin America to have
                put to a popular vote the contentious
                question of whether or not to sign such
                a treaty.

Significant People, Institutions, Places, and Events

Abolition of the Army. The armed forces of Costa Rica were abolished on December 1, 1948, by José Figueres acting as head of a provisional junta that had taken power after Figueres's faction won the civil war of that same year. The armed forces had never been very strong in Costa Rica, and Costa Ricans are almost unanimously proud now to have no army or navy and that their country has proclaimed itself neutral (1983). In the absence of the armed forces, policing duties are divided among many different entities.

Alajuela. This is the one of the most important cities in the Central Valley and is the capital of the Alajuela Province. The city, which lies to the west of San José, was founded in 1782. The Juan Santamaría International Airport is now located there, as is the principal monument to the national hero after whom the airport is named. The city's soccer team, La Liga Deportiva Alajuelense ("La Liga"), is usually one of the top two teams in the country and has fans throughout Costa Rica.

Aqueductos y Acantarillados (AyA). The Costa Rican Institute of Aqueducts and Drainage was founded in 1960. It is the arm of the government responsible for providing clean water and sewage services. Because of its success in bringing potable water to almost the entire country, public health improved greatly in Costa Rica during the last decades of the 20th century. The AyA has done a much poorer job of providing for the disposal of urban sewage, more than 97 percent of which currently enters watersheds untreated. The country, with a loan from the Japanese government, hopes to begin to address this problem by constructing a system of sanitary sewers and waste treatment plants beginning in 2007.

Arenal Volcano. This is an active volcano in the north-central region of the country. In 1968, before volcanoes in Costa Rica had been scientifically studied to any great extent, Arenal suddenly erupted, killed numerous people, and wiped out a whole town. On clear days, the volcano still stands out as a perfect cone shape, and from the national park area at its base, one can occasionally hear boulders as they bounce down its steep sides. At night, it is sometimes possible to see red-hot lava issuing from the faraway crater. Despite (or perhaps because of) this continued volcanic activity, Arenal and the large man-made reservoir at its base have become important tourist attractions in recent years.

Arias Sánchez, Óscar (b. 1941). Arias, a member of a prominent coffee-growing family in Heredia and a graduate of British universities, was president of Costa Rica from 1986 to 1990 and was awarded the Nobel Peace Prize in 1987 for defying the interventionist policies of the United States and negotiating a peace plan together with his fellow presidents of Central America. After a controversial change in the constitution allowing for reelection, he was again elected president in 2006. Together with his brother, Minister of the Presidency Rodrigo Arias Sánchez, Óscar has worked thus far in his second term for passage of the Dominican Republic–Central American Free Trade Agreement (DR-CAFTA).

Cahuita. This town on the southern Caribbean coast is populated mainly by the descendants of Jamaican immigrants. In 1970, a national park was created on land adjacent to the town; it protects not only the land but also an important coral reef just off the shore. In 1979, Paula Palmer, a Peace Corps volunteer living in Cahuita, published *What Happen: A Folk History of Costa Rica's Talamanca Coast,* which is still the best introduction to Afro-Caribbean life in Cahuita and its neighboring towns on the coast. Today, Cahuita's national park and distinct culture make it an important tourist attraction.

Caja Costarricense de Seguro Social. Founded in 1943, the "Caja" administers the public health care system through its network of hospitals and clinics throughout the country. It has historically been one of the most respected public institutions, and it succeeded in greatly improving public health in Costa Rica. Since the economic crisis of the 1980s, it has seen a decrease in public investment and a resulting deterioration of service. Several corruption scandals have also diminished its reputation.

Calderón Guardia, Rafael (1900–1970). The son of a prominent physician, Calderón Guardia studied medicine in Belgium, where he was inspired by the social teaching of the Roman Catholic Church. In 1940 he was elected president with the backing of the traditional coffee elite, but quickly alienated those interests when he embarked upon an ambitious plan for social reform. Calderón is recognized as the founder of Costa Rica's social security system and system of labor laws and as the man responsible for the inclusion of social guarantees in the country's constitution. Following the defeat of *Calderonismo* in the Civil War of 1948, Calderón and his family went into exile. He returned to Costa Rica in 1958 and served in the Legislative Assembly. His son, Rafael Ángel Calderón Fournier, founded the Social Christian Unity Party in 1983 and was elected president in 1990. In 2004 he was arrested under accusations of corruption associated with the Caja Costarricences de Seguro Social founded by his father.

Calypso Limonense. Calypso music came to Costa Rica with the Afro-Caribbean immigrants to Limón Province. Using creole English lyrics, "calypsonians" (as these musicians are called) sing songs that tell the stories of life along the Caribbean coast. The most famous living calypsonian in Costa Rica is Walter Gavitt Ferguson, a resident of Cahuita. Ferguson's music has recently been recorded, and through the efforts of musician Manuel Monestel Ramírez and the band Cantoamérica, Costa Ricans in the Central Valley have come to know this wonderful part of their musical heritage.

Carrillo, Braulio (1800–1845). Carrillo was president of Costa Rica from 1835 to 1837 and from 1838 to 1842. He was one of the most important forces for the unification of Costa Rica after its independence from Spain. In 1838 he declared the country's independence from the ill-fated Central American Federation and, perhaps most importantly, began the promotion of coffee production. Yet, in his second term, he made himself a dictator, was overthrown, and was sent into exile. His name lives on in a very large national park to the east of the Central Valley. The most important highway running to the Atlantic port from San José crosses this otherwise undeveloped area and is also known as the "Braulio Carrillo."

Cartago. Cartago is another important city in the Central Valley and is the capital of Cartago Province. It was founded in 1564 and was the capital of Costa Rica throughout the colonial period. The capital was moved to San José in 1823, but Cartago is still the home of Costa Rica's patron saint, the Virgin of Los Angeles, and the site of an important pilgrimage every August. It is also the home of the Instituto Tecnológico de Cartago, one of Costa Rica's four public universities. The city has been destroyed several times by earthquakes, most recently in 1910. Colonial Cartago is brought back to life in Tatiana Lobo's novel *Assault on Paradise,* which is still in print and available in English.

Chang Díaz, Franklin (b. 1950). This scientist, educated in Costa Rica and at the Massachusetts Institute of Technology, is one of the most well-known and popular public figures in Costa Rica. He is the only Latin American to have traveled as an astronaut on U.S. National Aeronautic and Space Administration space missions. In 2005, he established Ad Astra Rocket, an important research laboratory in Guanacaste devoted to the development of plasma-powered rockets that are hoped someday to take humans to Mars.

Civil War of 1948. This was the last, and most violent, of a series of struggles over electoral fraud that had plagued Costa Rica since the 19th century. Alleging systematic fraud in the reelection of Rafael Ángel Calderón Guardia to the presidency, José "Pepe" Figueres launched a military action in April 1948, for which he had been preparing for several years. Through his contacts with a group known as the Caribbean Legion, dedicated to the removal of dictators in the region, Figueres imported arms from Guatemala and established a stronghold in the mountains of Talamanca. From there his partisans were able to launch successful attacks on weak government forces in San Isidro el General, Limón (by air), and Cartago. The battle lasted approximately six weeks and never reached San José, where it was feared that pitched fighting between *Figueristas* and armed elements of the government and Communist Party would end in a bloodbath. A peace agreement was signed at the Mexican Embassy guaranteeing the safety of communists and other partisans of Calderón. Contrary to the agreement, the Communist Party was declared illegal and was not permitted to participate openly in public life until the 1970s.

Duncan, Quince (b. 1940). Duncan was born in Limón, and spoke only English for the first eight years of his life. With the arrival of Spanish-language education after 1948, he was able to take advantage of the new educational opportunities offered by the Costa Rican state, and has become the most important Afro–Costa Rican literary and cultural figure. His novels, stories, and autobiographical accounts written in Spanish were among the first to reflect the experiences of the black citizens of Costa Rica.

Estado de la Nación. A project sponsored by the rectors of Costa Rica's four public universities, this is probably the most important compilation of economic and social development statistics and analyses published in Costa Rica. Every year social scientists and researchers analyze topics from education to the environment to tourism, evaluating the current trends and suggesting ways to improve the situation of the country in the future. It generally takes a critical stance toward the changes in Costa Rica since the economic crisis of the 1980s.

Fallas, Carlos Luís (1912–1966). His novel *Mamita Yunai* (1940), based on his experiences in the banana strike of 1934, is one of the best known in Costa Rica. He was also involved in politics, and his other novels deal with social problems of the era.

Figueres, Pepe (1906–1990). The son of Spanish immigrants, José "Pepe" Figueres led an interesting life in Costa Rica and abroad. In his youth, he spent four years working and studying in the United States. Upon returning to Costa

Rica, he devoted himself to farming and became prosperous before emerging on the political scene in 1940 as a virulent critic of President Calderón Guardia. Figueres was sent into exile in Mexico and returned to join, and ultimately to lead, the political and military movement that defeated the Calderonistas in 1948. Although a committed anticommunist, Figueres was an advocate of a "mixed economy." He was considered a leader of the "democratic left" in Latin America and was a declared enemy of the region's many right-wing dictators. He was twice elected president from the National Liberation Party (of which he was a founder). Figueres was influential in policy circles in the United States, particularly in the early 1960s when the Kennedy administration launched its progressive Alliance for Progress in Latin America.

Guanacaste. This is the national tree of Costa Rica, the *Enterrolobium cyclocarpum.* It is also the name of the northwest province of the country that is bordered on the north by Nicaragua and on the west by the Pacific. A portion of this region, the Nicoya Peninsula, was originally part of Nicaragua but was annexed to Costa Rica after independence from Spain. Geographically and culturally, it still has much in common with its northern neighbor, and ironically, considering the general low opinion of Nicaragua in Costa Rica, it is also the source of most of the folklore that Costa Ricans from the Central Valley recognize as their own, including the figure of the *sabanero,* or cowboy, as well as many traditional dances and costumes. In the last years of the 20th century and the first years of the 21st, the region has been transformed by a boom in tourism and the construction of large numbers of beachfront hotels and other attractions, often with a lack of planning that has led to various environmental problems.

Guayabo. This is Costa Rica's most important archeological site and is located near the town of Turrialba on the northeastern edge of the Central Valley. It was occupied as early as 500 B.C. but reached its high point in development about 500 or 600 years before the Spanish conquest. It is now a national monument, and from the careful excavations done there, visitors can get a good idea of what the ancient inhabitants' round houses, paved roads, petroglyphs, and irrigations systems were like.

Heredia. This is another important city in the Central Valley and is the capital of the Heredia Province. The area was first settled beginning around 1706; it was declared a town in 1763 and 10 years later took its present name. In 1973, the National University (Universidad Nacional, or UNA) was established here.

Instituto Costarricense de Electricidad (ICE). The Costa Rican Institute of Electricity is one of the most important autonomous institutions. It was established in 1949 to control and expand the electrical, and later the telecommunications, network of the country. It has been very successful in this effort: more than 98 percent of Costa Rica's residents have electricity, and access to telephone service is nearly universal. It is one of the institutions that many Costa Ricans fear will be threatened with privatization if DR-CAFTA is ratified. In 2000, a proposal for its partial privatization led to widespread protests, and the proposal was withdrawn.

Instituto Nacional de Seguros (INS). The National Insurance Institute is another autonomous institution that will face competition, and perhaps ultimately privatization, under the pending free trade agreement with the United States, DR-CAFTA. It was established in 1924 and sells all homeowner and car insurance in Costa Rica, as well as provides workers' compensation insurance. Valued for decades for its services to small farmers, businesspeople, and homeowners, the Institute's reputation has been tarnished in recent years by a number of corruption scandals.

Irazú. An indigenous word indicating a place covered with frost, this is still one of the most imposing volcanoes that can be seen from the Central Valley (even if its peak is no longer icy). The emerald green lake in its crater and the surrounding ash fields are now a national park easily visited by car from San José. Its eruption in 1723 destroyed most of the city of Cartago, and from 1963 to 1965 it intermittently rained a great deal of ash on the metropolitan area.

Keith, Minor (1838–1929). The nephew of Henry Meiggs, the famous builder of Andean railroads, Keith was an American entrepreneur who was awarded the concession to finish the first Costa Rican railroad to the Caribbean coast after some British investors were unable to complete the project. He also founded the powerful United Fruit Company after he discovered how profitable it was to plant bananas along the route of the new railroad and to export them to the United States. He became one of the most important foreigners in Costa Rica, and the name "Minor" is still a common one in the country.

Limón. This is Costa Rica's largest town on the Caribbean coast and the capital of the province of that name. Columbus landed near here on his fourth voyage to the New World, but during the colonial era, Matina was the most important port on that side of the country. Limón was not established as a port until 1865 and did not really begin to grow until the completion of the railroad from San José in 1890. The most important container port is now Moín, just north of the city of Limón, although Limón now receives a number of cruise ships and promotes itself as a tourist destination. A significant proportion of the population of the province and the city are descendents of Afro-Caribbean immigrants, many of whom originally came to work on the railroad or the banana plantations. The city has a distinct culture and cuisine because of this influence, but it is also one of the poorest areas in the country.

Manuel Antonio National Park. This is one of the most frequently visited parks in Costa Rica because of its beautiful combination of Pacific beaches, tropical rain forest, and white-faced capuchin monkeys (among other fauna). Located on the Pacific coast, south of the former banana port of Quepos, its relatively accessible location has led to the construction of many hotels and other tourist services. While improving the economy of the area, this mostly unplanned development has also threatened the natural environment and animal populations that the tourists come to see.

Ministerio de Ambiente e Energía (MINAE). The Ministry of Environment and Energy was established to protect and regulate the use of Costa Rica's natural resources. The SINAC (National System of Conservation Areas), a branch of the MINAE, is responsible for administration of the system of natural parks and protected areas. This task has become more difficult in recent years as budget cuts have made maintenance and expansion of parks more difficult, ironically at the very moment when more and more tourists began arriving in hopes of visiting them. The Ministry and its problems are a central theme in Ana Cristina Rossi's popular and controversial novel about a woman struggling to save a protected area on the Caribbean coast, *La Loca de Gandoca* (The Crazy Woman of Gandoca).

Monteverde. Now one of the most frequently visited private nature reserves in the country, this highland cloud forest area northwest of the Central Valley was originally settled by

Quakers from Alabama. They left the United States because of their objections to the Korean War and established dairy farms here in the 1950s. Because of their abiding interest in the preservation and restoration of the natural environment in this region, this has become an important area for scientific study, as well as for eco-tourism. In addition to a famous cheese and ice cream factory started by the original Quaker colonists, a number of other private reserves have been established in the area, along with many hotels, restaurants, and other services catering to visitors.

Morazán, Francisco (1792–1842). Morazán was born in Honduras and served as president of the Central American Federation beginning in 1830. He was overthrown in 1840, but with hopes of recovering his power, he invaded Costa Rica, seized power there in 1842, and tried to raise an army to fight for the Federation. Most citizens of Costa Rica were not in agreement with this plan, and he was overthrown and executed in San José in 1842. A large park in downtown San José bears his name.

Nicas. Nicaraguans call themselves "nicas," just as Costa Ricans call themselves "ticos." However, since Nicaraguans have been arriving in Costa Rica in large numbers—first in the 1970s as refugees from civil unrest in their country, and since then looking for jobs—it has acquired a pejorative connotation when used by Costa Ricans. Many (though not all) ticos try to blame the nicas for every negative issue, from job losses to an increase in crime to a decline in quality of the schools, situations for which the Nicaraguans are not responsible, but rather are a result in many cases of lack of public investment in Costa Rica.

Nicoya Peninsula. This peninsula is found on the northwestern Pacific coast just south of the border with Nicaragua. Before the arrival of the Spanish, this was an area of relatively large settlements of indigenous peoples speaking languages related to those of Mesoamerica to the north. It was also the site of the first Spanish incursions into the region in the early 16th century; the Spanish found some gold, but even more slaves. In the last few years, it has been the site of tourist incursions, though some of the resultant development of tourist services and attractions has been poorly planned and has caused environmental degradation. The Nicoya Peninsula is also home to the oldest church in Costa Rica and several national parks, the most well known being those established to protect sea turtles that arrive on the peninsula to nest.

Osa Peninsula. This peninsula juts out of southwest Costa Rica into the Pacific Ocean just north of the border with Panama. It is home to the Corcovado National Park. It is still one of the most remote areas of the country and contains large areas of unspoiled rain forest. In recent years, however, is has begun to draw many tourists, and with the planned addition of a large marina and an airport, it looks soon to draw even more.

Oxcarts. With their teams of enormous oxen, these were once the off-road vehicles of choice in Costa Rica. They were used in particular to haul coffee from the Central Valley across the mountains to the Pacific port of Puntarenas. In some highland areas—particularly the San José suburb of Escazú—they can still be seen at work. Painted with bright colors and intricate geometric designs, they have now become one of Costa Rica's most visible folkloric symbols. In 2005, the United Nations declared the carts part of the world cultural patrimony. Every year in San José, Costa Ricans celebrate *"el día del boyero"* (the day of the oxcart driver), and the carts and drivers parade through the streets of the city.

Partido Acción Ciudadano (Party of Citizen Action). The PAC is universally identified with the presidential candidacy of Ottón Solís, who forced the elections into an unprecedented second round runoff in 2002 and came within 18,000 votes of defeating Óscar Arias and the National Liberation Party (PLN) in 2006. Solís, a former PLN minister, left the government in protest over the first round of neoliberal reforms. He and the PAC are strongly identified with opposition to the free trade agreement with the United States and with efforts to create a new sort of politics. Solís has firmly resisted the country's traditional practice of patronage and promises of public works and other projects in exchange for votes. Two of the most important PAC leaders are women. Epsy Campbell, of Afro-Caribbean descent, was Solís's vice-presidential running mate in 2006 and is now the president of the PAC; Elizabeth Fonseca is the leader of the PAC in the Legislative Assembly.

Partido Liberación Nacional (National Liberation Party). A central tension has defined the PLN since its founding in 1951. On the one hand, it was created as the electoral vehicle for the victor of the Civil War of 1948—José "Pepe" Figueres. On the other hand, Don Pepe and his associates were committed to the notion that Costa Rica needed to move from a political culture dominated by caudillos to one driven by ideas and institutions. The PLN won the elections of 1953 and has since provided the country with several legislative majorities and six presidents. The PLN continues to call itself a social democratic party, is affiliated with the Socialist International, and takes credit for building the Costa Rican welfare state. However, recent forays into neoliberal reform have made the party's current ideological orientation hard to pin down and have generated defections to the Partido Acción Ciudadana. The internal politics of the PLN are also unclear. As in most Costa

Rican parties, it is assumed that strong personalities (Don Pepe until his death in 1990 and Óscar Arias today) have more influence than institutional mechanisms like formal party conventions.

Partido Unidad Social Cristiana (Party of Social Christian Unity). Founded in 1983 by Rafael Ángel Calderón Fournier, the PUSC raised the first effective opposition to the PLN and ushered in an era of two-party politics. Like its rival, the PUSC relied on loyalties forged in the 1940s, but it also traded on the more enduring resistance of Costa Rica's business groups to what was perceived as excessive government intervention in economic matters. Inheriting the mantle of his father, Calderón Guardia, Calderón Fournier won the presidency in 1990 and built the PUSC into a national party. From 1998 to 2006, the party controlled the presidency and a plurality in the Legislative Assembly. Following the influence-peddling scandals that landed ex-presidents Calderón Fournier and Miguel Ángel Rodríguez in jail, the PUSC suffered a stunning loss in the 2006 elections and has nearly disappeared from the political scene.

Poás Volcano. Another of the large volcanoes visible from the Central Valley, Poás is most easily accessible from the city of Alajuela. Its accessibility made it one of Costa Rica's earliest tourist attractions and later one of its most popular national parks, despite the fact that the volcano is still active and the park must sometimes be closed when the crater emits more than the usual amount of steam and gases.

Presbere, Pablo (d. 1710). Presbere was the leader of an Indian revolt in the southern region of Talamanca in 1709 that killed a number of Spanish priests and soldiers. The revolt was brutally suppressed, and Presbere and many of his followers were taken off to Cartago. Many died along the way;

some, including Presbere, were tried and executed; others were sold into slavery. A monument to Presbere is located in the plaza of the city of Limón.

Puntarenas. This is Costa Rica's largest port town on the Pacific coast and the capital of Puntarenas Province. Caldera was the main port on the Pacific until the mid-19th century, but Puntarenas then became a stop for steamships traveling between San Francisco and Panama. It is now more important as a tourist town and a departure point for tours to the southern tip of the Nicoya Peninsula, and Caldera has again become the most important working port.

Sala IV. Also known as the "constitutional chamber" of Costa Rica's supreme court, the Sala IV was established by the Legislative Assembly in 1989. Perhaps unexpectedly, the Sala IV became one of the most important checks on government power and one of its most overworked institutions. It has jurisdiction in all except electoral matters. Citizens can approach the court to seek protections (*amparo*) from government actions and to question the constitutionality of laws. Minority legislators have also made considerable use of the Sala IV to rule on the constitutionality of parliamentary procedures used by the majority to push laws through the Legislative Assembly.

San José. San José was founded in 1736. By the end of the colonial period, it was the most economically important towns and was finally made the capital in 1823, although rivalry among the towns of the Central Valley continued. With the coming of the coffee boom in the second half of the 19th century, it solidified its position not only as the center of government but also as the country's cultural, educational, and economic hub. Visitors were impressed with its beauty, nestled among the green coffee fields. The city grew very rapidly in the last half of the 20th century; it now has a population of more than two million and most of the social problems of any Latin American city (crime, urban deterioration, overcrowding, slums, suburban sprawl, lack of green space, etc.). Unfortunately, it can no longer be said to be particularly beautiful. San José is also the home of Saprissa, one of the two premier soccer clubs in Costa Rica.

Santamaría, Juan (1831–1856). The hero of the Battle of Rivas during the war of the National Campaign, he was a humble soldier who sacrificed his life to set fire to the building where William Walker's troops had holed up. Because Costa Rica lacks any heroes or heroic deeds from the period of its independence from Spain, Juan Santamaría has become an even more important symbolic figure than his one deed might seem to warrant. The international airport is named after him, and a large statue of him stands there, another adorns a plaza in Alajuela. Juan Santamaría and the victory at Rivas are celebrated every year on April 11.

Talamanca. This region in the southeastern and south-central parts of the country contains both the southern coastal area (with beach towns like Cahuita and Puerto Viejo) as well as high mountainous areas. It has always been rather inaccessible. It was never entirely conquered by the Spanish in the colonial era, and it is still one of the poorest areas of the country, in many parts still lacking in roads, schools, and hospitals. On the coast, there is a large Afro-Caribbean population. The highlands are home to indigenous groups such as the Bribri and Cabécar, who often live in very isolated settlements. The isolation of this region has meant, however, that much of the natural environment has been preserved. It contains the Cahuita National Park on the Caribbean, the Gandoca-Manzanillo Wildlife Refuge south of Puerto Viejo, and the Chirripó National Park, which contains Costa Rica's highest peak. It also makes up part of the Amistad International Park, which crosses over into Panama to provide a large uninterrupted corridor for wildlife.

United Fruit Company. This powerful company was founded by Minor Keith in 1899 after he realized the profitability of exporting the bananas grown along the new railroad line to the Caribbean (which, conveniently, he had the concession to finish building). It was against United Fruit that the Costa Rican banana workers went on strike in 1934. The company expanded its operations to other Latin American countries where, as in Costa Rica, it tried to maintain a monopoly on the production of bananas and earned a reputation for ruthless business and labor practices. For many Latin Americans, it became the symbol of the perceived economic imperialism of the United States. It was bought by Standard Fruit in 1969.

La Virgen de los Angeles. She is the patron saint of Costa Rica, and her statue is housed in the Basilica of the city of Cartago where it is the object of an important pilgrimage every August. According to tradition, in 1635 an Indian woman, Juana de Pereira, found a small black statue of the Virgin in a kind of grotto with a spring, and she took it home with her. It reappeared, however, where she had found it and was soon credited with several miracles. It was decided to build a church on that spot. In fact, many churches were built there over the years, and they were all destroyed by earthquakes. The large, white wedding cake of a church that sits there now dates to 1921.

Walker, William. In 1854, when Nicaragua was embroiled in one of its many 19th-century civil wars, an American adventurer, or "filibuster," William Walker took advantage of the situation, sailed from New Orleans with a mercenary army, and managed to take over the country. He had his eye on the rest of Central America as well, imagining that it might be annexed to the United States as an extension of the southern slave states. Juan Rafael Mora, president of Costa Rica, motivated the other countries of Central America to unite forces to get rid of Walker. This was the origin of what is known in Costa Rica as the National Campaign. In 1856, the Costa Rican forces defeated Walker at Santa Rosa in Guanacaste (now a national monument) and then at Rivas, Nicaragua. Walker held out for another year, but was finally defeated by the combined Central American forces in 1857.

Costa Rican Language, Food, and Etiquette

LANGUAGE

As with many other characteristics, in their use of the Spanish language Costa Ricans are very proud of their "idiosyncrasies." One of the most notable of these is the use of *vos* rather than the more common *tú* for the second person singular "you." This form is used in some other Central American countries as well as in Argentina, but it is not common elsewhere, and most students of Spanish do not learn it. *Vos* is apparently more closely related to the now-archaic forms that would have been used by the Spanish when they arrived to conquer the New World in the 16th century, and it remained common only in the most out-of-the-way corners of the empire. *Vos* is really the simplest form of "you" and is constructed in the present tense by removing the final -r from the infinitive form of the verb and adding an -s. Thus, many of the worst irregular forms of the verb (the bane of so many beginning Spanish students) are avoided. The accent is written on the last vowel: *poder* becomes *podés; hablar* becomes *hablás.* There are also slight variations in the past and imperative forms of the verb.

The difficulty is not so much, however, in how to form the verb with *vos,* but when to use it. Most Costa Ricans, in fact, do not use it, preferring the *Usted* form for "you." In most Spanish speaking countries, *Usted* is reserved for formal situations. Not so in Costa Rica. One hears it everywhere: between co-workers, good friends, and even family members. *Usted* is used by children to address adults, as well as vice versa, and children and teenagers use it when talking among themselves. Even dogs and cats are addressed "formally." Although these are situations where in other Latin American countries the use of *Usted* would sound rather funny, this is the form *ticos,* as Costa Ricans are known, seem most comfortable with. Although certain people (particularly university students and professors) do use *vos,* a foreigner is always safest using *Usted* when addressing Costa Ricans. Because the more universal *tú* is heard often in Costa Rica in movies and on television (whose content is largely imported), Costa Ricans also know this form and will generally forgive a nonnative speaker its use, even in situations where they might feel offended by another tico presuming to use a familiar form of address.

Costa Rica also has vocabulary and usage that is unique to the country. Some words that may have bad connotations in other Spanish-speaking countries have a different, perfectly polite meaning in Costa Rica. The following are just a few of the best known and often heard of these *tiquismos.*

Adios   Although literally this means "goodbye," it can also mean "hello" when passing acquaintances and even strangers on the street. In that context, it may be more frequently heard than *hola* (hello).

Chunche (m)   This is an all-purpose word for that little thing whose name is forgotten, or that never even had a name at all: a whatchamacallit, a thingy, a gizmo (pl. stuff, junk).

Coche (m)   This is not the word that Costa Ricans use for car. Car is always *carro* or *auto.* A *coche* is a baby carriage or the buggy at the supermarket.

Con mucho gusto   You're welcome. Costa Ricans always use this expression rather than *de nada,* the expression common in most other Spanish-speaking countries.

Diay (excl.)   Imagine that! Gosh; oh, well; hey, what can you expect? This is a multipurpose exclamation that is peculiarly Costa Rican.

(Por) Dicha Fortunately, thankfully, luckily. A frequent response to the question "How are you? (*¿Cómo está usted?*)" is "I am well (*estoy bien*), *por dicha.*"

Güila (m/f) A child.

Hueputa An obscene, but frequently heard, exclamation technically calling into question the legitimacy of one's birth and the virtue of one's mother. This term expresses anger and sometimes simply reflects a reduced vocabulary (see entry for *maje*). Its impact can be softened for use in a vein similar to "darn it!" by saying *puchis.*

Jodido/a (adj) Although this has an obscene meaning in Spain, Mexico, and other Spanish-speaking countries, it does not have this connotation in Costa Rica. It simply means to be in a sticky situation or to have a problem.

Jupa (f) Head. *Romperse la jupa* (literally, "to break your head") means to think a lot or to worry a lot about something.

Macha/o (adj) A nickname for a fair or blond person; often used by men calling attention to a woman (especially a foreigner) in the street. This is just one example of the Costa Rican (and, more generally, Latin American) custom of referring to people by their physical characteristics. North Americans may feel insulted if they are called *gordo* (chubby), *flaco* (skinny), *negrito* (dark-skinned or black) or *chino* (Asian), and sometimes these terms are meant insultingly. But often, that is not actually the intention, and these can even be affectionate nicknames.

Maje (m) Literally, dummy, but used by young people (often compulsively) when talking to their friends as something akin to "dude" or "buddy."

Nica (m/f) Someone from Nicaragua. The Nicaraguans call themselves this, but it usually has a pejorative connotation if Costa Ricans use it to refer to Nicaraguans.

Pendejo/a (adj) Timid or scared. In Mexico, this is an obscene insult, but in Costa Rica it has a much softer meaning.

Pipa (f)   Literally, a coconut, but figuratively, a brainy person.

Pura Vida (adj)   Cool, great, OK, I agree; can also be used as a greeting. This phrase appears on lots of tourist souvenirs but is also used very frequently by Costa Ricans, both young and old.

Salado/a (adj)   Literally, salty, but figuratively it means "too bad" or "tough luck."

Sele (f)   Short for *la selección,* the Costa Rican National soccer team, (i.e., those who were selected or made the cut for the team).

Si Dios quiere   God willing. Many Costa Ricans will tack this on, somewhat superstitiously, to their response to any statements (i.e., "see you tomorrow") that imply certain knowledge of the future.

Tico/a (adj)   Costa Ricans' name for themselves. It supposedly comes from their habit of making diminutives by adding -*tica* or -*tico* to a word.

Torta (f)   A problem or difficulty. *Jalarse una torta* means to get in trouble, to have a problem.

Tuanis (adj)   Much the same as *pura vida* but not heard as frequently.

Upe (excl)   Hello, anyone home? This exclamation is called out approaching a house where no one answers a knock on the door, there is no bell to ring, or if the door is open but nobody is around.

Vacilón (adj)   Something that is pleasing, cool, neat, interesting.

Viera (excl)   Just imagine!

Zaguate (m)   A dog, especially a mutt or a street dog.

FOOD AND BEVERAGES

Costa Ricans from all parts of the country are almost unfailingly dedicated to their typical national dishes, their *comidas típicas,* even if they do not eat them all the time.

Tamales are eaten almost exclusively at Christmas; *chicharrones* might only be a special weekend treat. The most truly typical dish, the one that is on almost everyone's plate every day, is rice and beans. In most of the country this is *arroz y frijoles,* but in the traditionally English-speaking Caribbean region, it becomes "rice-and-beans" (in English) and is cooked with coconut milk, giving it a distinctive flavor. Caribbean food, besides using coconut milk, also uses more chile and can be spicy—especially in comparison with most of the food in the rest of the country, which is generally very bland. (This may be a relief to some travelers who have come to think that all Latin American countries have food as spicy as Mexico's.) The traditional diet of the residents of the Pacific northwest region of Guanacaste has much in common with that of Mesoamerica (the region north from Nicaragua to Mexico) and features more corn than in other parts of Costa Rica.

On the whole, however, Costa Rica's foods have been "globalized" over the last 20 years. In most of the larger towns, there is just about any American fast food one could want; it can be found on almost every corner of San José. Chinese food can be found in almost all towns of any size. However, there are still a number of dishes peculiar to Costa Rica of which Costa Ricans are proud and which visitors ought to try.

Common Costa Rican Dishes

Agua dulce   This hot drink may be served in lieu of coffee. It is a local brown sugar (*tapa de dulce*) sold in a cone-shaped lump dissolved in hot water or hot milk and has a flavor of molasses.

Aracache, yuca, and other roots   Thanks to its South American indigenous heritage, Costa Rican cuisine still uses a number of root vegetables with which United States and European visitors will probably not be familiar. These are often served in soups or as *picadillo* (a kind of hash served as a side dish) or, in the case of yuca, deep fried.

Bananas and plantains   Unsurprisingly, Costa Rican cuisine features an enormous variety of these. There are several varieties of the regular sweet yellow bananas. Also available is the large, green, starchy plantain that may be fried into round, crunchy *patacones,* boiled in soup, or served stewed as a side dish. Stranger varieties are also worth trying, such as the small, sweet red banana that tastes of raspberries and is, on the Caribbean coast, baked into a kind of empanada called *patty.*

Caribbean food   This is probably the most distinctive regional cuisine in Costa Rica (but to many highland Costa Ricans it still seems very exotic, and many have never tried it) and was brought to the country by immigrants from Jamaica and other Caribbean countries. Besides the pastry-like *patty,* which can be filled with sweet bananas or with spicy ground beef, a number of seafood dishes use the very hot *chile panameño.* Seafood is also used in a number of soups, some with coconut milk. One of the most delicious is *rondon,* whose name allegedly comes from "run down"— meaning that traditionally it might have contained a great variety of seafood or other meats, anything that one might be able to "run down."

Casado   This might be said to be the Costa Rican version of the "blue-plate lunch special." It is supposedly called a "marriage" because it always brings together the two staples of rice and beans, usually black beans. Besides rice and beans, a casado usually has a bit of cole slaw with tomato, a picadillo of potato or some other root vegetable or the bland, squash-like *chayote,* and a few pieces of cooked plantain. A serving of chicken, pork, beef, or fish, or for vegetarians, an egg, is the main dish.

Chicharrones   These are savory squares of fried pork served without sauce, but usually accompanied by slices of sour orange to squeeze over the meat. They are often served as bar food (*bocas*), one of various items (fried plantains or yuca, beef brochettes, etc.) that were traditionally served free with the purchase of drinks. Bars still serve bocas, but they are almost never free.

Chilero   Along with salt and pepper, many restaurants may put this jar of spicy marinated chiles, onions, and other vegetables on the table for those who want to add spice to their food.

Coffee   Most Costa Ricans are very fond of the drink that first made their country's fortune back in the 19th century. Many people still have the custom, either at home or at work, to take a break for *cafecito* at mid-morning or late afternoon. Either sweet or salty snacks may be served with coffee. Electric coffeemakers are now more popular, but at some restaurants, one may still see coffee prepared in the traditional way where it is placed in a kind of cloth sock in a wooden stand and boiling water is poured through it into the waiting cup.

Fruits   Costa Ricans enjoy an enormous variety of fruits. Some are well known (pineapple, blackberry, watermelon, cantaloupe, mango, papaya), while others are more exotic: *cas, maracuyá* (passion fruit), *guayaba* (guava), *tamarindo* (tamarind), *marañón* (the fruit of the plant that produces the cashew nut), *guanabana* (soursop), *carambola* (star fruit), *mamón chino,* etc. These fruits are served most often in delicious drinks, *refrescos naturales,* blended with either milk or water. Unlike in some other Latin American countries where fruit drinks are rapidly losing ground to soft drinks, Costa Ricans are still very enthusiastic about their home-made refrescos, and with good reason.

Gallo   This is Costa Rica's version of the taco. It is usually a very small tortilla served alongside some kind of stuffing—chicken, beef, picadillo, beans, etc.—but without any salsa.

Gallo pinto   Not to be confused with a gallo, *gallo pinto* is Costa Rica's traditional and omnipresent breakfast food.

Usually served with eggs and maybe with bacon or sausage, a thick piece of white cheese, or a sort of Costa Rican sour cream (*natilla*), it is basically yesterday's rice and beans re-fried with spices, bell peppers, and parsley. It also is usually flavored with Costa Ricans' favorite bottled salsa, the ever-present Salsa Lizano, a kind of modified Worcestershire sauce that is to be found on almost every restaurant table and in every kitchen cabinet.

Guaro   This clear sugarcane liquor is usually marketed under the brand name Cacique. At the time of this writing, the production and sale of *guaro* is still a government mo-nopoly. Guaro is typically drunk straight, or mixed with juice or soda. It is also substituted for other *aguardiente*-like liquors in cocktails. The Brazilian *caipirinha,* prepared with Brazil's cane alcohol, might be made with guaro and called a *guaipirinha.*

Olla carne   This is a very popular beef stew, literally, "pot of meat." Meat is served in broth with stewed potatoes, yuca, plantain, corn, and other vegetables. Sometimes these vegetables are served alongside for the diner to add to his or her own soup.

Pejibaye   This is the fruit of a native palm plant, which for millennia was one of the staple foods of the indigenous peo-ples in this region of the tropics. In Costa Rica *pejibayes* are still very popular and can be bought ready-boiled from many supermarkets. They have a beautiful orange-red color and a nutty but bland taste. They are often served with mayonnaise.

Tamales   Costa Rican tamales are savory rather than spicy and are served wrapped in banana leaves. Each packet (they are usually served in twos) contains the *masa* (corn meal) that is their base; a little piece of roast pork, roast chicken, or beans; slices of carrot; red pepper; and maybe a green bean. The most interesting aspect of tamales is that they are a holiday phenomenon. The ingredients are in such demand that every year around Christmas, the price of these very common items increases notably. The whole family may be enlisted to help in the long and complicated process of assembling dozens and dozens of tamales.

ETIQUETTE

Although Costa Rica may seem extraordinarily exotic in its flora and fauna, and does have its own distinct historical tradition, it is a Western culture, and as such does not have rules of etiquette that would seem overly strange or demanding to visitors from North America or Europe. That said, Costa Ricans do have their own way of doing things. They are usually exceedingly polite. Friends as well as new acquaintances are greeted with a kiss (for women) and a handshake (between men). Inquiries are made as to how everyone is. In the morning, *¿Cómo está?* may become *¿Cómo amaneció?* (literally, how did you wake up this morning?). The most polite answer is, *Bien, por dicha* or *bien, gracias a Dios* (very well, thank goodness). Ticos also tend to invoke God's will in saying goodbye. It is very common to hear not just *¡hasta lunes!* (see you Monday!), but also added to that, *si Dios quiere* (if God wills it).

Besides being generally polite, ticos are also very concerned with avoiding conflict. Although this may be a reflection of their inherently peace-loving and democratic natures, it can also itself be the source of conflict. People want to, as Costa Ricans themselves say, *quedarse bien,* or leave a good impression. This desire may, for example, lead co-workers to paper over today some difficulty or disagreement that will only come back to haunt them in the future. It may lead the auto mechanic to neglect to return one's calls instead of having to admit that he is unable to fix the problem because the needed part will not arrive for two weeks. Good manners are nice, and conflict is generally a bad thing, but the polite, yet passive aggressive behavior that an exaggeration of these qualities can provoke can be quite frustrating.

Another manifestation of politeness is the custom of calling almost everyone by the honorific *don* or *doña*. This is similar to the old custom in the southern United States of calling people "Miss" or "Mister" along with their first names. A boss at the office, for instance, might be called don Gilberto rather than Señor Odio. This is an acceptable address for almost any acquaintance, co-worker, or employee who is not a particular friend of the speaker's. If the name of the person being addressed is not known, he or she may be called simply *don* or *doña*. If the person addressed is young or, almost regardless of age, if he or she is working in a restaurant or a store or in some other service profession, he or she will be called rather generically *muchacho* (boy) or *muchacha* (girl).

Just as is the case wherever good manners are highly esteemed, sometimes the appearance is more important than the fact. This may mean that unlike in some other Latin American countries, hospitality to strangers is a nice attitude to adopt, if it does not really have to be taken too seriously. Costa Ricans themselves joke that ticos love to invite people to their houses, but they never give out the address. Thus, the form of the polite invitation is maintained, while the actual visit may never take place. If, in fact, one does visit a Costa Rican's home (on a social or commercial call), it is polite to say *con permiso* (with your permission) when stepping through the door.

Costa Ricans are private people; family always comes first, before almost every other obligation. It is usual for children to live at home even after they are grown; they usually do not leave home until they get married. This seems to be the custom for economic reasons and because of the high value placed on family ties. Some children do not leave home even after marrying and having their own children. If there is room, they simply build a house on the same lot as their parents and raise their own family there. Families tend to cluster in certain parts of town or on certain streets. *Calle*

Díaz may be the name of a street because it is where all the Díazes live (or lived at some time in the past).

One area in which the Costa Ricans' courtesy consistently fails them, however, is behind the wheel of a car. Many drivers are aggressive, rude, and unpleasant in traffic. Costa Rica has a terrible record of injuries and deaths in traffic accidents (see sidebar in chapter 4). It has been suggested that very bad driving may be due, at least in part, to the relative anonymity that one has in a car. It is almost certainly also due to the fact that the roads in Costa Rica are so badly maintained and that traffic at rush hour in San José becomes almost hopelessly snarled. While the number of cars on the road has increased exponentially in the last 20 years, the road network has not been substantially expanded, nor, in many cases, have modern conveniences like traffic lights been added at busy intersections. In any case, many, if not most, ticos tend to ignore traffic laws when it suits them. They also know that so few transit police are on the road that it is not very likely they will ever be caught. This rather selfish calculation does not, of course, do anything to lessen the threat they pose to other drivers and to pedestrians.

Costa Rica–Related Organizations

Since Costa Rica has become such a popular tourist destination, a great deal of information can now be found on the World Wide Web about the country, not all of it reliable. Probably the best source for links on the Web related to Costa Rica (or any other Latin American country) is the LANIC site run by the University of Texas (www.utexas.lanic.org/). It lists information by country as well as theme and covers aspects from tourism to resources for academic research. A good source for maps of Costa Rica is Maptak (www.maptak.com/), which has physical and political maps of the entire country and of the various regions and cities, including an interesting satellite map. Good general information about who is doing what in Costa Rica is available in Spanish at the Web site of the major national newspaper, *La Nación* (www.nacion.com/) and in English at the Web site of the *Tico Times* (www.ticotimes.net/).

BUSINESS AND ECONOMICS

Association of Residents of Costa Rica
www.arcr.net/

This is an association for foreigners living in or thinking of moving to Costa Rica. It has information not only about doing business in Costa Rica but also about immigration requirements, tax questions, and cultural issues, as well as links to other useful sites and to various books about life in Costa Rica.

Costa Rican American Chamber of Commerce
www.amcham.co.cr/

This association of Costa Rican and U.S. business interests is very active in the business world in Costa Rica. Its Web site provides much useful information about doing business in Costa Rica—including policies on legal, labor, and export requirements.

CANATUR (Costa Rican Tourism Board)
www.canatur.org/

This is the business association for the tourist sector in Costa Rica. It works to promote Costa Rica as a tourist destination, but its Web site also provides general information for tourists to Costa Rica, including useful information like official holidays and the phone numbers for hospitals and museums. It has links to statistics about tourist arrivals in Costa Rica (in Spanish).

CULTURE, EDUCATION, AND EXCHANGE

CATIE (Tropical Agricultural Research and Higher Education Center)
www.catie.ac.cr/

Since the 1970s, the campus of this university, oriented toward sustainable agriculture and resource management, has been located in the town of Turrialba. Yet it has its roots even further back, in the 1940s when Costa Rica and other Latin American countries had a great interest in promoting agricultural research and development. This is now not only an important research center with students from all over Latin America, but it also offers tours of its botanical gardens and facilities to the public.

EARTH University
www.earth.ac.cr/

This university also has an international student body that comes to its campus in the town of Guápiles (east of San José) to study agricultural sciences of the tropics and sustainable development. It invests in research, but particularly emphasizes the business side of promoting good agricultural practices.

ICADS (Institute for Central American Development Studies)
www.icads.cr.com/

There are many excellent Spanish schools in Costa Rica, but this institute offers Spanish language programs as short as two weeks for anyone interested in learning Spanish, as well as semester-long study abroad credit for undergraduate students. It has volunteer opportunities and field study projects, both of which are in keeping with its socially and politically progressive focus.

INCAE
www.incae.ac.cr/EN/acerca/

This business school, whose campus is located west of San José, was founded through the cooperation of various Central American countries and with the ongoing assistance of Harvard Business School. It offers master's degrees in business-related areas and executive training programs.

Museo de Arte Costarricense (Costa Rican Museum of Art)
www.muar.go.cr/

This is Costa Rica's most important art museum. It is housed in the building that used to be the airport terminal in the Sabana Park in downtown San José—which is interesting to see if only to realize how airport terminals have changed. Its Web site is only in Spanish, but it shows interesting photos of works in the collection, as well as information about exhibits and activities.

Museo de Cultura Popular (Museum of Popular Culture)
www.ilam.org/cr/museoculturapopular/
This museum is run by the National University in the Central Valley town of Heredia. Its Web site is available in English and Spanish and contains photos of the traditional Costa Rican house that has been preserved at the museum. The museum also actively promotes the rescue and preservation of traditional culture by sponsoring activities and workshops on topics such as traditional food, construction techniques, and children's toys.

Museo Nacional de Costa Rica (National Museum of
Costa Rica)
www.museocostarica.go.cr/
This is the country's most important anthropology and history museum. Its Web site is available in Spanish and English (the translations are strange, but understandable). Nice photos of much of its collection are provided on the Web site, as well as information about temporary exhibits, activities, and research at the museum.

Universidad de Costa Rica (the University of Costa Rica)
www.ucr.ac.cr/
This is Costa Rica's largest, most important university. Its main campus is in San Pedro, a suburb of San José, and it has branch campuses throughout the country. Its Web site is available only in Spanish, but it provides information about undergraduate and graduate programs of study, research being undertaken by its faculty, and campus activities.

University for Peace
www.upeace.org/
This university, located in the town of Ciudad Colón near San José, was established by the United Nations for the promotion of tolerance and international understanding through the study of peace and conflict. It has an international student body studying for graduate degrees in areas such as peace education, peace and conflict studies, sustainable development, and international law.

University of Kansas Study Abroad
www.studyabroad.ku.edu/
Although there are now many study abroad programs for undergraduates in Costa Rica, this was one of the first available. It offers a program of direct enrollment in the UCR that allows students a greater immersion in Costa Rican culture and education than might be had in other programs.

THE ENVIRONMENT

Some information provided in this section overlaps with the previous section, but because Costa Rica is well known now in large part because of its commitment to its national parks and environmental preservation, this topic seems to merit its own section. Included here are only a few of the many national and international organizations working toward these ends.

Asociación ANAI
www.anaicr.org/
This organization has worked on the Caribbean coast of Costa Rica since 1978 promoting not only conservation of marine resources (especially turtle protection) and sustainable agriculture, but also community involvement and

management of conservation and development projects. It also offers eco-tours of the Caribbean area and volunteer opportunities. The Web site has much information about its projects, including downloadable reports.

Caribbean Conservation Corporation (CCC)
www.cccturtle.org/
This nonprofit organization was founded in 1959 to protect the sea turtles of the Caribbean coast. It has worked for the passage of legal protections and the establishment of refuges for the turtles. Its Web site contains much information about the research and environmental education that the group promotes. It also has maps that show where satellite-tracked turtles are swimming in various parts of the world. The CCC also has a volunteer program for people interested in sea turtle conservation.

INBio (National Institute for Biodiversity)
www.inbio.ac.cr/
This research center was established in 1989 to study and inventory the country's great biodiversity. It also created a park near San José where visitors can experience many of the different bioregions of the country. Its Web site has a great deal of information (much of it in English) on its publications and an online biodiversity data bank.

Kids for Saving Earth
www.kidsforsavingearth.org/
This nonprofit works with the OTS (see below) to involve children in contributing to preserve rain forest resources in Costa Rica. Its Web site has Costa Rican nature photos and provides free environmental education curricular material for teachers and parents, and activities for kids.

Organization for Tropical Studies (OTS)
www.ots.ac.cr/
    This institution was founded in 1963 through cooperation between U.S. and Costa Rican universities. It now runs several very important biological research stations that also offer opportunities for undergraduate study abroad and graduate research, as well as ecotourism. Its Web site also has a number of good online resources, such as a searchable database and links to other sites concerning the Costa Rican environment and research.

Rainforest Alliance
www.rainforest-alliance.org/
    This nongovernmental organization works around the world on conservation, ecotourism, and sustainable agriculture projects and has one of its main offices in San José. It has been particularly successful in certifying companies that adopt environmentally sound practices. Its Web site has much information on all the organization does, including reports of its conservation projects in Costa Rica (and other Latin American countries) and up-to-date newsletters.

Tropical Science Center
www.cct.or.cr/en/menu_cct.html/
    The organization focuses on research and environmental planning and, importantly, has been involved in the preservation of the Monteverde Reserve since the early 1970s. It also offers courses in plant identification for nonscientists. Its Web site provides summaries of its research as well as information about how to visit Monteverde.

COSTA RICA'S GOVERNMENT REPRESENTATIVES IN THE UNITED STATES

Costa Rican Embassy
211 S Street, NW

Washington, DC 20008
Phone: (202) 234-2945, (202) 234-2946
www.costarica-embassy.org/

Consulates General of Costa Rica
Washington, DC
2112 S Street, NW
Washington, DC 20008
Phone: (202) 328-6628
E-mail: consulate@costarica-embassy.org

Atlanta
1870 The Exchange, Suite 100
Atlanta, GA 30339
Phone: (770) 951-7025
E-mail: consulte_ga@costarica-embassy.org

Chicago
203 N. Wabash Ave., Suite 702
Chicago, IL 60601
Phone: (312) 263-2772
E-mail: crcchi@aol.com

Houston
3000 Wilcrest, Suite 112
Houston, TX 77042
Phone: (713) 266-0484
E-mail: consulate@sbcglobal.net

Los Angeles
1605 Olympic Blvd., Suite 400
Los Angeles, CA 90015
Phone: (213) 380-7915, (213) 380-6031
E-mail: costaricaconsulatela@hotmail.com

Miami
1101 Brickell Ave., Suite 401-N
Miami, FL 33131
Phone: (305) 871-7487, (305) 871-7485
E-mail: consulate_mia@costarica-embassy.org

New York
225 W. 34th St., Suite 1203
New York, NY 10122
Phone: (212) 509-3066, (212) 509-3067
E-mail: costaricaconsul@yahoo.com

TOURISM

In many ways, tourism is what Costa Rica is all about these days, and so an overabundance of tourism information is available on the Internet. Seemingly every airline and every tour company offers a special package deal. All of the major guidebook companies (i.e., Fodors, Lonely Planet, Frommers) as well as many lesser-known publishers offer a book about how, where, and why to travel to Costa Rica. One of the best of these is *The New Key to Costa Rica* (see annotated bibliography below). Here, we list some lesser-known tourist options that may not have gotten much publicity, but deserve more.

ACTUAR (Asociación Costarricense de Turismo
Rural Comunitario)
www.actuarcostarica.com/
   For rural community-based lodging and tours in all parts of Costa Rica, ACTUAR is one of the best bets. Its aims to support community development, conservation projects, and women's and indigenous organizations by offering tourists a large range of options that allow visitors to see beautiful and sometimes remote areas of the country. It has

a very good Web page with many pictures and descriptions of the activities that are available, which include both natural and cultural offerings. It also has an office in downtown San José, where you can drop in for advice on how to see what ACTUAR calls the "real Costa Rica."

CODECE (Asociación para la conservación y desarrollo sostenible de los cerros Escazú)
www.codece.org/

This organization was formed 20 years ago to protect and preserve the water resources, landscape, and rural culture of the mountains of Escazú, a wealthy suburb of San José where many expatriates make their home and where real estate development has been very fast and mostly uncontrolled. To support these aims, the group offers interesting tours in this area on which visitors can hike the countryside, learn about organic farming and the tradition of mask-making, try traditional foods, and even take a ride in a painted oxcart.

COOPRENA
www.turismoruralcr.com/

This organization is a cooperative promoting the rural and ecotourism offerings of its members. Its Web site details the lodges and the tours available and the cooperative's aim in supporting small-scale tourism that respects and even contributes to conservation efforts.

KéköLdi Indigenous Reserve
www.kekoldi.org/

The home of the Bribri people in the southern Talamanca region is host to this project that focuses on environmental concerns and, at the same time, offers unique opportunities for visitors. It is one of the few places in the world apt for observing, at certain times of the year, the migration of birds of prey. The residents of the reserve also offer rain forest tours, tours of a local project of iguana restoration, and talks on indigenous culture, as well as opportunities for longer-term volunteer projects.

Sarapiquí Conservation Learning Center
www.learningcentercostarica.org/
     This nonprofit project in the northern Caribbean region unites a commitment to conservation with community outreach and environmental education programs, while also offering activities for tourists. Tourists can learn about the programs the center sponsors; participate in home stays and home visits in the community; participate in local reforestation efforts and other service learning projects; and even take art, cooking, or dance classes.

Tirimbina Rainforest Center/Centro Neotrópico Sarapiquí
www.tirimbina.org/; www.sarapiqui.org/
     These adjacent institutions, located only an hour-and-a-half away from San José in the Atlantic lowlands, offer excellent opportunities to learn about the rain forest and the indigenous culture that once inhabited it. In addition to a small but excellent museum of indigenous cultures, an indigenous burial site, and a chance to learn (and taste!) all there is to know about chocolate, a long hanging bridge guides visitors at canopy level into the well-maintained trails of the 300-hectare forest reserve. The Tirimbina Rainforest Center offers excellent educational tours, as well as opportunities for research and volunteering. Both centers offer lodging ranging from elegant to adequate.

Annotated Bibliography of Recommended Works on Costa Rica

GEOGRAPHY AND HISTORY OF COSTA RICA

Blake, Beatrice, and Anne Becher. 2006 [1993]. *The New Key to Costa Rica* (18th ed.). Berkeley, CA: Ulysses Press. Although mainly a guidebook with recommendations for hotels, restaurants, and things to see, this book also places tourist options in ecological and geographical context and gives a useful description of what ecotourism ought to encompass and rates hotels and attractions that comply with sustainable criteria. The authors provide a historical summary, cultural insights, and practical information for travel and life in Costa Rica.

Coates, Anthony, ed. 1997. *Central America: A Natural and Cultural History*. New Haven, CT and London: Yale University Press. This collection of essays by geographers, biologists, and historians puts Costa Rica in its Central American context in all of these areas of study. The authors address not only the far geological past of the isthmus and more recent historical events but they also look to the future in discussions of ecological sustainability and regional conservation.

Forsyth, Adrian, and Ken Miyata. 1995. *Tropical Nature: Life and Death in the Rain Forests of Central and South America*. New York: Touchstone. Although this collection of short essays on natural history is meant to be an introduction to tropical biology in general, many of the observations were drawn by the authors from their experience working in Costa Rica. It is an extremely well-written and interesting account meant for nonspecialists, and it covers everything from trees to bugs to birds. Also included is a useful appendix of tips for travel in the tropical rain forest. This book is highly recommended for anyone planning a trip to the tropics, as well as for armchair travelers and naturalists.

Hall, Carolyn, and Héctor Pérez Brignoli. 2003. *Historical Atlas of Central America.* Norman, OK: University of Oklahoma Press. The maps and illustrations in this book are beautiful as well as enlightening, and the clearly written text emphasizes the fascinating historical development of Central America as a region of which Costa Rica is only one part. Covering the period from pre-Columbian times to the present, this regional focus helps to place the economic, political, and social development of Central America into very useful context. This book is much more interesting and much better illustrated than your average atlas; it is really a great short course on the entire history of the region.

Leitinger, Ilse Abshagen, ed. and trans. 1997. *The Costa Rican Women's Movement: A Reader.* Pittsburgh: University of Pittsburgh Press. This book is an interesting collection of essays, personal histories, and case studies of the situation and experiences of Costa Rican women up through the 1990s. The selections address everything from history to art to women's cooperatives to women's health issues. Although perhaps it occasionally ranges too broadly (and may now be a little out of date) this is the best collection for understanding the great variety of women's experiences in Costa Rica and their plans for the future in a society where they hope to be treated as equals and appreciated for their unique contributions.

Lobo, Tatiana. 1998. *Assault on Paradise.* Asa Zatz, trans. Willimantic, CT: Curbstone Press. This is a historical novel by a Chilean writer who has lived in Costa Rica for many years. She weaves colonial history and indigenous heritage into a vivid account of the Spanish conflict with the native peoples and the role of the Catholic Church and religion in the colonial era. It even features a love story. The author skillfully incorporates her research in such a way that sheds a great deal of light on the Costa Rican past, but never becomes didactic.

Molina, Iván, and Steven Palmer. 1998. *The History of Costa Rica: Brief and Up-to-Date with Illustrations.* San José: University of Costa Rica. Available in English and Spanish, this is the best short history of Costa Rica from pre-Columbian times to the end of the 20th century. As the title says, there are great illustrations, and the authors (a U.S. and a Costa Rican historian) provide not only lots of information but also an interesting critical perspective on the country's historical development.

Molina, Iván, and Steven Palmer. 2004. *A Costa Rica Reader: History, Culture, Politics.* Durham, NC: Duke University Press. This is a more recent compilation of historical documents and essays by the authors of the brief history. Part of a series of readers on various Latin American countries, the collection also covers the period from the Spanish conquest to the start of the 21st century. Its thematic organization allows the editors to turn their attention to everything from popular culture to coffee production, while providing enough context to make it interesting to the nonspecialist.

THE ECONOMY OF COSTA RICA

Clark, Mary. 2001. *Gradual Economic Reform in Latin America: The Costa Rican Experience.* Albany, NY: State University of New York Press. This is the most complete academic account available of Costa Rica's slow-motion experience of neoliberal reform in the 1980s and 1990s. While it tends to accentuate only the positive potential of the reforms, it does an excellent job of revealing the intricacies of policy making in Costa Rica and of explaining the obstacles the country's unique system of "checks and balances" puts in the way of rapid change.

Edelman, Marc. 1999. *Peasants against Globalization: Rural Social Movements in Costa Rica.* Stanford, CA: Stanford University Press. This anthropological study uses both fieldwork and a theoretical framework to analyze the impact of the economic crisis of the 1980s on peasants in Costa Rica. The author discusses how rural peasants first organized and then protested the cutbacks in government services and the changes taking place in the marketplace before ultimately having to begin to accommodate themselves to the globalization of Costa Rican society and the economy.

Honey, Martha. 1994. *Hostile Acts: US Policy in Costa Rica in the 1980s.* Gainsville, FL: University of Florida Press. Together with her husband, Tony Avirgan, Martha Honey reported extensively on the Central American crisis of the 1980s from her home in Costa Rica. In engaging journalistic language, this book tells the story of U.S. efforts to bring Costa Rica into the fight against the Sandinistas in Nicaragua and to use its financial leverage to push neoliberal reform. For an accessible account of the "parallel state" in the 1980s, this is unbeatable.

Robinson, William. 2003. *Transnational Conflicts: Central America, Social Change, and Globalization.* London: Verso. Set in a challenging, but enlightening, theoretical discussion of globalization, this book sheds light on what occurred in Central America after the economic crisis of the 1980s. For those interested in how their clothes are made or where their winter vegetables are grown, or why Costa Ricans are worried about becoming more like the rest of Central America, this book is well worth the time and effort.

Sick, Deborah. 1999. *Farmers of the Golden Bean: Costa Rican Households and the Global Coffee Economy.* DeKalb, IL: Northern Illinois Press. This is the best introduction to what life is like today for the small-scale coffee farmers upon whom so much of the country's democratic self-image is based. Sick lived in two small towns on Costa Rica's 20th-century coffee frontier in the southern mountains. Her book clearly describes daily life and strategies for survival of the coffee farmers in times when the market for coffee is uncertain. She addresses the advantages and disadvantages for the farmers of joining a cooperative and why many are choosing now to migrate to the United States. This is a good, concise introduction to the world behind one's daily cup of coffee.

Vandermeer, John, and Ivette Perfecto. 2005 [1995]. *Breakfast of Biodiversity: The Political Ecology of Rainforest Destruction.* Oakland, CA: Food First. This book takes you from your breakfast table to the Sarapiquí region of Costa Rica, where the bananas on your cereal may very well have been grown. A good example of "political ecology" analysis, this book makes the connections between international markets for tropical fruits and foreign loans and the destruction of the rain forest. It also looks critically at the many nature reserves that attract tourists to the country and asks if fencing off pristine fragments of forest is, in the long run, best for the ecosystem and for the people who must live in it.

COSTA RICAN INSTITUTIONS

Allen, William. 2001. *The Green Phoenix: Restoring the Tropical Forests of Guanacaste, Costa Rica.* Oxford: Oxford University Press. This book is an interesting, detailed account of the restoration of a portion of dry tropical rain forest on the northwestern coast that is now incorporated into the Guanacaste Conservation Area. The author describes not only the biological but also the bureaucratic and fundraising challenges faced by American and Costa Rican scientists determined to rejuvenate a region decimated by years of uncontrolled farming and ranching.

Evans, Sterling. 1999. *The Green Republic: A Conservation History of Costa Rica.* Austin, TX: University of Texas Press. This is a comprehensive, but rather too optimistic, account of the history of the establishment of the National Parks System. Although the author rightly praises the determination of scientists and administrators to protect the country's natural heritage and promote tourism in the parks, he neglects to point out that the existence of these parks does not necessarily guarantee that most Costa Rican citizens live in anything even close to a "green" nation.

Holden, Robert H. 2004. *Armies without Nations: Public Violence and State Formation in Central America, 1821–1960.* Oxford: Oxford University Press. This book puts Costa Rica's famous 1948 decision to abolish the army in a more realistic light than one will encounter in the travel literature. It compares Costa Rica to its more militaristic neighbors, using a careful historical approach to explore why force and an institutionalized army played a less prominent role in Costa Rica even before 1948. The author shows how even after that date the country did not cease to seek weapons or military cooperation with the United States in the Cold War era.

Wilson, Bruce. 1998. *Costa Rica: Politics, Economics, and Democracy.* Boulder, CO: Lynne Rienner. This is a concise but thorough account of Costa Rica's institutional development by one of the most dedicated students of the country. Wilson is a particularly good source on the Sala IV of the Supreme Court and the ways in which its emergence in 1989 has affected both policy making and citizen action in Costa Rica.

COSTA RICAN SOCIETY AND CONTEMPORARY ISSUES

Biesanz, Mavis Hiltumen, Richard Biesanz, and Karen Zubris Biesanz. 1999. *The Ticos: Culture and Social Change in Costa Rica.* Boulder, CO: Lynne Rienner. This is an interesting, if idiosyncratic, description of Costa Rican history, society, and institutions. Discussing such varied topics as education, leisure, and religion, it is the latest installment of an ongoing discussion about Costa Rica that members of the Biesanz family have been holding since the publication of *Costa Rican Life* in 1944. The authors not only provide a great deal of information but also try to give the reader an insight into Costa Rican character and personality.

Palmer, Paula. 2005 [1979]. *"What Happen": A Folk-History of Costa Rica's Talamanca Coast.* 3d ed. Miami: Distribuidores Zona Tropical. This is an oral history of life on the Caribbean coast and one of the best books on any aspect of Costa Rican history and society. Palmer allows the Jamaican immigrants and their descendents in the region to tell much of the story in their own words. And they have a lot to say not only about the distinctive history, music, food, and customs of the area, but also more broadly about race relations in Costa Rica. This new edition is very attractively designed as well.

Ras, Barbara, ed. 1994. *Costa Rica: A Traveler's Companion.* San Francisco: Whereabouts Press. This is not a travel guide, but rather a collection of short stories by Costa Rican writers. It offers a good selection of work by some of the country's best-known authors, which is particularly nice because Costa Rican literature is not widely available in English translation. The book is organized by geographical regions in order to give travelers to Costa Rica a taste of culture and scenery from all over the country, and in the process it throws some light on the national character and history.

Sandoval-García, Carlos. 2004. *Threatening Others: Nicaraguans and the Formation of National Identities in Costa Rica.* Athens: Ohio University Press. This is an account of the way in which negative stereotypes of Nicaraguans have played into Costa Rica's persistent sense of exceptionalism, and also have conveniently diverted attention from deepening domestic problems by laying the blame for the degradation of public institutions (and particularly public safety) at the feet of the "nicas." The book is challenging on several levels, particularly when it explores the way all identities are reinforced by stereotyping the "others" we encounter, and when it suggests that we move beyond our habitual construction of separate—and always "exceptional"—national identities.

Sawchuck, Dana. 2004. *The Costa Rican Catholic Church, Social Justice, and the Rights of Workers, 1979–1996.* Waterloo, Ontario, Canada: Wilfrid Laurier University Press.

This is the only recent work available in English on the contemporary Catholic Church in Costa Rica. The author is honest about her "liberationist" theological stance, but nonetheless puts forward a careful account of the tendencies and institutions within the church and their very different approaches to the question of labor relations. For a concise (if not unbiased) account of "solidarism," a worker-management relationship that is advancing very rapidly in Costa Rica with the help of some church-sponsored institutions, this book is particularly helpful.

Stocker, Karen. 2005. *"I Won't Stay Indian, I'll Keep Studying": Race, Place, and Discrimination in a Costa Rican High School.* Boulder, CO: University Press of Colorado. This is an anthropological study of the interactions between the residents of an indigenous reservation and a nearby small town, particularly of the difficulties young people from the reservation face in trying to finish their education. Using participant observation methods (she lived in the area and taught at the school), the author illuminates many of the problems of discrimination faced by indigenous students and, one imagines, by many young people who are perceived to be in some way "different."

Index

Note: Page locators in italics reference sidebars in the text.

About the Authors

Meg Tyler Mitchell is an independent scholar living in San José, Costa Rica. She holds an MA in European history from The College of William and Mary and a PhD in Latin American Studies from Tulane University.

Scott Pentzer lives in San José, Costa Rica, where he is the director of Latin American Programs for the Associated Colleges of the Midwest. He holds a PhD in Latin American Studies from Tulane University.